CLASSIC WALKS OF
THE WORLD

Edited by Walt Unsworth

The Oxford Illustrated Press

© 1985

Walt Unsworth Via delle Bocchette,
The Lidder Valley, The Pennine Way,
Tour du Mont Blanc, The Ascent of
Kilimanjaro, The Everest Trek
Erica Penfold The Milford Track
Martin Collins Tour de la Vanoise
John Hunt A Traverse of the Pindos
Mountains
Hamish Brown The Cordillera Blanca
Trek
Kev Reynolds The Pyrenean High
Route
Christopher McCooey A Traverse of
the North Alps
Duncan Unsworth The Corsican High
Level Route
Dennis Kemp The Circuit of
Annapurna
John Gillies The Cordillera Huayhuash
Trek
Chris Townsend The John Muir Trail
Alan Rouse The Concordia Trek

Printed in England by J.H. Haynes &
Co Limited

Reprinted 1986, 1987

Published by:
The Oxford Illustrated Press, Sparkford,
Near Yeovil, Somerset

Haynes Publications Inc
861 Lawrence Drive,
Newbury Park,
California 91320.

ISBN 0 946609 14 4

CONTENTS

INTRODUCTION

Two hundred and fifty years ago people regarded mountains in an altogether different light from the way we do today. In the East they were looked upon as the homes of Gods; in the West, the haunts of dragons. Either way they were best left alone, the people prey to the powerful fear of the unknown.

In Europe, the change in attitude came about fairly swiftly, as a strong wind blew an Age of Enlightenment through the second half of the eighteenth century. Men looked at mountains with fresh eyes and saw beauty there, which the painters and poets of the Romantic movement tried to capture. Jean Jacques Rousseau thought he saw even more: man's salvation in a return to Nature. Hard on the heels of these poets and philosophers came the scientists, who looked harder and closer than anyone else.

The work of all these men, displayed or written up and published, proved immensely popular. The scientists in particular opened the public's eyes because they not only ventured into remote valleys, but actually climbed to the top of some of the highest mountains. That there were hardships and dangers was apparent from some of their stories—but they were dangers which could be understood. There were no dragons.

This is not the place to go into the development of mountaineering or mountain exploration. Suffice to say that the mountaineering pioneers were great walkers as well as climbers. It was said that the Rev. Charles Hudson, who died in the Matterhorn tragedy of 1865, could average 80km (50 miles) a day: not a feat many present-day mountain walkers would like to emulate! The Tour of Mont Blanc was already a firm favourite at that time, although the five leisurely days now recommended from Chamonix to Courmayeur was reckoned to take three in those days and (says a contemporary guidebook) 'a strong walker can do it in two'. Our predecessors were hardy walkers—women as well as men.

The combination of the German and Austrian Alpine Clubs in 1897, with a total membership of 17,000—more than all the other Alpine Clubs put together—brought a new dimension to mountain walking. A comprehensive network of mountain huts was established throughout the Eastern Alps, where members could stay overnight for a very small sum. This made hut-to-hut touring a practical pursuit, and to further this

aim, individual sections of the club improved paths and safeguarded dangerous sections with cables. Blobs of paint, known as 'waymarks', were daubed on trees or rocks at irregular intervals to assure the walker he was following the right path. Some of this 'improvement' was overdone, and was criticised at times by mountaineers, who failed to appreciate that the club was catering for the majority of its members who were not climbers in any technical sense but happy berg-wanderers. The most popular of these high-level routes were given names, like the Heilbronner Weg and Jubilaums Weg in the Allgauer Alps, both of which were established before the turn of the century.

Shortly after this some waymarked trails were opened in the wilderness areas of the United States. The Long Trail, for example, stretching for 420km (263 miles) across the Green Mountains of Vermont to the Canadian border, was opened in 1910. In remoter parts of the world, certain 'safaris' or 'treks' became standard for the more adventurous local *sahibs*—the ascent of Kilimanjaro in what was then German East Africa, and the Lidder Valley in Kashmir, are two obvious examples.

Walking tours in Britain benefited from the establishment of the Youth Hostel Association in the 1930s; an idea which had originated in Germany and was similar in many ways to the Alpine club hut system. Unfortunately, access problems caused by private landlords who held vast areas of moorland sacrosanct for grouse shooting and public bodies like the various water boards and the Forestry Commission, made the creation of long-distance paths in Britain a difficult business. It was not until 1965 that the first long-distance footpath—the Pennine Way—was officially opened, after some thirty years of negotiation. There are now ten 'official' long-distance paths in England and Wales, with three more in Scotland.

On the Continent of Europe a big boost was given to long-distance walking by the *Comité National des Sentiers de la Grande Randonnée*, which from 1947 began to establish a system of long-distance footpaths known as *la Grande Randonnée* throughout France. The GR system is now extremely extensive and linked with routes in other countries. The GR5, for example, extends from the Dutch coast to the Mediterranean. A system of simple refuges, *gîtes d'étape,* exists along the routes.

Just as the advent of the railways in the 1850s brought about the Golden Age of Alpine exploration, it was the arrival of the wide-bodied jets and cheap air travel which opened up the remote corners of the world to the walker. Thirty years ago it was inconceivable that anyone from Europe, America or Japan could spend their summer vacation trekking in the Himalaya or the Andes, whereas now it is commonplace. Political restrictions apart, all the hidden places of the world are now open to the walker, from the jungles of New Guinea to the frozen wastes of Alaska.

Out of the hundreds of walks which are nowadays available, some have gained international recognition as being amongst the best in the world. It is from these that the contents of this book have been chosen. For the most part they are well-defined routes, either because that is the official policy, as in the case of the Pennine Way, or because it would be difficult, even impossible, to go any other way, as in the Concordia trek. Some few, like the Pindos walk, are much more flexible and the practice of creating *variantes,* or alternatives, to established routes has grown considerably in recent years. Sometimes this is just change for change's sake, but sometimes the motives are more altruistic —a desire to protect a worn path, for instance. In very few cases are the *variantes* a scenic improvement on the original—which is why the original was chosen in the first place, of course.

Sadly, the very popularity of some routes is having damaging ecological effects on the land and even the people who live there. Parts of the Pennine Way have been so badly eroded that the paths have to be reinforced artificially. On the Everest trek, the time-honoured wood fires of the Sherpas are giving way to paraffin stoves because the valley has been stripped of usable wood. The way into the Nanda Devi Sanctuary, which is truly one of the classic walks of the

Above: **The Berliner Hut in the Zillertal Alps of Austria. With the combination of the German and Austrian Alpine clubs in 1874 a chain of huts was established enabling walkers to plan long tours.** (Photo: W.A.Comstive.)

Left: **Path erosion is a serious problem in some places. This Welsh path has been repaired in a 'natural' manner.** (Photo: W.Unsworth.)

5

world, is not described in this book because the authorities have closed the Sanctuary to tourists, to prevent further ecological damage.

It is a sad catalogue, but not a cause for utter despair. In my experience only a few walks are seriously affected and those only in certain parts. Many walks, even some popular ones, are not affected at all. The authorities responsible throughout the world are alerted to the dangers of human erosion and are taking steps to see that the damage is repaired—or better still, prevented.

Deliberate vandalism is fortunately rare, though there is the occasional graffiti of the 'Kilroy Was Here' variety on some walks. The most unusual examples are to be found on the black shaley plateau below Kilimanjaro's Kibo Hut, where idiots have gone to extraordinary lengths to spell out their names in stones. One wonders what motivated them to attempt Kilimanjaro in the first place.

A more serious problem is litter. Litter is one of the great scourges of our time, not confined to long-distance walks by any means, as a trip to any roadside lay-by will quickly demonstrate. On walks, however, the trouble is often more concentrated, more visually offensive, and this is particularly so at camp sites. Cleaning up operations are done from time to time—as I write this the Nepalese are undertaking a cleaning up of the Everest trek and the Peruvians are about to spend 60,000 dollars cleaning up the Inca Trail—but the real answer lies in educating both walkers and porters in better waste disposal habits. Sadly, it is not something for which I hold out much hope.

* * *

I think it was that great explorer Bill Tilman who once said that all you needed for an expedition was to put your boots on and go. He didn't mean it literally, of course. What he meant was that if you sit at home trying to calculate all the risks, all the costs, all the bother—why then, you'll never go at all. And though Tilman was speaking of hardships beyond anything contemplated in this book, the same principle applies. A positive attitude is the prime requirement of anyone considering attempting a long-distance walk: it will get you there and it will see you through.

This doesn't mean you should be foolhardy. The coat must be cut according to the cloth, as the saying goes. Let me give just two examples. On the Via delle Bocchette in the Dolomites, the path threads its way across some horrendous precipices and would obviously be a terrifying ordeal for anyone who suffered from vertigo, whereas that same person might be quite happy on the Pennine Way or the Milford Track. Again, anyone who doesn't like carrying a heavy backpack would not enjoy the John Muir Trail, because backpacking is the only way to do it, but he or she might enjoy the Everest Trek if a Sherpa were hired to carry the load. A sense of achievement might be felt once a fine walk has been completed, but it is much more important to have a sense of enjoyment whilst it is actually taking place.

Anyone who is a regular hill walker will have a pretty good idea of his or her own limitations. Anyone who is *not* a regular hill walker would be advised to try it out for a weekend in some hills near home before embarking on a costly journey half way round the world to attempt something they may not enjoy. In walking you have to work for your enjoyment but then, by some curious alchemy, the effort itself becomes enjoyable and you feel at one with the hills, appreciating to the full their true magnificence. For the price of a ticket anyone can take the cable car to the top of the Brévent and from there view the whole panorama of the Mont Blanc range across the Chamonix valley—but that person will never appreciate Mont Blanc in the same way as someone who has walked around it on the Tour of Mont Blanc.

You need to touch, to smell, to hear the mountains as well as see them. To touch the warm, rough rock; to smell the new mown hay of an Alpine meadow; to hear the roar of a distant avalanche. That is what walking is all about. There is, too, a social element, especially in lands which have cultures very different from our own. To be invited into a Sherpa home to drink tea laced with rancid butter is an honour not given to everyone—though you soon learn that the quicker you drink it (most Westerners find it repulsive) the quicker they fill the glass again! Sitting round a camp fire with Kashmiri porters you will almost certainly be passed the *hookah*, for at least a symbolic puff of friendship. It will probably be hashish. And so it goes on and as time passes you will discover that the human race is not so very different in different parts of the world: mostly friendly, but you can be cheated in Kathmandu or robbed in Cuzco, just as readily as in London or New York.

The Pennine Way has been run in four days from end to end. My own first reaction to this is, *why?* But then again, *why not?* Many of the walks in this book have been subjected to record-breaking attempts and if that is where the pleasure lies for some people, then good luck to them. One remembers John Ruskin, who in the last century, criticised climbers for turning God's cathedrals, the mountains, into soaped poles such as might be found in a bear garden.

The mountain marathon runners are turning them into racetracks, but who are we to be elitist about it? What damages the cathedral more, a marathon runner or a cable car?

It is, however, a different point of view and not one we are concerned with in this book. The walk's the thing, leisurely, enjoyable. Super fitness is not required, but obviously anyone who spends fifty weeks of the year behind a city desk and expects to go straight out and knock off the Tour of Mont Blanc or the Pennine Way, is not going to enjoy it much. At best he or she will have a rough time for the first few days. On the other hand, arduous training is uncalled for. A long walk over some local hills once a month is really all the training that is necessary.

Here's a list of the walks arranged in order of toughness, from the least arduous to the most arduous. The contents follow the same order. It is totally subjective, open to any amount of argument, and ignores special factors such as extreme exposure and the possibility of altitude sickness. It's a fun list—but with an element of truth in it:

Walk	Remarks
Via delle Bocchette	Extremely exposed
Milford Trek	Voracious midges
Lidder Valley	Slight risk of altitude sickness
Tour de la Vanoise	A good introduction to alpine walking
Pennine Way	Arduous in bad weather
Pindos Trek	Tricky route-finding
Punta Union	Some risk of altitude sickness
Tour of Mont Blanc	Cols under snow in bad season
Pyrenean High Route	Long and arduous
Japanese Alps	Language problem – maps, signs etc
Corsican High Route	Reputed to be toughest GR
Kilimanjaro	Risk of altitude sickness
Everest Trek	Risk of altitude sickness
Annapurna Circuit	Risk of altitude sickness
Cordillera Huayhuash	Some risk of altitude sickness
John Muir Trail	Tough backpacking exercise
Concordia Trek	Risk of altitude sickness, Dangerous paths

Altitude sickness, which in its extreme form is pulmonary oedema and cerebral oedema, has been known to occur as low as 3000m (10,000ft), though 4500m (15,000ft) is more usual. It is not a symptom of a lack of fitness or otherwise, for it seems to strike the fit and less fit, male and female, young and old with complete impartiality. In its milder forms many walkers who go to altitude suffer from it: headaches, lack of appetite, even Cheyne-Stokes breathing, which occurs in sleep, and is very frightening to a companion who might be lying awake listening to it! It consists of rapid heavy breathing which builds to a climax then suddenly stops, giving an impression of sudden death. In fact, it is quite harmless.

The two oedemas are far from harmless—they are certain killers unless something is done about them pretty quickly. As always, prevention is better than cure and the real answer is proper acclimatisation to altitude. This can only be achieved by ascending slowly, with time out to acclimatise, that is, remaining at the same altitude for a rest day, whilst your body metabolism catches up. In fact, it is possible to go higher for a few hours (say to climb a local hill) so long as a return is made back to the same base for the evening.

The oedemas are due to a build up of excess body fluid in the lungs (pulmonary) or the brain (cerebral). In the last few years a drug with the market name of Diamox has been available on prescription, and has proved very effective in reducing the risk.

The chief problem is recognizing the symptoms for what they are, and not pressing on in the hope that things will improve. A constant headache, puffy features, blue coloration round the lips, frothing—these are danger signals. The only certain cure is to descend to lower altitude as quickly as possible. Recovery is remarkable, but sadly, anyone who has suffered from altitude sickness is likely to do so again.

* * *

A number of trekking companies offer guided tours along many of the walks which are in this book. For the novice, and especially for anyone going to the Himalaya or Andes for the first time, a guided tour offers distinct advantages. The pre-tour information will include advice on inoculations, visas, money changing, and kit. The travel arrangements and accommodation will be arranged by the firm's local agent, as will trekking permits, porters, tents and food. In fact, as Bill Tilman said, all you have to do is put on your boots and go!

Most firms include in the package a little general sight-seeing before or after the trek. For example, on the Everest trek it is common to include a day in Delhi or a visit to the Taj Mahal at Agra; the Lidder Valley trek will almost certainly include a stay on the houseboats of the Dal Lake, and some of the Peruvian treks include a visit to Machu Picchu.

A comprehensive service like this doesn't come cheap, of course, but most firms offer good value for money. There is certainly less frustration: obtaining a trekking permit in Kathmandu, for instance, can be time consuming. In addition, an unwary traveller can become involved in incidental expenses which soon erode any savings on a tour price.

Yet cocooned against the harsh realities of foreign travel, the traveller does not experience it to the full. Some see this as a disadvantage: they maintain that the hassles and frustrations are part and parcel of the total experience, not to be missed. They prefer to go it alone.

Cheap flights to most destinations are advertised in the quality papers and tourist offices will advise on health regulations, visas and travel within the country concerned. They usually know nothing about mountain walks, however, and are not so helpful when the trip involves leaving their country for another. I remember the Swiss tourist assistant in Geneva who assured me that she had no idea how one could reach St. Gingolph from Geneva. St. Gingolph was just across the lake, in fact—but it was in France!

The individual traveller (and in this I include groups of friends who are organising things for themselves) should have no difficulty in picking up porters when required, though they may be of variable quality and will certainly need careful supervision. The most reliable porters usually have regular employment with the commercial trekking companies.

Even the idea of porterage is anathema to some walkers, however. They prefer to backpack; to be totally reliant on themselves and their equipment, nothing else. The problem is, of course, that this involves carrying very heavy loads, especially if food has to be carried as well. Particularly at high altitude, many walkers would find this too much for them to bear. Only the very fit and very experienced should contemplate this method for the Himalaya or Andes.

On the John Muir Trail in California, backpacking is the only alternative; food and fuel have to be included. On the Via delle Bocchette, the method is not really applicable, and on the Concordia trek it is virtually impossible. All the others can be backpacked with varying degrees of comfort.

* * *

Our Victorian forefathers were tough old birds. They would happily sit out a night bivouac at high altitude dressed in the same sort of clothes they wore on the grouse moors. Nowadays we are not so hardy, nor need we be, since modern technology has provided an excellent range of gear for the outdoors.

In walking gear, as in most things in this life, you gets what you pays for, and it pays to buy the best quality you can afford. Comfort and reliability are essential for peace of mind, if nothing else; a trip can be ruined by gear which is inadequate for the job or which malfunctions. Occasionally it might even be dangerous, but it will certainly be frustrating and if the trip has meant a journey to distant lands, costly. I can never understand the mentality of people who happily pay £500 for an air ticket, then try to save £5 on a pair of boots.

All the walks in this book can be done wearing the same basic walking gear one might use in the Lake District or Wales. There are plenty of books on the market describing walking gear, though equipment has changed so much recently that a book more than five years old is probably out of date in its recommendations. The outdoor magazines carry regular features on new gear as well as plenty of adverts showing what is on offer, but here are some suggestions incorporating both new and old:-

Boots

No need to go clumping around in heavy mountaineering boots these days. The new breed of lightweight walking boots is superbly comfortable. Satisfactory for all the walks except possibly the Concordia trek. A vogue has developed for walking in training shoes, but these don't protect the ankles and are miserable on snow patches. Take along a pair as reserves.

Most treks do not require heavy mountaineering boots. Superb lightweight boots such as these shown here are much more comfortable.
(Photo: Inter Footwear Ltd.)

Shell Clothing

Polyurethane anoraks (or cagoules, or alpine jackets) and overtrousers keep rain out but they also keep body moisture in, so you end up wet just the same! Various branded materials have recently been developed which claim to overcome this problem, the best known being Gore-Tex. Argument rages as to just how good these materials are at their job; some outdoor experts swear by them, others are less enthusiastic. My son, who describes the Corsican walk, always wears Gore-Tex; I prefer my tried and trusted double Ventile jacket.

Whatever the material, an alpine jacket with plenty of pockets and a good hood is more adaptable than an anorak or cagoule.

Breeches

Climbing breeches are more comfortable in rough country than ordinary slacks, though not essential. They have no loose flappy trouser legs to catch in the undergrowth or snag on rocks and socks can be turned down in warm weather. For the overseas walks where daytime temperatures can be very high, lightweight breeches are needed, not the heavy tweeds so common in Britain. Shorts may be preferred: but mountain weather is notoriously fickle and if shorts are worn, a pair of breeches or slacks should be carried in the rucksack, just in case.

Warm Wear

One problem on many walks is the extremes of temperature likely to be encountered. You can swelter one day and face a snowstorm on the next. In fact, the weather can even change hour by hour. In addition, at high altitude, night time temperatures plummet—on the Everest trek, for example, it is not unusual for frost to form on the tent at night.

Apart from the usual sweaters, the following should be considered: 4-season sleeping bag (if camping), thermal underwear, duvet jacket, balaclava, woollen gloves. You are likely to wear *none* of these on the Via delle Bocchette and *all* of them on the Everest trek!

Rucksacks

The rucksack is another item of gear which has undergone considerable changes recently.

Machu Picchu, Peru. This is the end point of the three-day trek along the Inca Trail but commercial treks to other Peruvian mountain areas often take time out to visit this famous Inca city. (Photo: W.Unsworth.)

Above left: **Many treks can be done by backpacking, but the heavy loads involved are not to everyone's taste.**

Above right: **A modern lightweight tent – the Phoenix Phreerunner.** (Photo: Phoenix Mountaineering Ltd.)

Hip bands and variable strap adjustment make them much more comfortable and efficient load carriers. The external framed sack is now something of an anachronism, though some backpackers still prefer it. Packing a rucksack is an art born of bitter experience—most people carry far too much!

On treks where porters or mules will do the load-carrying a kit bag makes a useful alternative for the bulky gear, along with a small 'day sack' for personal items.

Camping Gear

On a commercial trek all the camping gear, except for a sleeping bag, is provided by the company. The design of tents, like much else, has changed radically in recent years, with tensioned hoops replacing poles in some. It is essential to have a tent which will withstand the rigours of a mountain storm, yet be suitably lightweight. Fortunately there are numerous models to choose from—none of them cheap! For the remoter quarters of the globe it is useful to have a multifuel stove.

First Aid

In addition to the usual first aid kit, it may be necessary to carry anti-malaria pills and Diamox for high altitude. Two common causes of complaint not usually met with at home are the sun and stomach disorders.

It is glorious to revel in unlimited sunshine, but it does have its dangers. Especially at altitude the UV rays can cause severe blistering, and it creeps up unnoticed! A good *high altitude* barrier cream should be rubbed on all exposed areas of flesh and a lip-salve used also. The old fashioned glacier cream is effective but horribly tacky and there are pleasanter alternatives nowadays. On extensive snow patches this sunburn prevention is doubly important. Eyes can be protected by sun glasses.

Tummy upsets, accompanied by diarrhoea, are almost inevitable in some countries. It is often caused by a reaction to a different climate and unusual food. Lomotil and kaolin-morph help to kill the pain and reduce the diarrhoea.

Two factors are important in reducing such infections to a minimum. Firstly, there should be strict personal hygiene, which also includes such things as peeling fruit before eating it and resisting the temptation to buy cooked goodies from market stalls. No water should be drunk (or teeth cleaned in it) unless it has been properly boiled—which is why tea is a safer drink than coffee, because the water for tea has to be boiled whereas for instant coffee it only needs to be hot; not at all the same thing! And finally—don't forget the toilet roll!

These notes on gear are not meant to be comprehensive, because that would almost require a book in itself. They are meant simply to indicate some of the recent developments and to highlight some differences between walking at home and abroad.

* * *

Any one of the walks in this book will provide an unforgettable experience, perhaps it may even be the trip of a lifetime. It is good to have something to remember it by in later years; to recall again the joys and pains, the people and places. A simple diary of events is one obvious way of doing this, illustrated by on the spot sketches. There is an intimacy about a personal diary and sketch book which is unique.

Photography

For most walkers, however, photography is the chief way of recording a trip. A recent survey in *Climber and Rambler* magazine showed that an incredible 94% of readers owned a camera and 60% of those were *actively* interested in photography as a hobby. It seems as though the mountains bring out the photographer in us all!

Perhaps in the years to come video will take over as the ultimate record of our experience, but the cameras will have to become a good deal smaller and lighter before that happens on a large scale. For the present the 35mm camera is the favourite. It is a good choice: the larger formats are too bulky for most people to bother with, the smaller ones are not really good enough.

Keen photographers do not need me to tell them what they require in the way of equipment. Suffice to say that even a moderate outfit of a camera body and three various length lenses, plus film and all the bits and pieces, adds considerably to the weight carried and that is a factor to be borne in mind. A modern zoom lens can reduce this, and is handier to use, though some photographers claim you can't get the same quality from a zoom as you can from lenses of different focal lengths. Actually, most people would be hard put to tell the difference.

Another consideration often overlooked is that good photography takes time. There are occasions when we all have to take 'shoot and run' pictures, hoping for the best, either because we are trying to capture a fleeting incident or because we ourselves can only pause momentarily, but most photographs—and especially landscape photographs—need to be composed and the exposures bracketed. This can easily add an hour on to the day's trek.

Perhaps keen photographers should only go walking with other keen photographers. I remember how I used to go walking with my son when he was in his early teens and how he used to chafe and moan at the delays caused by my photography, when all he wanted was to be up and away across the hills. The irony is that he later became a professional photographer!

Because most of the walks are in remote areas it is necessary to take adequate supplies of film. Think how frustrating it would be to do the Everest trek, each day of which reveals astounding mountain scenery which simply *has* to be photographed, only to discover that by the time you reach the world's highest mountain you've run out of film! It happens, believe me. Better take too much than too little, the chances are you will never pass that way again.

But what about the walker who is not particularly keen on photography; who simply wants a record of his or her holiday? It seems to me that a modern automatic 35mm compact camera of good make is entirely adequate. They are light in weight and small in size, easily slipping into an anorak pocket. They won't do everything of course—you can't alter the focal length and in some situations, like bright snowfields with glinting highlights, they can be temperamental, but for most subjects they produce excellent results. A UV filter will help to protect the lens from damage.

It is well to remember though that it is the camera which is automatic, not you. Before setting out on the holiday of a lifetime, learn how to use it. Learn how to load it under difficult circumstances (in rainy weather for example), learn what it will do and what it won't do—how close can you focus on flowers, for example? How accurate is the viewfinder— not 100% probably? What about sunset shots—or even moonlight shots, if you steady it on a wall? Push it, push it all the time until the camera is as familiar as your own fingers.

Familiarity with the camera extends also to the film. Different makes of film have slightly different characteristics and more consistent results are obtained by keeping to one sort.

I would recommend dedicated photographers to take along a few rolls of black and white film, especially if they have access to good printing facilities or can afford one of the specialist

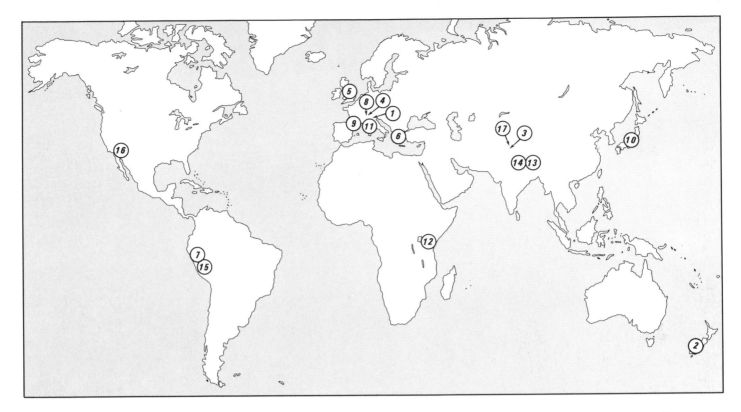

commercial firms who undertake this work. There is something undeniably satisfying about a good black and white enlargement: at its best, this photography is an art form and the lack of colour enhances the sculptural qualities of the mountains.

For most of us, however, it has to be colour and the prime consideration is whether to go for prints or slides. It really depends on what you intend to do with the pictures once you have them. If the intention is to simply keep a record, then an album of prints, suitably captioned, is the most convenient way of doing it. If, on the other hand, you want to relate your adventures to the local walking club or Mothers' Union, then obviously you need slides. You also need slides (transparencies or 'trannies' in the publishing world) if you intend to submit your masterpieces to magazines.

Until the age of electronics takes over in photography (and it is not far away) transparencies are the most universal method of photography. It is possible, at a certain cost, to have either colour prints or black and white prints reproduced from them.

* * *

The seventeen walks described in this book have been chosen not only for their intrinsic merit but also for the variety of experience they offer. In duration they range from three days to three or four weeks, so that they are normally possible during a usual vacation period. The very long walks, like the GR5 from Holland to the Mediterranean or the Pacific Crest Trail in the U.S.A. which take many weeks to complete, are deliberately excluded because relatively few walkers will ever have the opportunity of attempting them.

Some of the place names mentioned suffer a variety of spellings in various maps and books. Within these pages the names are consistent and of a commonly accepted spelling, readily recognisable. It seems a pointless exercise in a book like this to try and evaluate the various forms of a name.

* * *

And now, as Bill Tilman said, just put your boots on and go!

Above: **The seventeen walks described in this book.**

Far left: **Walking through the woods of Mount Horrid on the Long Trail, Vermont. This 425-km route across the Green Mountains to the Canadian border was established in 1910.** (Photo: W.Unsworth.)

Walk 1 ITALY: The Via delle Bocchette
by Walt Unsworth

An Airy Walk in the Brenta Dolomites

The long valley of the Adige in northern Italy runs south from Bolzano to Trento like a broad trench, hot and shimmering in the summer sun. To the east lie the Dolomites, whose fantastic limestone towers and walls are like no other mountain region on earth, whilst to the west rise the snowy peaks of the Presanella and Adamello groups. Sandwiched between the Adige and

After the Campanile Basso the Bocchette route crosses to the western face of the Cima Brenta Alta where it makes a delicate traverse of two gullies, the second of which is shown here.
(Photo: W.Unsworth.)

these latter there is another small mountain chain; a limestone ridge left over from the Dolomites and of such startling appearance that it catches the breath. It is known simply as the Brenta.

The main Brenta ridge is some 20km (12 miles) long but only a few kilometres wide. A walker could cross quite easily from west to east, say from Madonna di Campiglio to Molveno, in a day, and a splendid walk it would be. However, the real joy of walking in the Brenta is to follow it along its axis, north to south. At first glance this seems scarcely possible, for the whole ridge is a complex series of steep crags and startling pinnacles, obviously designed by God for the rock climber, not the walker, and it would indeed be impossible but for one thing——the *via ferrate*.

A *via ferrata* ('iron way') is an adaptation by man of the curious weaknesses common in limestone. Nature has laid down the rock like the layers of a sponge cake, albeit one which has been distorted by rough handling. Some of the layers, being stronger than others, are more resistant to weathering, so that frequently a ledge is left where an upper softer layer has worn back from a lower harder one. Such a ledge might well run right across the face of a cliff, providing a narrow but exposed path: in some places a couple of metres wide, in others no more than a few centimetres. Obviously such a path has its dangers and to help overcome these a stout wire is stanchioned to the rock face as a sort of handrail.

However, this is not the whole story. The ledges are seldom continuous for very long. Ancient geological movements have fractured them so that a ledge may end at one fracture point, only to continue fifty feet higher. On a *via ferrata* such breaks are overcome by iron ladders bolted to the wall between ledges. Some such ladders are only a few metres long—others have over 300 rungs!

By linking ledges like these together (and it must be confessed, by using the occasional stick of dynamite where a good route was thwarted by the odd rock bulge) it is possible to create a *via ferrata* of considerable length. They are to be found throughout the southern limestone Alps, especially in the Dolomites, but they find their highest expression in the Brenta where *via ferrate* and paths are linked together in an exciting network of routes.

The walk that follows forms the crux of the whole system: a series of routes which make up the famous Via delle Bocchette. There are several variants to this exciting walk, but I have chosen a continuous journey which initiates the walker gradually into the system. It is by far the shortest walk in this book but in some ways it is the most serious. A head for heights is absolutely necessary because the ledges are frequently narrow and the exposure is extreme. In bad weather or early and late in the season when there might be snow lying on the ledges, the Via delle Bocchette becomes a serious mountaineering expedition. Care too is necessary in thunderstorms because the ladders and steel cables make excellent lightning conductors. On the other hand, the route involves only one steep uphill slog of any length: mostly it is horizontal or even downhill!

Day 1: Campiglio to Alimonta Hut

The centre for this walk is the large village of Madonna di Campiglio which lies in the valley of the same name on the west side of the mountains. In winter a popular ski centre, Madonna di Campiglio has lost any old world charm it might once have had: it is modern, smart and very upmarket.

A short distance north of the village on the main road is the bottom terminus of the Grostè cable car which rises in two stages to the Passa del Grostè (2442m, 8012ft); a gap which divides the main Brenta ridge roughly in half. The northern half is seldom visited; all the interest lies in the superb rock formations of the southern half.

Anyone who has ethical objections to using the cable car is welcome to walk up from the village in a rather steep three-hour slog, but from the upper terminus a well marked path leads gently downhill below the ridge, across stony slopes, to the foot of the Torre de Vallesinella where it turns a corner and climbs to the Tuckett Hut. The walk takes about two hours and if you have timed it right you will arrive at the hut just in time for lunch.

The Tuckett Hut is splendidly sited on the edge of a high crag overlooking the moraines of the Tuckett Glacier. There are superb views of the adjacent peaks and out across the Campiglio valley can be seen the Adamello–Presanella ranges floating like white clouds in the distance. Behind the hut the sheer walls of the Castelletto Inferiore (2601m, 8530ft) shoot skywards. Only a few metres away there is a second hut, the Sella, which seems to be seldom utilised,

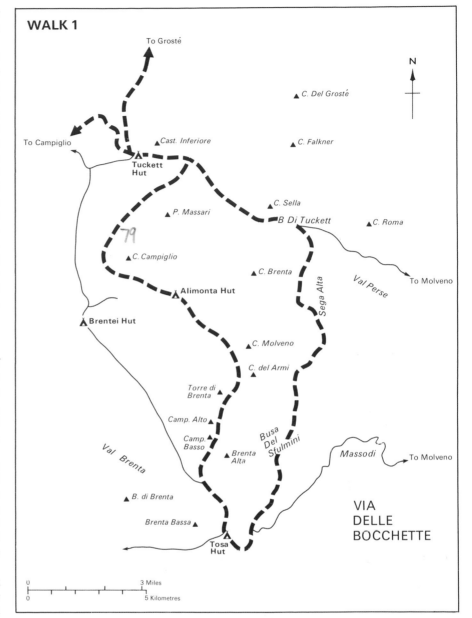

WALK 1

To Grostè

▲ *C. Del Grostè*

To Campiglio

▲ *Cast. Inferiore*

▲ *C. Falkner*

Tuckett Hut

▲ *C. Sella*

▲ *P. Massari*

B Di Tuckett

▲ *C. Roma*

79

▲ *C. Campiglio*

▲ *C. Brenta*

Val Perse

△ *Alimonta Hut*

Sega Alta

To Molveno

△ *Brentei Hut*

▲ *C. Molveno*

C. del Armi ▲

Torre di Brenta

Camp. Alto ▲

Camp. Basso

Busa Del Sfulmini

Massodi

To Molveno

Val Brenta

▲ *Brenta Alta*

▲ *B. di Brenta*

Brenta Bassa ▲

△ *Tosa Hut*

VIA DELLE BOCCHETTE

0 _____ 3 Miles
0 _____ 5 Kilometres

although the Tuckett Hut, like most Brenta huts in summer, is often crowded.

The start to the walk has been easy, but on the next leg comes the first introduction to a *via ferrata*. The Sentiero SOSAT is reached by crossing the narrow cwm below the Tuckett Glacier which is the small glacier descending from the col in the ridge above. The crossing is sign-posted and a rough track leads to a series of short limestone walls climbed by a few ladders. The going is not difficult and before long you find yourself traversing an amazing block field, where some of the stones are the size of a garage. The waymarking is fairly good, but the scrambling round the blocks makes progress fairly

Distance: 24 km (15 miles).
Time required: 3 days.
Type of Walk: A good head for heights essential: extremely exposed.
Base: Madonna di Campiglio. Nearest airport Milan or Venice.
Start: Madonna di Campiglio.
Best Time of Year: July – August inclusive.
Maps: Kompass Wanderkarte 073, Dolomiti di Brenta, 1:30,000
Guidebooks: *Via Ferrata: Scrambles In the Dolomites* by Cecil Davies (Cicerone Press).

15

slow. The views out across the valley are superb.

Suddenly all this changes. The route dives into a rock crevasse and emerges on the brink of a profound abyss. The change is so sudden, so startling, that one is momentarily shocked.

The sense of shock is reinforced when you realize that the way ahead is that thin thread of a path you can see clinging precariously to the cliff face opposite. But how do you even reach it? Progress seems impossible.

A series of cracks and chimneys provided with steel cables lead down a steep wall. Here and there a ladder, or sometimes a few stanchions, help out on the tricky bits. The drop below doesn't bear thinking about. The route takes a diagonal line into the recesses of a deep gully, where it ends on a platform formed by an enormous chockstone. The situation is sensational, entombed between gigantic walls of rock: there are few places that can offer the ordinary mountain walker an experience to match it.

From the chockstone stance two ladders, each of 30m (100ft) lead up the opposite wall of the gully. Unlike the earlier ladders these are really vertical and seemingly endless! However, they do eventually give out onto a curious overhung ledge carved into the walls of the Cima Mandron. Great care is needed in leaving the ladders for the ledge since the overhanging rock is quite low and for a few feet at least it is necessary to crouch as you edge along. But things soon get better. The ledge is much wider than it seemed from a distance and leads easily to a sharp corner from where there is one of the finest views in the Brenta.

The first thing to catch the eye is the towering Cima Tosa (3173m, 10,405ft) with its snow-covered summit and long ice gully. It is the highest peak in the range and is seen to real advantage from this point, across a wide, stony cwm. In the bottom of the cwm, looking like a doll's house from this height, is the Brentei Hut, whose guardian is Bruno Detassis, one of the most famous climbers in the Brenta. Bruno has been responsible also for extensions to the Via delle Bocchette, a route he regards as 'the longest and finest high-level path in the Alps'.

At the head of the cwm rise the famous towers of the Sfulmini group: the massif Torre di Brenta (3008m, 9866ft) and the impossible needle of the Campanile Basso (2937m, 9635ft). From here they are not seen at their best and there will be much better views from them on the morrow.

A short ladder leads from the ledge down to a path which climbs up steadily to a large limestone pavement on which is situated the modern and very comfortable Alimonta Hut. This is the base for the night. According to the guidebook the Sentiero SOSAT from the Tuckett Hut to the Alimonta Hut takes two and a half hours, but most people will probably need a bit longer than that. Even so, you should arrive at the hut in plenty of time for one of the Alimonta family's splendid meals.

Day 2: Alimonta to Tuckett Hut

An early start next morning will see you crunching steadily through the crisp snow of the little Sfulmini Glacier towards an impressive notch in the ridge known as the Bocca d'Armi. The ascent, which takes about half an hour, is neither steep nor difficult.

Just before the crest of the col there is a distinctive flying buttress, tower-like, standing out from the huge walls of the Torre di Brenta, which marks the start of the central and most impressive section of the Via delle Bocchette. You step from the snow of the glacier straight onto a vertical ladder and climb a series of ladders to the top of the tower, only to discover that it really *is* a flying buttress! A bit of balance is necessary at this point, for the ridge connecting the tower with the parent mountain, though short, is narrow and unprotected.

Before long, however, you reach a comfortable ledge equipped with a cable, which leads across the sheer face of the Torre and round the corner. For the first time you are on the eastern side of the range, with views across to the Adige and the distant Dolomites. The more immediate circumstances are sensationally exposed: here indeed is the 'fly on the wall' syndrome so often experienced by rock climbers but seldom by walkers—and never like this! But it is safe enough: the ledge is quite broad (seldom less than a metre) and there is a good cable for its whole length.

It is the beginning of a remarkable traverse, unparalleled in the Alps. For a long way the route is virtually level, across the red and grey limestone walls of the Torre di Brenta, the Sfulmini, the Campanile Alto, to the little shattered rock tower of Sentinella where a delicate descending scramble is made down to the foot of the Campanile Basso—the famous 'Guglia di Brenta'. This celebrated tower of rock has been in view for some time before you actually reach it: it acts like a magnet, drawing you steadily on, fascinated by its impossible shape.

The route goes around the back of the Guglia onto the western face of the Cima Brenta Alta where it crosses a couple of gullies. It is narrow and tricky at this point—technically the most difficult part of the whole walk—but steadiness and care will see you safely through and it is only

a matter of a few metres. Before long the ledge broadens out again and leads without further trouble to a good path winding up to a distinctive gap in the ridge, the Bocca di Brenta (252m, 8370ft). All the way up to the col there are splendid views of the Crozzon di Brenta (3118m, 10,227ft) and Cima Tosa.

Just beyond the col, on a rocky knoll, can be seen the large Pedrotti Hut which is reached by an airy path. Once again, as with the Tuckett Hut, there is a secondary hut nearby—the old Tosa Hut, built as long ago as 1874 when the Brenta was first being explored by mountaineers. The Pedrotti Hut should make a convenient resting place for lunch—the time taken from the Alimonta Hut being three or four hours.

From the hut a worn path zig-zags down some rock outcrops to the start of one of the oldest *via ferrate,* the Sentiero Orsi, which traverses below the ridge on the eastern side. After the exhilarating exposure of the morning's walk, the Orsi seems a little tame, for it is just like walking along a path in the Lake District or Wales. The views to the east make up for any lack of excitement, however, especially the huge rock walls of the Croz dell Altissimo (2339m, 7670ft) across the wooded Valle delle Seghe. Before long too, the towers and pinnacles which you traversed earlier come into view; a whole panoply of fantastic peaks, including of course, the remarkable Guglia. Certainly they are seen at their comprehensive best from here: one of the finest views in the limestone Alps.

The path continues without difficulty until it is possible to leave it momentarily and walk along a rocky ridge to the Naso (2527m, 8288ft). This promontory is obvious and the diversion, which only takes a few minutes, is well worth while if only to reinforce the grandeur of the views which surround you.

After the Naso the Orsi path shows a bit of bite. A large, boulder-filled gully cuts down the mountainside and has to be crossed. It is steep and care is required in route finding, but there is no real technical difficulty.

Beyond it is a broad ledge known as the Sega Alta. It is like a slot in the rock, massively overhung and the wall below dropping sheer to the valley. It turns out to be quite wide but the exposure is real enough for all that. Before long it emerges onto the block fields below the Bocca di Tuckett.

One of the most pleasant features of the walk during the past two days has been the total absence of hard up-hill slogs. The ascent to the Bocca di Tuckett makes up for this! The climb to the col is a very steep grind of over 1000m (3250ft) mostly on loose limestone scree—how

Above: **Iron ladders on the Sentiero SOSAT. A *via ferrata* is made up of ledges and paths joined by ladders and protective cables.** (Photos: W.Unsworth.)

Far left: **The Cima Tosa (left) and Crozzon di Brenta (right) tower over the Brentei Hut.**

It takes four to five hours from the Pedrotti Hut to the Tuckett Hut by the Sentiero Orsi, so that all in all it has been a fairly hard day. For this reason it is better to plan to stay the night at the Tuckett Hut.

Day 3: Tuckett to Campiglio

Return to Madonna di Campiglio in the morning, either by the delightful paths through the woods to the Rifugio Casenei and the Vallesinella or, girding your loins yet again, by the fairly recently constructed *via ferrata* known as the Sentiero Alfredo Benini which traverses the ridge from the Bocca di Tuckett to the Grostè cable car station. (Time required is about three hours.)

The walk which I have described encompasses the original Via delle Bocchette, but so popular have the *via ferrate* become over recent years that there are now all sorts of variations and extensions, some easier, some harder. It would be easy to spend a week or more in these delectable mountains traversing back and forth along these exciting paths.

In high summer the route described should be perfectly within the capabilities of experienced mountain walkers with some scrambling ability. It must be emphasised that exposure is considerable—much, much more than on a usual mountain walk—and the special *via ferrata* protective system should always be employed (see inset). In my opinion, this walk is not suitable for small children.

Via Ferrata Protection

The steel cables adorning the ledges of a *via ferrata* are not there simply as handrails. They are intended to be used for self protection in the event of a slip. The method employs a long loop of climbing tape which is tied around the waist so as to leave two loops of 18 inches dangling in front (see diagrams). A karabiner is clipped to each loop and one of these is attached to the via ferrata cable. When passing a stanchion the second karabiner is clipped to the wire beyond the stanchion *before* the first one is removed, thus ensuring protection at all times. The loops can also be employed to safeguard ladders in a similar fashion. The diagrams should make this clearer.

A chest harness of the sort used by climbers, to which two loops like those described above are attached, is even better protection, but it is unlikely that many walkers will have such expensive equipment. Due to the increasing popularity of these walks, special 'via ferrata kits' are now available in some climbing shops. The tape loop around the waist is quite adequate for the Via delle Bocchette.

Above: **The Campanile Basso. This splendid rock tower is a showpiece of the Brenta.**
(Photo: R.A.B.Keates.)

Left: **The safety belt recommended by the C.A.I. on a *via ferrata*.**

Far right: **As the route crosses the walls of the Torre di Brenta the rock scenery becomes increasingly spectacular.**
(Photo: W. Unsworth.)

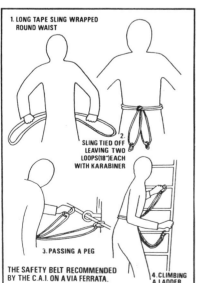

1. LONG TAPE SLING WRAPPED ROUND WAIST

SLING TIED OFF LEAVING TWO LOOPS(18")EACH WITH KARABINER

3. PASSING A PEG

THE SAFETY BELT RECOMMENDED BY THE C.A.I. ON A VIA FERRATA.

4. CLIMBING A LADDER

steep is indicated by the fact that here and there steel cables are laid to help the walker pull himself up! It seems endless, but eventually the col is reached and the snowy upper edge of the Vedretta di Brenta Inferiore, perhaps better known simply as the Tuckett Glacier. The glacier is quite a harmless one and is descended on the right hand side to meet a path which leads directly to the Tuckett Hut.

Walk 2 NEW ZEALAND: The Milford Track
by Erica Penfold

Across the Fiordland Mountains and Past One of the World's Highest Waterfalls

The most beautiful walk in the World—so some consider the Milford Track but being in the Fiordland of the South Island of New Zealand with an annual rainfall of about 250 inches, the 'beautiful' description is rather dependent on the weather. Certainly the Walk can be labelled 'an experience' and is a must for visitors to that part of the country.

The discovery of the Milford Track was made in 1888 by Quintin Mackinnon who finally found a route over the saddle between the Clinton and Arthur Rivers. A search for such a Pass had occupied explorers for years in the hope of obtaining access from the interior to the Milford Sound on the West Coast. With surrounding valley heads proving insurmountable, this finally left the Clinton Valley in the East and Roaring Creek, a tributary of the Arthur River in the West. The Maoris in fact knew of this route but though the early explorers must have been passed this information, for some unknown reason these valleys were the last to be explored.

Milford Sound was made known by a whaling captain called John Grono who is supposed to have named the Sound after his birthplace Milford Haven in Wales, along with other local places that were also given Welsh names such as the Cleddau River, Pembroke Glacier and Llawrenny Peaks.

Looking back down the Clinton Valley from the Mackinnon Pass. (Photo: N.Z. High Commission.)

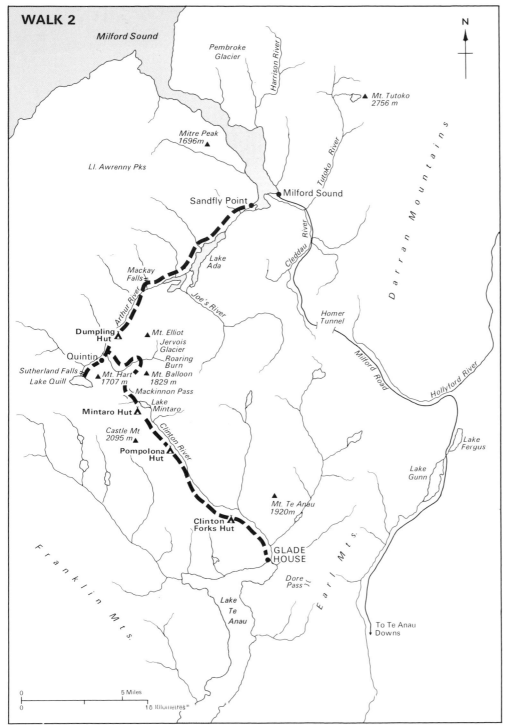

Distance: 52km (33 miles).
Time required: 5 days.
Type of Walk: Rocky surfaces, steep climbs and descents, many river crossings. You need to be reasonably fit.
Base: Te Anau, South Island, New Zealand.
Start: Glades House, Lake Te Anau.
Best Time of Year: November–March.
Guidebooks: *Milford Trails* by William Anderson (A.H. & A.W. Reed). *The Companion Guide to The South Island of New Zealand* by Errol Brathwaite (Collins.)

After this discovery in the early 1820s, Milford Sound became known to seafarers as a safe harbour from the storms at sea with magnificent scenery an added lure. Later, surveys by boat were made of the New Zealand coastline and the Sound was considered as a possible port to serve the South West Coast with tourists coming to view the spectacular scenic attractions. But a route also had to be found heading inland.

Donald Sutherland was the first settler at Milford in 1878. Having visited the Sound several times while working on a Government steamer, he became so impressed with the beauty

21

of the scenery that he went ashore and made a rough hermit's life for himself exploring the area. After a while, John Mackay, a mineral prospector, joined him and on one of their particularly tough excursions along the Arthur Valley, they came upon a fantastic waterfall dropping from an incredible height in the mountains. They had found the Sutherland Falls. However, because of the apparent sheer wall of mountains forming the head of the Arthur Valley, they thought there was no way of getting over them.

Some ten years later, C.W. Adams, Chief Surveyor of Otago, sailed into Milford Sound to explore the surrounding countryside and made a concentrated effort to find a route overland to the Clinton Valley and Lake Te Anau. His small party and Donald Sutherland were following the track cut earlier by Sutherland to the Falls, when one of the men mentioned he had seen some black swans fly over the mountain range. Knowing these birds cross at the lowest point, he believed the gap through which the swans had come could be the pass they were all seeking.

Meanwhile, across the mountains, Quinton Mackinnon, a surveyor, and Ernest Mitchell were exploring the Clinton Valley for the sought-after pass. After weeks of hard slogging and cutting a trail, they finally found a saddle that seemed passable, the one in fact that the swans had been seen to fly over, at the head of the Clinton Valley. With the rain falling and visibility poor, they felt their way carefully up and over the pass (now known as the Mackinnon Pass) meeting with Donald Sutherland's tracks on the other side. The route from Te Anau to Milford had been found.

The Milford Track is 52km (33 miles) long and a generous 5 days (one a free/rest day) are allowed for its enjoyment. To avoid overcrowding, the number of walkers is limited on the departures from Glades House and there are two ways of undertaking the walk. The first is an organised trip with the Government Tourist Board where groups of about 35 are taken by a leader, staying at huts with the luxuries of showers, heating, bedding and meals provided by hut staff. Using this accommodation, the only items the walker has to worry about are clothing and personal requirements which can be carried in hired packs. These should include walking boots or stout shoes, waterproofs and

Far left, top: **The view towards Quintin from the Mackinnon Pass.**

Far left, bottom: **On the track between Clinton Forks and Mintaro.**

Right: **A walker on the Milford Track pauses by the Clinton River.** (Photos: Erica Penfold.)

The high rainfall of Southland is reflected in the Old Moss Beard hanging from trees along the Milford Track.
(Photo: N.Z. High Commission.)

warm clothing for the very changeable weather that can be experienced, a torch and plenty of insect repellant–though it cannot be guaranteed that any amount of the latter will be sufficient!

The second way of doing the Walk is to become one of a group of twelve 'Freedom Walkers', arranged through the Fiordland National Park Board in whose ground the Milford Track lies, with the difference being that all requirements for the trip (clothing, food, cooking utensils and sleeping bags) have to be carried and overnight stops are in the spartan National Parks Board huts.

Though the Milford Track is within the capabilities of most reasonably fit people, the rocky surfaces, steep climbs and descents, and crossing of rivers without bridges can make it quite an exciting hike. As the area also has one of the world's highest annual rainfalls, flash flooding can turn this hike into a nerve racking and dangerous expedition.

Day 1: Glades House to Clinton Forks Hut

On the first day the launch is taken from the town of Te Anau or from where the bus passengers board at Te Anau Downs, across Lake Te Anau to the start of the Track at Glades House, a voyage of about two hours. Already there is a little of the feeling of the splendour and remoteness that lies ahead, with the steep wooded mountain slopes leading down to the lakeside which has a beautiful stillness about it.

The Tourist Board walkers stay their first night at Glades House which stands in a large clearing at the end of the Lake, but the 'Freedom Walkers' have five miles to cover to reach their first hut at Clinton Forks. From Glades House you cross a swing bridge over the Clinton River, the first of several bridges and in better condition than many, and are faced with a large sign '33 Miles—Good Luck'—the beginning of the Milford Track.

Following the left-hand bank, the Track takes you on an easy path through thick beech forests and then alongside the clear Clinton River with its stony beaches and tempting pools. For the fisherman, regret at not adding a line to his pack must be great as the trout swing their way lazily along, unaware of what their fate would be in a more frequented river. If the weather is warm and you have the courage for a dip, the unexpected coldness takes your breath away. It can also be here that you are first reminded this part of New Zealand is renowned for three things: the spectacular scenery, the heavy rain and the sandfly—a tiny black insect that bites like the midge and makes life decidedly unpleasant. A swarm of the perishers can soon find you a tasty morsel (in between the thickly coated repellent). The locals might call New Zealand 'God's Own Country' but for what purpose He placed sandflies in such a gorgeous spot, has everyone beaten!

Clinton Forks hut is situated in a glade with grand views of the Earl Mountains behind. Like the other two Parks Board Huts to come, it consists of four rooms with eight bunks in each (no mattresses, only hessian hammocks) and a common area in the centre of the hut with a wood stove. Wood has to be chopped and water fetched from a river or from the rainwater tank attached to the side of the hut. If possible most cooking is carried out before dark falls after which the only light available is from candles which also have to be carried in. Living conditions after a rainy day with everyone trying to dry dripping clothes over the stove while the evening meal is being cooked, become quite interesting. Shortly after dark, and to everyone's relief, the sandflies decide to turn in, but instead the smoke billowing out of the stove soon has eyes streaming. There is a special knack to get those stoves working well. The next problem is how to avoid thinking of a possible call of nature in the night as the privy is outside, usually round the back, up the narrow footpath, over the mound, among the trees, fifty yards from the hut! A somewhat difficult job to find in a hurry in the middle of a black night!

Day 2: Clinton Forks Hut to Mintaro Hut

The next day is 13km (8 miles) to Mintaro Hut (or a little less to the Tourist Board hut at Pompolona)—another easy walk though finishing with a pull up to the hut. Except for the ascent of Mackinnon Pass, a climb of 1000m (3400ft), due to be done on the third day, most of the Track is along the valley floors. The mountain sides, covered with forests and thick bush, tower above with Castle Mountain at 2095m (6872ft) standing supreme as it reaches to the sky. The valley floor though, is soft and gentle with its numerous hues of green foliage shrouding the Track. Moss and lichen coat the trees and long vines hang from the branches to the ferns below. The sunlight glinting through this mesh makes the scene quite wierd. All that is needed is the three witches from *Macbeth* and the setting would be complete.

On leaving this enclosed part, the canyon opens out to give a two-mile stretch of fairly open country through which the now smaller Clinton flows. The thick bush becomes scrubland with only the pampas-like grasses waving their brushes high. In the far distance, the head of the valley can be seen as the mountains close in with their seemingly sheer walls, and any pass appears most unlikely.

Although flat and comfortable to walk along, the valley floor gradually steepens and the sides close in again for the pull up to the hut at Lake Mintaro, mirror-like except for where the Clinton River falls on its journey from the source in the mountains. In the undergrowth at night the kiwi, the rare National bird, has been known to hunt while the weka (woodhen) is often seen. However, you have to watch out when the keas (mountain parrot) put in an appearance. These fearless and nosey birds are known to demolish camps and shred packs (even boots) with their sharp beaks—a guard over equipment is advisable.

If the weather is good and the walk from Clinton Forks to Mintaro has not taken too long, the temptation to climb up to Mackinnon Pass is very great, especially as the following day the weather could dramatically change, hiding the views of the spectacular scenery surrounding the Pass. With packs left at Mintaro Hut the climb can be made easily and quickly.

Day 3: Mintaro Hut to Dumpling Hut

The hardest part of the walk is the 14km (9 miles) from Mintaro Hut, over the Pass to Dumpling Hut. On crossing the Clinton River by another swing bridge, the long slog to the top of the Pass begins. The ascent is made along a

The Sutherland Falls, fed by Lake Quill, are reputed to be the third highest in the world. They are reached by a detour from the main trail. (Photo: Erica Penfold.)

path that zig-zags its way ever upwards through the mountain beech and ribbonwood which gradually thins until the treeline is reached near the summit. Though a steady walk with head down will allow the Pass to be reached more quickly and comfortably, there are 'strategically' placed rocks where a pause can be made to admire the surrounding scene and sounds!

Eventually, the path opens out onto the plateau of the Pass with tussockland replacing woodlands. The views are spectacular, revealing the steep sided valleys on either side with Lake Mintaro glistening in the Clinton Valley and the mystery of the Arthur Valley, 600m (2000ft) below, still to come. The simple stone cairn of the Mackinnon Memorial somehow enhances the grandeur of the peaks with cone-shaped Mount Balloon at 1800m (6000ft) standing sentry over it in the East. Mount Hart at 1700m (5600ft) towers at the western end of the saddle

and Mount Elliot with its Jervois Glacier makes a forbidding sight, more so in winter when it regularly throws avalanches down into the valley below. In fine warm weather the dangers are hard to appreciate. The alpine flowers and grasses hold your attention, except for the occasional bird fluttering away, and time passes unnoticed. However, when the weather changes, and it can very suddenly, the Pass can be a different place as the sky darkens and cloud creeps in covering the peaks and hiding the edges of precipices and their hundreds of feet drops. The wind strengthens turning into a howling gale which for the walker makes an upright stance impossible and the raindrops come like bullets against your face. Refuge in the shelter hut on the Pass comes as a welcome break in the struggle against the elements though you get a reminder of what is happening outside each time a new arrival turns up, opens the door and then strains to close it behind him.

The hut is shared by both the Government Tourist Board and the National Parks Board. Each group, if they arrive at the same time, should stay on their own side of the hut to make their cups of tea and have refreshments, but everyone mingles exchanging their impressions of the walk so far. Feeling cosy and warm after the drink, it takes courage to heave on the packs and face the elements outside again, but once the first hundred yards or so are covered to reach the downward track and the relative quietness and shelter of the entry into Arthur Valley, enjoyment of the surroundings returns.

For a while, as the path zig-zags downwards under the awesome eye of Mount Balloon, there seems to be a wilder appearance in the rough undergrowth until you get down into the beech forest again. After crossing Moraine Creek by another swing bridge, beside the main track on the left hand side, is a small sign marked 'Arthur's Track' which is a short alternative route. This narrow path is very rough, steep and slippery with the protecting rails gratefully grabbed to help keep balance. The undergrowth is thick and close, with brilliantly coloured mosses in every shade of green and the series of waterfalls leading down to Linwood Falls, sparkle white against the green backcloth. The atmosphere and strangeness of this route makes the outside world seem very far away.

Just before rejoining the main track, a crossing of the upper section of Roaring Burn has to be made by a swing bridge which, when I used it, was in dire need of repair. It was very old and rickety and had obviously served its users well but was now most precarious to cross. Half the wire framework was hanging loose while planks of wood along the walkway were missing.

The high point of the Milford Track – walkers climb up towards the Mackinnon Pass.
(Photo: N.Z. High Commission.)

Clinging on to the sides, which seemed to spread further apart the harder I gripped them, it made the long strides I had to take from one remaining plank to the next appear like part of a circus act. Even my tired, nervous, breathing had to be held in check in order to avoid the bridge's swinging even more with each bouncing step. All the time the waters below were rushing towards Roaring Burn, a thought which was best left at the back of the mind. Certainly the unexpected adds to the excitement of any such walk!

Back on the main Milford Track, the way gradually leads down to the next overnight stop for the Government Tourist Board walkers at Quintin Hut which is reached by a swing bridge where one person only is allowed to cross at a time. Two miles further on, Dumpling Hut is the resting place for the Parks Board walkers. Though the itinerary has to be altered sometimes, an extra day is usually allowed at these huts either to revel in a day of rest or to take gentle walks in the vicinity; a visit to the famous Sutherland Falls being the highlight.

Quintin is the operation centre of the Track along the Arthur River valley and after the remoteness experienced up until this point, all the activity taking place is a little unexpected at first. The resident staff have to cater for the regular groups passing through, providing them with their hot meals, bedding in the large dormitories and guides along the Track as well as catering for the staff employed in maintaining the Track. As with all the staffed huts, provisions have to be brought in regularly. The early explorers carried their initial requirements on their backs and hopefully replenished any food by fishing or catching game. Later when the track became more negotiable, pack horses and then horse-drawn wagons were used. In recent times along the Clinton Valley, and certain sections in the Arthur Valley, tractors have replaced the horses where the track is wide and well established and in the late 1960s an airstrip was made at Quintin. The helicopter is now a regular visitor if a somewhat disturbing one, as its chattering noise shatters the peace of nature.

Day 4: Rest Day

For those staying at Dumpling Hut, there are no hot showers or prepared meals to spoil them! About 45m (50 yards) from the hut is a nice quiet stretch of the river where a cold dip can be taken and even if you cannot wallow for too long, at least it acts as a refresher. Unfortunately no sooner have the numerous layers of insect repellent been chipped off, than, spying naked bodies exposed to the elements, the sandflies swoop. With fumbling fingers clothes are quickly replaced and the inevitable repellent once more plastered on the bits still exposed. How do you gain immunity from the blighters?!

Although when doing a walk like this, you always hope for good weather in order to get the best out of the views and avoid having to wear cumbersome waterproofs which produce a swishing noise at every movement, the most dramatic time to see this Fiordland is in fact in the rain. The steep mountain sides become sparkling waterfalls, every nook and cranny collects water and shoots it down, swelling the river below. Yet not an hour after the rain stops, the falls fade and the river goes back to normal level. Earthquakes have occurred in the Milford Track region and cyclones have been known to drop their water load there, sometimes making life dangerous and uncertain. If caught out in such conditions, decisions have to be made quickly as the scene can change in moments.

Mitre Peak is one of the attractions of Milford Sound. (Photo: N.Z. High Commission.)

27

Walkers preparing to set out from Quintin Hut. (Photo: N.Z. High Commission.)

What was a trickling stream crossed by large stepping stones suddenly becomes a fast flowing river. The stepping stones disappear as the water plunges over them making the crossing a major ordeal. Holding hands with other members of the group, gives support as you gingerly stretch out a foot to find the stones. If not found then wading through waist-high water is often the alternative. And the time you take in making a crossing carefully, probably means the next stream to be crossed is getting even deeper. Some of the streams have wooden bridges spanning them and these are covered with chicken wire which gives better adhesion when wet. If the waters are flowing over the top the only way the bridge can be found is by tripping over the first plank!

Parts of the Track are very close to the river and after long spells of rain the river has been known to rise over 9m (30ft) above its usual level, flooding the Track. This makes it necessary to take to the bush for an alternative route to reach the next higher part of the Track. That bush has been the doom of pioneers who lost their way. The undergrowth is a tangle of roots and old leaves, low trees and hanging vines. The water dripping from above causes less direct danger than that walked over or waded through. A slip on a protruding root can result in a broken limb with a rescue party not easily called to assist. Softened by the heavy rain, the soil on the steep slopes moves and landslides occur in varying degrees. Once a particularly large one halted only about 30m (100ft) from Quintin. With all the debris, sometimes strewn high in the trees, detours have to be made or steps cut through a fallen tree–it is a full time job to keep the Track well maintained.

The Sutherland Falls, fed by Lake Quill, are thought to be the third highest falls in the world at 580m (1904ft) and in fact drop in three leaps; the first being 248m (815ft), the second 228m (751ft) and the third 103m (338ft). They lie about a mile from Quintin and as they are approached, the great thundering noise gets louder. In dry weather the three leaps can easily be distinguished as they drop finely into the pool below, but when rain has flooded Lake Quill, the water falls in a single, deafening sheet with spray forcing you back to admire the sight from a distance.

Day 5: Dumpling Hut to Sandfly Point

The last day's walk is an 18km (11 mile) stretch which at first follows the right hand bank of the Arthur River. As with the Clinton River, fish can be seen swimming in the clear waters amongst the stones and with the wildness of the high country being left behind, the scenery becomes gentler and the difficulties of the early explorers are forgotten. Again the mountains tower above you, their steep slopes clad in dark green forest while the pebbly beaches of the river make convenient resting places for you to soak up the surroundings, providing the rains have passed on and the river receded to normal levels.

At Boatshed, you cross the river once more to the left bank by a swing bridge where debris and foliage still cling from the last flooding. Here the Track leaves the river for a short while in order to branch into the thick bush leading to the attractive Mackay Falls, named by John Mackay—Donald Sutherland's mining companion.

Returning to the river, the Track skirts Lake Ada, a beautiful mountain lake about 5km (3 miles) long, and then you are on the last mile to the end of the Track at Sandfly Point from where the launch is taken to Milford. As the name suggests, Sandfly Point has a large resident insect population, making any previous encounter a minor event compared with their greeting here. During the wait for the launch, constant movement is necessary and to an accompaniment of slapping and cursing, the launch's eventual arrival is welcomed by everyone. The short boat trip to Milford shows off Fiordland in all its glory with the mountain sides rising sheer from the waters and then Mitre Peak, rearing up to 1695m (5560ft) at the end of the range, comes into full view. Only then does the full realisation that you have completed the Milford Track hit you and any hardships, aches, pains and blisters endured cannot take away the pleasure of having seen this part of New Zealand.

Walk 3 KASHMIR: The Lidder Valley
by Walt Unsworth

A Walk Through the Deodars to the Kolahoi Glacier

The story goes that when the great Mogul emperor Jahangir lay on his deathbed he was asked if there was anything he specially desired. 'Only Kashmir', he replied.

It is not difficult to understand what he meant, for Kashmir is a lotus land beyond comparision: a fertile land inhabited by a gentle people, with forests, mountains and lakes in abundance. It is not unlike an enlarged version of the English Lake District or a Switzerland transported on some magic Kashmir carpet to the heart of Asia.

Kashmir lies in the north-west corner of India, and this geographical fact accounts for both its beauty and its sorrow. It has always been surrounded by war-like neighbours who have from time immemorial ravaged the land. Even today the old feudal state of Jammu and Kashmir is partitioned by the cease-fire line of the Indo-Pak wars of the recent past, so that the whole of Baltistan and the great bend of the Indus is now in Pakistan territory. What remains to India is the Vale of Kashmir and the remote provinces of Ladakh and Zanskar.

Camping at Lidderwat is on a huge marg or meadow, large enough to hold a regiment.
(Photo: W.Unsworth.)

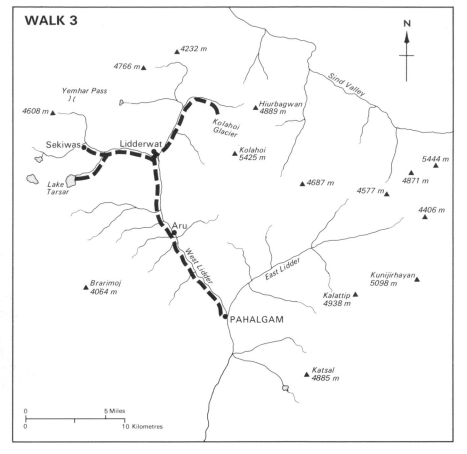

WALK 3

4232 m

4766 m

Yemhar Pass

4608 m

Sekiwas

Lidderwat

Hiurbagwan
4889 m

Kolahoi
Glacier

Kolahoi
5425 m

Sind Valley

N

5444 m

4687 m

4871 m

4577 m

4406 m

Lake
Tarsar

Aru

West Lidder

East Lidder

Kunijirhayan
5098 m

Brarimoj
4064 m

Kalattip
4938 m

PAHALGAM

Katsal
4885 m

0   5 Miles

0   10 Kilometres

Distance: 80 km (50 miles)
Time required: 6 days
Type of Walk: Not too strenuous but a high route with a slight risk of altitude sickness.
Base: Srinagar.
Start: Pahalgam.
Best Time of Year: May – October.
Map: Trekking Route Map of Jammu and Kashmir Sheet 1. 1:250,000 (obtainable in Srinagar).
Guidebooks: *Sonamarg Climbing and Trekking Guide* by J.A. Jackson (Srinagar).
Kashmir, Ladakh and Zanskar by M. and R. Schettler (Lonely Planet Publications).

Despite this division and the restrictions imposed in some parts by the military, there is still an immense amount of wild country open for the trekker. From south-west to north-east the main divisions of the country are: the Pir Panjal range, which rises to over 4700m (15,415ft); the Vale of Kashmir, rich and fertile and where the capital Srinagar lies; the main Himalayan range with mighty peaks like Nun Kun (7135m, 23,402ft) and Kolahoi (5425m, 17,794ft); the long and lonely Zanskar Valley; the Zanskar range, rising to some 6000m (19,680ft) and the Indus valley of Ladakh, with its romantic capital Leh, once one of the great staging posts of Central Asia.

The monsoon has little effect this far west. The rains coming up from India beat against the Pir Panjal, water the Vale of Kashmir and spend themselves against the Himalayas. Beyond there—in Zanskar and Ladakh—the land is like a vertical desert; a moonscape of mountains, red, grey and ochre, reflecting the meagre three inches of rain which fall in an average year. These eastern lands are not known as Little Tibet for nothing—quite apart from the religion, (which like Tibet is Lamaist Buddhism) Ladakh is high and bitterly cold in winter. The little town

of Dras (3094m, 10,150ft) below the dramatic pass of the Zoji La, is reputed to be the coldest town in Asia, and the unfortunate Indian soldiers stationed there probably agree!

In winter too, snow can fall anywhere in Kashmir—even in Srinagar—and the hill station of Gulmarg in the Pir Panjal is probably the best ski resort in India.

In summer, the opportunities for trekking are as immense as they are varied. From the key centres of Gulmarg, Sonamarg and Pahalgam a large number of tours are organised, whilst further east in Zanskar and Ladakh there are treks which are as tough as anywhere in the world. In recent years Zanskar has been a fashionable objective for trekkers owing to the world-wide distribution of a superb television documentary which claimed it was 'the last kingdom on Earth'.

As you might expect, unaccompanied backpacking in Zanskar or Ladakh is a pretty serious undertaking. The going is rough, to put it mildly, the passes are high, and there is little hope of assistance should things go wrong. In the rest of Kashmir, though remote in many respects, the overall burden is not so great and the backpacker could have a spendid trip. Indeed, for anyone who wants to avoid the altitude problems of Nepal, Kashmir would make a suitable alternative. The trek described in this chapter, for instance, would be perfectly feasible for a backpacker.

However, the traditional method of trekking in Kashmir is rather more luxurious. It is often combined with a stay on a houseboat on the Dal Lake at Srinagar, for just as the Nepalese visitor must explore Kathmandu, so too the Kashmir visitor must explore Srinagar and the Mogul gardens which stretch down to the Lake.

Srinagar stands on the River Jhelum and the Dal Lake. This latter is a broad sheet of water, fringed by trees and distant blue hills. At the town end the inhabitants have, over the centuries, built islands out of decaying vegetation, anchored them with trees and planted them with a variety of vegetables and flowers for the city. Between the islands is a network of waterways, which have turned Srinagar into a sort of Indian Venice. As in Venice, these canals are thoroughfares, alive with *shikari* boats being punted back and forth, but unlike Venice the waterways are also home for thousands of boat people.

In the time of the Raj, Kashmir was an independent state and the British visitors who found Srinagar's summer climate a delight compared with the heat of the plains, were not allowed to own land there. To get round this they joined the boat people—except that they built houseboats which over the years became the last word in luxury, equipped with four or five bedrooms, bathrooms, dining rooms, living rooms—in fact, a regular little summer floating palace. And the tradition has continued, though nowadays the houseboats are Kashmiri owned and hired out to visitors. From the outside they resemble nothing so much as miniature Mississippi paddle steamers without paddles and carry garish names painted on huge headboards, which give them a rather tatty appearance—but inside they are a wealth of exquisitely carved woodwork and very comfortable.

The Dal houseboats are a unique experience and one not to be missed. As somewhere to recover from jet lag after a flight to India (or to recover from the rigours of trekking, perhaps!) they are ideal. An additional advantage is that the houseboat owner will almost certainly arrange your trek for you, should you wish. This not only saves a lot of hassle on your part, but you will probably get better porters as well.

Of all the treks in Kashmir that which goes up the beautiful valley of the West Lidder to the Kolahoi Glacier is the most famous. It is not a long or arduous journey—five or six days away from Srinagar will suffice, and the terrain is easy.

Day 1: Pahalgam to Aru

The trek begins at Pahalgam (2130m, 6986ft), some 95km (60 miles) from the capital, reached in a couple of hours by car, though by public transport bus the journey can take much longer. There are several buses a day in both directions. This popular little town nestles in a bowl of the hills at the junction of the East and West Lidder rivers, streams which are noted for trout fishing—though fishing is strictly controlled and a licence is required. The wide main street is lined with shops, hotels, banks, a tourist bureau and a post office. Tethered clusters of trekking ponies give it the air of a Hollywood western.

The pony is to Kashmir what the yak is to Nepal—a beast of burden. On trek everything is carried by pony, and each day at least some of these will depart early so that the next camp is ready and waiting by the time the trekkers arrive.

From Pahalgam the route crosses a broad alluvial plain to the entrance of the West Lidder valley. The track is broad and easily graded for the benefit of forestry trucks. Himalayan pines crowd the hillsides, broken only where some stream comes tumbling down a rocky nullah. Above the forests the peaks rise to high rocky crests, 4000—4500m (13,000—15,000ft) high.

For four hours the path climbs steadily, rising high above the true left bank of the river which can be glimpsed through the trees, white and tumbling in the valley bottom.

Suddenly, the valley divides. A large nullah leads off the main valley to the east and at the junction of the two streams lies the clustered hamlet of Aru (2414m, 7920ft), with, incon-

Top: **Pahalgam is the starting point for the Lidder Valley Trek.**

Above: **A typical trekking party in the Lidder Valley.**
(Photos: W. Unsworth.)

31

gruously perhaps, a very modern hotel. Half a mile up the nullah, above the hamlet, is a flat *marg* or camping ground, bordered by a clear running stream.

The *marg* at Aru is idyllic. The head of the nullah is blocked by a craggy peak, reminiscent of the Skye Cuillins, but below the campsite the eye travels down and outwards, over the cluster of chalet-like houses, into the deep forested depths of the Lidder and up again to the long mountain ridge up the other side, to Hodasar Bal (4056m, 13,307ft) and half a dozen other peaks of similar height but no names.

In bad weather or late in the season snow dusts the rocky faces of the Lidder mountains, and then the scene becomes strongly reminiscent of Switzerland; Zermatt as it might have been a hundred years ago.

Day 2: Aru to Lidderwat
From Aru a track climbs up a steep bank

above the camp site then makes a more gradual ascent through scattered forest, where the blue pine and silver birch mingle with the Himalayan maple in an ever changing forest pattern. Overhead the lammergeiers spread their enormous wings, tracing slow, graceful circles in the ascending thermals. Late in the season the track is busy with *gujars*, shepherding their flocks down the valley for the winter; plump brown sheep, fattened on the high hill pasture.

For four hours the path climbs steadily up the valley until it comes to a bridge over the river and the rest house at Lidderwat. Beyond the rest house is a *marg* large enough to accommodate a regiment, and conspicuously marked by a huge erratic boulder. It is a magnificent camp site.

Day 3: Lidderwat to Kolahoi Glacier to Lidderwat

At Lidderwat the valley divides again. The main branch runs north-east to Kolahoi, the other turns sharply west towards the lake of Tar Sar. It is feasible to explore both branches, and usual to tackle Kolahoi first.

The camp is left at Lidderwat ready for the return. A track which is fairly rough in places is followed up the true right bank of the river into an increasingly narrow valley. The peaks rear up on either hand and the tree line is soon left behind. As the valley turns to the right the Kolahoi Glacier comes into view. It takes about four hours to reach this point, and the altitude is almost twelve thousand feet so the going can be exhausting. The return journey takes two or three hours, and by the time you return to Lidderwat you will have had a very full day—about 25km (16 miles) at moderately high altitude.

Day 4: Lidderwat to Sekiwas

From Lidderwat next day the trek continues up the western valley, which rises steeply at first and is soon beyond the tree line. The main path continues on the true left hand bank of the stream towards the distant Yemhar Pass (4049m, 13,280ft) and the Sind Valley, but at a distinct bend in the river a minor track crosses to the other bank and climbs steeply towards a group of pointed peaks. These throw down long humpy spines towards the valley, each of which has to be crossed until, almost at the last moment, Tar Sar Lake comes into view (3962m, 12,995ft). The lead coloured water, high and lonely, combines with the rocky peaks around it to give an impressive picture.

By following the outflow from the lake, and contouring across some rough scree slopes it is possible to reach the main stream again and

follow it up to yet another junction known as Sekiwas (3430m, 11,250ft) where there is a good camp site.

Days 5 and 6: Sekiwas to Pahalgam

Compared with the delightful *margs* lower down, Sekiwas is a barren, inhospitable place surrounded by bare, stony hills. There are obvious ways through the hills over high passes, of which the Yemhar is the best known, but it is usual to turn back at Sekiwas and return to Pahalgam. Late in the season the passes may be closed by snow in any case and Sekiwas itself may well prove to be a snow camp.

The retreat is rapid. Down to Aru in one day, then next day on to Pahalgam and back to Srinagar.

Above: **The hamlet of Aru. This is what Zermatt must have been like a hundred years ago.**
(Photo: W.Unsworth.)

Far left, top left: **Late in the season snow can lie on the higher parts of the valley. These trekkers are climbing up towards the mountain lake called Tar Sar.**
(Photo: W.Unsworth.)

Far left, top right: **Walking through the pines towards Kolahoi.**
(Photo: W.Unsworth.)

Far left, bottom: **A shikara on the Dal lake, Srinagar.** (Photo: W.Unsworth.)

Walk 4 FRANCE: Tour de la Vanoise
by Martin Collins

Through the Mountains of France's first National Park

France is wonderful walking country. Its surface is etched with a network of footpaths over all kinds of terrain. The more challenging long-distance trails are prefixed 'GR', short for *Sentiers de Grande Randonnée* and one such, crossing the French Alps from Lake Geneva to the Mediterranean, has become a classic mountain journey. It is known as *La Grande Traversée des Alpes : GR5* and passes through superlative alpine scenery, equalling the best in western Europe. Fifty kilometres (30 miles) south of where the trail skirts Mont Blanc, it reaches an area of quite exceptional beauty—a diamond in a necklace already hung with pearls—the Vanoise.

Easily imagined if not remembered, the Vanoise is an archetypal alpine landscape. Cradled between the upper valleys of the Arc and the Isère, it lies in Savoie, nudging Italy to the east, and provides habitats for an extraordinary diversity of plant and animal life. It is also densely mountainous, with 107 summits over 3000m (9840ft) and La Grande Casse rising to 3852m (12,635ft). There are dazzling peaks and glaciers, meltwater torrents and deep gorges, ski slopes, forests and ancient villages, all connected

Distance: Approx 75 km (46 miles)
Time required: 5 days
Type of Walk: Previous experience of mountain walking and a good level of fitness required
Base: Landry, in the Isère Valley, France.
Start: Landry.
Best Time of Year: July – September (NB: much snow early season).
Maps: I.G.N. Carte Touristique, 1:25000, nos. 235, 236 & 237.
Guidebooks: *Walking the French Alps: GR5* by Martin Collins (Cicerone Press).

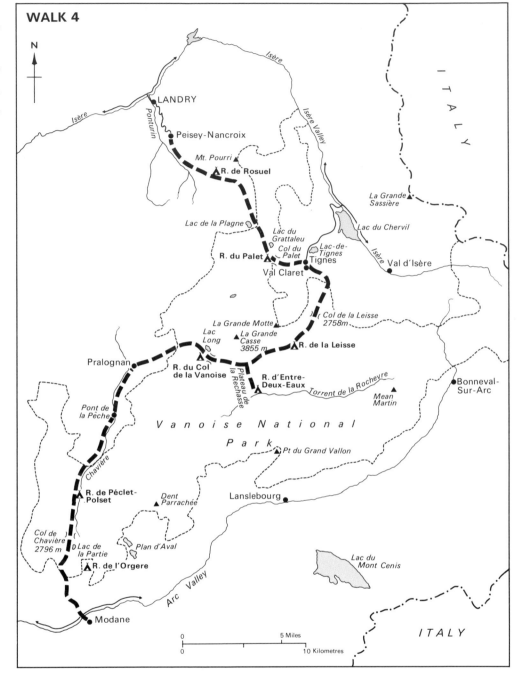

WALK 4

by numerous waymarked paths. It would be quite possible to wander in the Vanoise for weeks and never retrace one's steps, except perhaps to return to a base or a *refuge*. But to taste the real flavour of this fascinating region one should make the high-level crossing, the GR5/55. It is not the easiest *variante,* nor always the most hospitable, requiring previous experience of mountain walking and a good level of fitness. However, it penetrates to the very heart of the Vanoise, to its wildest reaches, its most stunning viewpoints. Depending upon the

weather, the walker's pace and choice of overnight halts, it will take from four to six days.

Day 1: Landry to Refuge du Palet.

The Isère river, our true starting point, flows west towards the mighty Rhône, cheek by jowl with road and railway. To the north lies *Le Versant du Soleil*, 'Hillside of the Sun', a group of communes whose sheltered, south-facing aspect deprives them of long-lying snow for a profitable winter sports industry and whose declining agricultural population has had to diversify to survive. To the south of the Isère, by contrast, we see some of the largest ski centres in the world: long-established meccas like Val d'Isère and new ones like Courchevel's Trois Vallées complex which have the situation, technology and capacity to attract winter visitors by the thousand. The region is also a great producer of hydro-electric power—'white coal'.

The Ponturin torrent rises high in a bowl of mountains to the south-east, its lower valley steep and densely wooded where it joins the Isère. The path up from the old Tarentaise village of Landry cuts off long road dog-legs, climbing in damp, deep shade. It is easy to drive by car or bus up the hairpins of the little D87 and reach the Rosuel *refuge* with barely a sideways glance. But you would miss much.

A short detour left leads to the small town of Peisey-Nancroix and its handsome, slender church. Accustomed to a cosmopolitan and discriminating winter ski trade, it is a more sophisticated place than the summer visitor might expect; and there are exciting views of peaks and high, forested slopes through bunting strung across its narrow streets.

Hereabouts the Ponturin tumbles picturesquely over boulders between pine trees as if posed for a calendar, and the GR5 is never far from its flowery banks. Beyond a good camp site in forest, the path emerges at Les Lanches hamlet in a broad upland basin. Farming here is simple, the technology antique – some hay, a few goats and cows. Signs forbid the unauthorised collection of snails. The little barns and chalets constructed from organic materials seem to have grown from the soil itself, like large cubiform fungi.

You cannot mistake the Refuge de Rosuel. It announces with a flourish the prestigious Parc National de la Vanoise, though the boundary proper is a little way on. The architecture of the *refuge* is a marriage of traditional materials with modern design and its great grassed, wave-shaped roof is an innovative solution to the problem of snow damage: snowslides from the slopes above simply pass over it without resistance.

From here, the Col du Palet is about four hours distant. It is a long, ambling ascent, nowhere especially steep and the popular trail is plainly waymarked. But try to choose good weather: in mist or threatening storm, much of the easy charm of the ascent is lost and there is very little shelter.

The route rises diagonally across stony hillside towards a dramatic narrowing of the valley. Clattering noisily from the ledge of cliffs opposite, down a hundred vertical metres, is the Cascade de la Gurraz, its waters channelled in

an 8km (5mile) underground gallery to the Tignes hydro-electric scheme. When it comes to civil engineering, the French are not known for their timidity!

For a while the GR5 is held between rocky walls before reaching a flatter area where larch makes a meagre stand and the bones of the earth show through thin turf. In the unfolding views ahead, most conspicuous of all will be the snowy dome of La Grande Motte, like a white beacon, as we mount successive levels of altitude towards the Col du Palet.

After passing the smart timber Chalet du Berthoud used by duty wardens, the path approaches a large sign bearing the National Park regulations. At a casual reading they might

The path climbs up the valley of the Leisse past La Grande Motte. (Photo: M.Collins.)

Above: **Tignes-le-Lac, built for skiing, looks incongruous in summer, like a misplaced resort from the Côte d'Azur.**
(Photo: M.Collins.)

Far right: **The descent to Pralognan crosses the shallow Lac des Vaches on a curious causeway.**
(Photo: W.Unsworth.)

ciative and responsible.

Farther on, boulders give way to marshy levels, the vestiges of a lake choked by alluvial deposits. Paths go off left for Mont Pourri (the *refuge* can be discerned high on a ledge of mountainside) and, in a little while, for the Col de Sachette and Tignes. Beyond the Chalets de la Plagne, surrounded by ancient dock-infested enclosures, the trail threads easily up through rock outcrops, revealing ahead and below a deep green lake—the Lac de la Plagne. In fine weather this lofty viewpoint is an exquisite place, suspended between valley and the high tops. Marmots abound on grassy banks, watching us humans with cautious curiosity before giving that piercing, whistle-like warning cry and ducking out of sight. From mid-October to mid-April, when snow cover at this altitude is heavy and persistent, they hibernate in communal burrows as deep as 3m (10ft) and as long as 10m (32ft), living off body fat. In late May or early June, up to six naked, blind young are produced and, thanks to conservation measures, population levels seem quite healthy.

The ruins of Chalet de la Grassaz stand back obscurely beside a huge stone-strewn grassy depression, all that remains of another ancient lake, progressively silted up with material washed down from higher slopes by the action of storm water, frost and melting snow.

Altitude 2335m (7658ft) and the final approaches to the Col du Palet unfold ahead. Depending upon the time of year and the severity of the preceding winter, there will be banks of snow to cross above about 2500m (8200ft). Where drifts have recently melted, the earth, starved of warmth and light, will be lifeless, dark, still spongy with ice-cold water. Yet growing miraculously at the very edge of the receding snow can be found a tiny and unbelievably delicate purple flower—the Alpine Snowbell. And within days, other flowers and grasses will respond to the sun's generous summer heat by bringing colour and life to favoured slopes for a few short weeks.

The gradient becomes steeper, until quite suddenly stony ground gives way to the clear, shallow waters of Lac du Grattaleu. On a fine summer's afternoon, the southbound walker will have passed a steady stream of people descending to cars and accommodation in the Ponturin valley. And when the last *'Bon soir'* has been exchanged, these upper reaches towards the col will seem remote and empty. But the emptiness is illusory for, as often as not, families will still be lingering in the sunshine over a late picnic, having come up the easy way in less than two hours from Tignes-le-Lac. Ten minutes away to the south-east stands the Refuge du

seem restrictive and authoritarian: no dogs allowed (even leashed) and no picking flowers, for example. The twin objectives of the Park's philosophy are to attract tourism and its revenue into the Vanoise and to protect an outstanding natural resource from damage and exploitation. The two are sometimes hard to reconcile and such rules of conduct as are laid down by the Park authorities for visitors, enforced by fines, are simply an acknowledgement that not everyone's response to natural beauty is appre-

Palet, a good place to end the day, lined outside with *randonneurs* catching the last of the sun.

Day 2: Refuge du Palet to Refuge de la Leisse.

The lake's outlet is crossed and a knoll climbed just to the south. Here it is time to pause and take a retrospective look before the Ponturin valley is obscured for good behind rising ground to the north. Over a foreground of old snowfields and barren rock, the route falls away from greys and browns to verdant green, until it disappears into the now distant, diminutive cleft above the Rosuel Refuge.

Trending east, the path reaches the Col du Palet. No graceful saddle this, but a spacious level of white stone at 2652m (8698ft), bearing an inauspicious cairn and pole and some wooden signs. From its broad summit, views are restricted to higher terrain. In the north sprawls the snowy Bellecôte massif and its Matterhorn-like neighbour L'Aiguille d'Aliet, conspicuous since leaving Landry. But there is a richer treat yet in store. As the wide track is followed east off the col, the great massifs of Italy's Gran Paradiso National Park are ranged on the horizon ahead. Although our route soon veers away to the south-west, the borders of the Vanoise and Gran Paradiso are coincident for 7km (4 miles) in the east. Over-hunting of the bouquetin, or mountain ibex, led to the concept of a protected reserve and to the establishment of the Gran Paradiso National Park in 1922. The French were slow to follow. Forty years were to elapse before the Vanoise National Park was inaugurated in July 1963, the first within France. But at last bouquetin, chamois, marmots and many other species could enjoy protected status and flourish.

Beside the descending path are curious snow-filled hollows and in stony crevices, even on the path itself, glow the luminous blue stars of the tiny Spring Gentian. It is as well to savour such jewels. In no time at all, one is on down the track and, at a corner where seconds before knuckles of limestone blocked off the valley view, suddenly it is there : a cityscape, all tower blocks and car parks, ski tows and access roads—Val Claret. And the desecration does not end there : ski lifts radiate across slopes shaved bare and scarred by bulldozed pistes.

Such pronouncements are, of course, somewhat subjective and should skiing be the reader's metier, he will not share the sentiments they embody. However, the walker on GR5 has just experienced what an effective policy of conservation can really achieve. That the trail temporarily leaves the National Park is his misfortune certainly, but he can hardly be blamed for

drawing comparisons. The pity is that ski development and environmental protection are irreconcilably at odds. No doubt Val Claret and nearby Tignes-le-Lac look smart enough under snow, and it would be worse than sour grapes to wish to deny skiers their sport and developers their profit. However, the fragile ecosystems pay a heavy price in erosion and during the summer months the ugly buildings, ski-lift hardware and barren pistes are, at best, a disturbing, unpleasant visual intrusion.

For one reason or another, Tignes-le-Lac may need to be visited, although the route spares us the necessity by striking off right at one teleski and following another, the Grande Balme, down rough ground to a bridge over the Retort stream. Tignes-le-Lac is an extraordinary place in summer, with an echo of the Côte d'Azur in its smart hotels and shops, its bars and casinos, its windsurfing and acres of tennis courts. Perhaps only the mountain walker, for whom the resort is merely an incidental, a comma in a sentence, will fully appreciate the incongruity of its setting. In its defence, it should be said that the lake, an inviting ring of clear, turquoise water, is quite delectable.

Summer skiers take the Grande Motte telecabin lift to permanent snow on the glacier 1000m (3280ft) above. Walkers on GR55 climb east beneath the small Bollins teleski, past the Chalet de la Leisse and up along the northern slopes of the Paquis valley above the Retort stream, which more or less coincides with the Park's boundary. Swinging up past rock outcrops and tiny lakes, the path rises over to the Chalet de Prariond and thence to a path junction. Just beyond the ridge to the east lies one of the skiing world's premier playgrounds above Val d'Isère and it is a simple detour to catch a glimpse from the Col de Fresse.

With civilisation now an hour and a half's hike behind and the National Park re-entered, an impression is increasingly gained of penetrating wild, unsullied mountain country. To the west lies the loftiest terrain in the whole Vanoise and the eastern skyline is monopolised by a long ridge connecting the Pointe du Lavachet, above Tignes, with Pointe de la Sana some 24km (15 miles) south. Dominated by the Grande Motte glacier, the going gets steadily rougher and crosses patches, often larger fields, of late-lying snow. This snow, in common with that on other high sections of the trail, will lie all summer and waymarking takes the form of small cairns instead of the familiar flashes of red and white paint. The trace of footprints will be clear enough in good visibility but cairns need to be carefully watched for in mist.

Col de la Leisse, at 2758m (9046ft), can be reached in two hours from Val Claret; it is another one and a half to the Leisse *refuge*. The descent due south from the col is no less rugged, but below Lac des Nettes there are grassier, more hospitable levels frequented by marmots; the gradient eases and waymarking becomes clearer. Passing round the west shore of Plan des Nettes lake and the little dam at its southern corner, the path zig-zags down to the Refuge de la Leisse (2487m, 8157ft). It is one of a handful of shelters without a resident warden in season, but has basic sleeping and cooking facilities and space for nearly fifty bodies!

Perhaps, here, it is as well to remember that camping is not permitted within the National Park perimeter. Undoubtedly this restriction is designed to avoid problems of litter, hygiene and disturbance of wildlife associated with groups setting up camp for several consecutive days. A discreet and experienced backpacker, or a walker equipped to bivouac, is unlikely to encounter official harassment. Most continental walkers, climbers and skiers use *refuges*—there are thirty or so in the Vanoise. Even though a peaceful night cannot be guaranteed, they do offer secure shelter, and during the busy months of July and August reservations can be made in advance.

Day 3: Refuge de la Leisse to Pralognan-la-Vanoise.

A little below the *refuge,* the Leisse torrent is crossed and its south bank followed in a slow, ninety-degrees arc down the deep 'V' of the Leisse valley. The torrent frequently flows beneath and through sizeable drifts of snow on the valley floor, carving out sinuous hollows and shallow arches. Surroundings are austere, even bleak, soaring cliffs and screes dwarfing the human traveller. But here, too, are marmots and high up amongst the crags and screes on the south-east flanks of La Grande Motte and La Grande Casse it is possible to spot chamois and bouquetin. Both are eminently shy creatures, inhabiting barely accessible terrain above about 3500m (11,500ft). Chamois live in groups of fifteen to thirty individuals, except for the solitary old male, and move with uncanny grace and sure-footedness on the dizziest of slopes. Bouquetin are found throughout the Alps, as well as in mountainous parts of north-east Sudan, eastern Egypt and the Arabian peninsula and are best recognised by their great curved, ridged horns, sometimes exceeding a metre in length. Neither species is usually encountered at close quarters, so an optical aid of some kind greatly increases the chances of observing them on mountainsides where they seem naturally disguised.

Far right: **Near the camp site at Pralognan is the spectacular Cascade de la Fraîche.**
(Photo: W.Unsworth.)

A little distance before the Leisse is re-crossed at the Pont de Croé-Vie, the Vanoise stream, opposite, falls to join it. Together they flow south, past the Entre-Deux-Eaux *refuge,* to meet with the Torrent de la Rocheure. But their aggregated waters no longer roar unfettered down the mighty Doron gorge which they once created. Instead, all but a trickle is diverted to generate electricity, travelling through 15km (9 miles) of underground galleries to Plan d'Aval, the lower of two artificial lakes above Modane.

(During the summer months, a four-wheel-drive passenger shuttle operates between Termignon in the Arc valley and the Entre-Deux-Eaux *refuge,* with obvious advantages for the GR55 walker who needs to reach the valley swiftly.)

The Plateau de la Rechasse falls away abruptly along its eastern edge and it is up the northern end of this steeply rising ground that our route climbs, an uncompromising 300m (984ft) ascent of zig-zags winding through snow-patched rocky bluffs. A memorial is passed to two army officers who died on the mountain, and higher up are the remains of a wartime blockhouse.

It is an uninvitingly gloomy, cellar-like building, pitch dark from a little way in and choked with frozen snow. Conceivably offering shelter, conditions would have to be foul indeed before most would resort to using it. But the ledge it was built upon has far-reaching views. To the south is the broad Plan du Lac shelf and, just visible, the head of the Doron gorge, whilst due east stands the impressive Pointes de Pierre Brunes. Yet the eye is drawn to the north-west, above the curving trench of the Leisse valley, where La Grande Motte, like a friend with a new haircut, momentarily defies recognition. Gone are the familiar ski slopes, that shining white dome of glacier, and in its place rises a squat tower of rock neatly capped with a snow cone. Unseen, unguessed at from the north, a long, graceful ridge wall hangs between La Grande Motte and La Grande Casse.

North-westwards now, GR55 passes close to where the Vanoise stream plunges through the plateau edge then, upstream, crosses it on stones as it flows out from wide, marshy shallows. The stream is meltwater from the icefall of the Rechasse glacier. A narrow neck of crevassed ice between two lines of cliffs on the left is all there is to see from the path. But up and beyond rests a vast weight of ice, held in uneasy suspended animation beneath the releasing influence of a southern European sun. From time to time, ice breaks from the leading edge and tumbles down as far as the lower screes. Even here the ice is unstable, continuing to topple and slide as it slowly melts.

Glacier de la Rechasse, Glacier de l'Arcelin, Glacier de la Roche Ferran, and farther south a dozen more in the Vanoise complex. They still imperceptibly shape the land but are hugely diminished since the times when they carved out whole valley sections. The Isère glacier alone once spread west beyond Chambéry and Grenoble and only began retreating some ten thousand years ago.

In places, the great scree fans and swirling rock buttresses of La Grande Casse almost reach down to the path as it wanders easily on past a rough wooden cross and skirts to the south of Lac du Col de la Vanoise and Lac Rond. Immensely impressive, the two west-facing glaciers of La Grande Casse slide into view: crevassed, contorted confections of white and green ice. Incredibly, winter ski routes descend the nearer Glacier des Grands Couloirs from the summit of La Grande Casse (3855m, 12,644ft) and from Pointe Mathews.

The Refuge du Col de la Vanoise (also known as Félix Faure after a French president) is one of the most popular in the region and during the summer accommodates up to 156 overnight guests, as well as serving meals and drinks (a plate of *frites* is almost *de rigueur!*) The hike up from Pralognan-la-Vanoise is one of *the* great Alpine excursions and on a good summer's day, walkers of every shape, size, age and level of fitness make the three-hour ascent, give or take an hour or two! Perhaps preferring to lie in the sunshine with a cool drink, or clamber around in search of wild flowers and take photographs, most continue no further. So there is a diurnal ebb and flow, a sort of human tide, and by six o'clock the last of the day-walkers are starting down. This is the time to linger if you can; to sit above Lac Long in the spreading silence, watching the brilliant high snows blush to coral-cream then pink in the dying sun. The evening air will be chilly—we are still at 2517m (8255ft)—and shadows lengthening. But even if the *refuge* is not chosen for an overnight halt, Pralognan is a straightforward two-hour descent.

The GR55 takes a well trodden path north-west, an ancient mule track following the glaciated valley of the Grande Casse. First over snow and earthy knolls past Lac Long, then down rough scree in an easy zig-zag, the route drops to a causeway of flat stones across the ankle-deep Lac des Vaches. Rock climbers scale the overlapping slabs on the big north wall of the Aiguille de la Vanoise opposite. A long wedge of bare rock from here, but end-on from just above the Glière forest some 300m (985ft) below, it resembles a slender, tapering blade like a shark's dorsal fin.

An upper stream feeding the Glière torrent is followed down past marmot burrows and soon Pralognan, yet to be glimpsed, can be sensed deep at the foot of the forested slopes ahead. Over the Pont du Chanton and on below is a fine waterfall across the valley, draining the Patinoire glacier and lake as the Vallonet stream. Cattle graze even higher than the Glière chalets and there is the most picturesque stretch of dry-stone-walled lane outside the Yorkshire Dales!

At Pont de la Glière we once again take temporary leave of the National Park—a technicality since we are never more than a few hundred metres outside. Legitimate by the letter, if not the spirit of National Park legislation, a little building development hugs the very perimeter, and it is no surprise after Val Claret to encounter more ski pistes and lift hardware. Ignoring a right fork to Mont Bochor, the trail submerges itself in patchy forest, parallel to the Fontanettes teleski and piste. From here, a stony lane through pretty Les Fontanettes and another woodland path lead straight down to Pralognan-la-Vanoise.

Other than the short detours to Peisey-Nancroix and Tignes-le-Lac, Pralognan is the only town on this high-level traverse. Cosmopolitan but retaining much of its original charm as a mountain village, its streets are busy winter and summer with visitors who come to walk and climb and ski. An open-air market will sell you cooked meats and fruit, bread and woolly socks, soaps and cheeses; or you can sit outside a bar and watch the rucksacked world go by. On a trek through uninhabited country, it is about as nice a place as you could wish to find to indulge yourself in a few of life's little luxuries!

Day 4: Pralognan-la-Vanoise to Refuge de Péclet-Polset.

A sectional profile along the GR55 shows Pralognan and Modane separated by a single, well-defined and considerable apex : the Col de Chavière. At 2796m (9170ft), it has the distinction of being the highest point reached by any waymarked GR path in the whole of France. Whilst the going is mostly without difficulty, snow often obscures the northern approaches and it is a very long day's hike indeed from Pralognan to Modane—some nine or ten hours of actual walking in reasonable conditions. The roadhead at Polset, above Modane, could be reached in eight, or a tent pitch found before that. Another solution is to use the Péclet-Polset *refuge*, four hours up from Pralognan, as a half-way house.

Leaving the town on a lane almost due south, the route enters the Isertan forest just beyond a municipal camp site and turns south-east above the Doron de Chavière. A metalled road runs up the left bank to a car park beyond Les Ruelles,

Top: **The Refuge du Col de la Vanoise nestles below the Grande Casse.** (Photo: M.Collins.)

Above: **The view en route to the Col de Chavière.** (Photo: M.Collins.)

but GR55 chooses to cross the Pont de Gerlon for a quieter walk on the other side, beneath the 1000m (3280ft) high steepnesses of Petit Mont Blanc. It is said that oats are still profitably harvested on this ribbon of arable land. Certainly the meadows are rich with wild flowers; the Vanoise is a botanist's dream, containing over two thousand species from true alpines to lush growth in the peripheral valleys.

Crossing the Chavière torrent for the last time at Pont de la Pêche, a broad rough track climbs south. It is still just low enough for silver birch and willow to grow, though the trees are squat and twisted. Height is gained gradually on a well graded track, curving gently south over tributary streams and past ruined chalets, with occasional glimpses of the grey and distant valley headwall.

At a grassy rise surrounded by Yellow Gentians, the Refuge du Péclet-Polset appears suddenly ahead above a great undercut vault of rock. It stands at 2474m (8114ft) and, like the Félix Faure on the Col de la Vanoise, is well patronised by walkers from Pralognan. In addition to providing eighty beds in season and serving meals and drinks, its popularity owes much to Lac Blanc. Twenty minutes on an easy path north-west leads to the lake, occupying a magnificent alpine setting bounded by cliffs and screes falling east from the twin Aiguilles of Péclet and Polset. Its waters are gathered, principally, from streams and rivulets draining the Glacier de Gebroulaz and contain mineral deposits of subtly beautiful colours.

Day 5: Refuge de Péclet-Polset to Modane.

Although the direct route by-passes the *refuge,* a detour passes round the building, contouring south over stony, snow-patched hillside. The two arms of path reconnect near a large pool where, even in August, snowdrifts may still extend underwater—pale, iridescent, swimming-pool blue.

Tantalisingly concealed until now, the final approaches to the col are revealed at last from a shaly hill: a wide, sloping basin of snow punctuated by dark islands of rock, hemmed in to the west by the screes and buttresses of the Dôme de Polset and to the east by elegant rock faces on the Cime des Planettes. Sketchily waymarked by small cairns and thus not easy to follow in poor visibility, a trodden line meanders ahead, seeking the easiest gradients, the firmest going. If the weather has been warm, this can prove a tiresome stretch, aslither in snow with the consistency of porridge. Within an hour of the *refuge* the gradient steepens, requiring

caution early in the season when this north-facing slope is still substantially snow-covered, and a sharp pull up loose ground leads to the narrow saddle.

Unlike Palet, Leisse and Vanoise, all cols by definition but expansive and indistinct, Chavière is the epitome of this mountain feature—an abrupt, physical divide. Climbing over its crest is to move from one valley system to another, to trade an old panorama for a new one—which is why cols are such exhilarating places, often more pregnant with hidden surprise than the gradually unfolding perspectives en route to a summit.

Col de Chavière is a fitting finale to the Vanoise traverse, with commanding views in all directions—Mont Blanc, the Vanoise glaciers and massifs, Mont Pelvoux, the Ecrins, Mont Thabor, Monte Viso and other, lesser, peaks and ridges. There is an hour's scramble west up to spot-height 2992m (9815ft) for a closer look at the Polset glacier, and for some way to the east the ridge is without difficulty. But the GR55, cairned as before, drops to the right then angles back south-east over shattered rock and more snowfields.

Lac de la Partie in its little *cirque,* visible at first, is lost behind intervening ground and in forty-five minutes a path junction is reached. The left fork takes the walker to the Refuge de l'Orgère and D106 road in just over two hours: less frequented, there is a greater chance of seeing chamois, bouquetin and marmots up towards the Aiguille Doran. The normal route forks right, crosses Le Grand Planay, drops into forest above the St. Bernard stream and converges on a minor road at the hamlet of Polset and the National Park perimeter.

The best now lies behind and what remains of the descent—700m (2295ft), an hour and a half at most—is by mule track and steep, jolting forest zig-zags to urban suburbs at Loutraz. Thus Modane is reached. It sits at 1000m (3280ft) on the frontier with Italy: a somewhat dour, functional sort of town, modestly industrial, and if not endowed with tourist attractions then at least providing shops, services and good international travel links.

Beautiful places the world over pay a high price for their popularity: erosion, pollution, problems of access. As yet, although a fragile and vulnerable enclave, the Vanoise National Park remains largely unscathed. Hopefully, its administrators will continue to resist pressures to develop its abundant natural resources; public opinion is increasingly on their side.

Walk 5: ENGLAND: THE PENNINE WAY
by Walt Unsworth

A Walk Along the Backbone of England

Down the middle of northern England there runs a long range of high moorland. It begins at the Tyne valley, just south of Hadrian's Wall, and continues without a break to the Derbyshire Peak District. These moors are the Pennines, which every schoolboy knows as the 'Backbone of England'—and with some justification, because not only do they occupy a spinal position on the map, but also, during the Industrial Revolution and for some time after, they were the backbone of our manufacturing wealth. Nowadays things have changed: we no longer need the power of the rushing streams, the softness of the acid peat water or the damp, thread-protecting atmosphere which was once so necessary for cotton spinning. Instead, the Pennine Moors have become popular for recreation: a vast playground for cities such as Sheffield and Manchester.

Though the 'Backbone of England' idea is a good aid to memory, it does have its faults. For one thing, it rather gives the impression that the Pennines are a single simple ridge line running from north to south, when in fact they are nothing of the sort. They have been worn away by erosion into separate groups of moors, divided by wide valleys. And they spread themselves, too. Only at the Stainmore Gap are they as narrow as 25km (15 miles); at their widest they are three times this distance. Within

Alston, in the Northern Pennines.
(Photo: W. Unsworth.)

45

Distance: 403 km (252 miles).
Time required: 16 days.
Type of Walk: Tough and challenging.
Best Time of Year: May – September.
Maps: O.S. 1:50,000. Sheets (south to north) 110, 109, 103, 98, 92, 91, 86, 80, 74.
Guidebooks: There are several guidebooks to this popular walk. Recommended are: T. Stephenson, *The Pennine Way* (HMSO). (The 'official' book includes the necessary maps.) C. J. Wright, *A Guide To the Pennine Way* (Constable) (Well illustrated and strong on historical detail.) A. Wainwright, *Pennine Way Companion* (Westmorland Gazette). (Finely detailed maps and diagrams. Unfortunately travels N – S.) Also recommended *Pennine Way Accommodation List*. Obtainable en route.

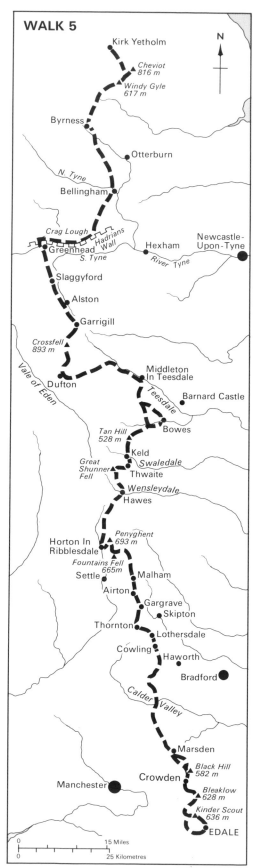

WALK 5

these boundaries the moors frequently rise to over 600m (2000ft) and the highest point is Cross Fell, (895m, 2930ft).

The geological upfold which formed the Pennines consisted of three principal layers. On top came the coal measures, then the millstone grit, and finally the core of limestone. Erosion has removed most of the first layer from the moors and in some places the gritstone has gone too, revealing the limestone. This has a profound effect on the landscape, for where the gritstone remains the moors tend to be barren and windswept, dotted with curiously eroded pinnacles known as tors. Peat hags abound and in early summer white tufts of cotton grass wave in the breeze. The limestone areas, on the other hand, have bright green, springy turf, with impressive crags of white rock. Occasionally there are outcrops of a different kind, like the basalt rocks which form the impressive High Cup Nick. It is these variations in the underlying rock which make the Pennine Way so fascinating, because the scenery changes so dramatically from day to day.

The Pennine Way was the brainchild of a journalist, Tom Stephenson, and was the first official long-distance walk in Britain. It actually took 42 years of negotiation before rights of way could be obtained for the whole of it, but it finally opened in 1965. It is usually walked from south to north, starting at Edale in Derbyshire and finishing at Kirk Yetholm in Scotland—a distance of 400km (250 miles). It actually goes further than its name suggests, beyond the real Pennines, by crossing Hadrian's Wall and entering the Cheviots.

Just because it traverses hills which are lower than most others described in this book, it should not be assumed that the Pennine Way is an easy stroll. The weather on the high moors can be pretty rough, even in summer when most walkers tackle the route. In winter, snow often lies deep and the winds are Arctic in their severity. It is still the toughest long-distance walk in England.

It is also the most popular. Unfortunately, this has led to some erosion of paths, particularly where the Way coincides with other popular access points, such as Edale. The authorities are doing their best to ameliorate wear and tear. Thankfully, at present, deterioration only affects a tiny fraction of the route as a whole.

Accommodation is not always easy to come by on the Pennine Way, especially in the Cheviots. Sometimes it may be necessary to quit the route to find a suitable sleeping place and, of course, such detours add to the distance one has to walk. A string of Youth Hostels serves it best so the description which follows is based on these: sixteen stages with a Youth Hostel at the end of each stage. Other accommodation is not always available if you follow these stages and backpacking might be the ultimate answer. Strong walkers could possibly combine some of the stages, but the going is not always easy, especially if the weather is not at its best.

The walk begins at the charming hamlet of Edale, tucked in a valley below the southern rim of the Kinder Scout plateau, which is the first of the moors to be tackled. It is a curious sort of mountain: a huge table, some 610m (2000ft) high with sharp escarpment edges around which strange black tors of millstone grit give it the appearance of a fortress. On top it is all peat and cotton grass, but the peat has been eroded in a haphazard fashion into long trenches known as *groughs*—some of them ten or fifteen feet deep—which make walking and navigation difficult.

Day 1: Edale to Crowden

The Pennine Way climbs to the plateau by the rocky defile of Grindsbrook and then heads straight across the groughs to meet the Kinder River where it flows between two low rock tors known as Kinder Gates. It is as tough an introduction to a long-distance walk as you are ever likely to meet anywhere—but don't despair, there is nothing else on the Pennine Way quite so frustrating as the groughs of Kinder and Bleaklow.

Unless you know Kinder Scout (and perhaps even if you do), you will need to use your compass to hit off the Kinder Gates, for there's little in the way of paths to help you. In bad weather the crossing can be traumatic; dangerous for the inexperienced. Exposure victims are quite common on these High Peak moors, even in summer.

There is, however, an alternative start which is longer but safer, and that is to follow good paths to the head of the Edale valley, climbing the steep zig-zags known as Jacob's Ladder to reach a moorland saddle called Edale Cross. From here a good track leads around the rim of the plateau to meet the original route at Kinder Downfall. This variant has the advantage of better views (there are none to speak of on the plateau) and straightforward walking but it does avoid the *groughs* and that is really what Kinder is all about!

Kinder Downfall is one of the scenic delights of the Pennine Way. The shallow Kinder River flows over the edge of a 30m (100ft) high crag into a rocky cwm—or at least, it tries to do so, for the rocks often funnel the wind towards the waterfall where the volume of water is so slight it is blown straight up into the air in a spectacular spume. If you have the good fortune to pass by on such a day you will see a sight that remains with you for the rest of your life.

From the Downfall the next objective is to cross the summit of the Snake Pass, a major road between Glossop and Sheffield which is frequently snowbound in a hard winter. Beyond lies Bleaklow, in the opinion of many the finest of the High Peak moors. Unlike Kinder it does have very distinctive summits and it is worth turning aside from the route to climb Higher Shelf Stones (620m, 2039ft) for the view it

Strong winds blow back the water from Kinder Downfall in a spume which can be seen for miles.
(Photo: M.R.Teal.)

Kinder Scout – the first great plateau crossed by the Pennine Way. (Photo: W. Unsworth.)

Day 2: Crowden to Marsden

The next two stages of the walk, though still across high gritstone moors, are not as strenuous or as spectacular as the first day. The route travels up the wide valley of the Crowden Great Brook passing the black pinnacles of Laddow Rocks, one of the earliest practice crags for rock climbers. From there it climbs Black Hill (580m, 1908ft), suitably named from the acres of bare peat which make up the top. The A635 is crossed and then more barren and boggy wastelands to Stand Edge, though it is much easier to follow the alternative route down the valley of Wessenden, with its reservoirs. This is not only more attractive than the original but leads straight down into the old mill village of Marsden, and a bed for the night.

Day 3: Marsden to Mankinholes

It seems as if there is no end to the bleak horizons when you continue on the following day. Rolling wastelands dotted with reservoirs, the hint of a distant village, the occasional road to cross—all austere browns, greens and greys. A special bridge, built for the Pennine Way, arches spectacularly over the M62 Trans-Pennine motorway and, by contrast, further on there is a Roman road at Blackstone Edge, demonstrating vividly how important this place has been as a crossing of the Pennines from the earliest times. Whether in fact the road really was built by the Romans is rather doubtful, but it is well preserved and worth seeing.

From the White House onwards towards Mankinholes the way follows the edge of two deep valleys; the Roch, which flows westwards to the Irish Sea and then the Calder which flows eastwards to the North Sea. The heads of the two valleys are separated by a ridge known as Summit; so named by the navvies who first pushed a canal through it in 1804, to connect Lancashire with Yorkshire. The vast reservoirs which the path skirts were originally built to feed the canal—each boat passing through the Summit locks required 742,500 litres (165,000 gallons) of water, and there were 50 boats a day in the canal's prime.

The bird's eye view down into these valleys, though industrial, is really quite spectacular. The walking is very easy—the easiest you'll come across on the whole route, in fact—because the path is man-made to service the reservoirs. Only beyond the Warland Drain does it revert to a natural moorland track again, with the curious needle-like monument of Stoodley Pike like a signpost on the horizon. At Withins Gate there is a flagged path known as the Long Stoup leading off the moor down to the charming little hamlet of Mankinholes which

affords. The diversion only takes minutes and then it is a mile or so to the twin summits of Bleaklow proper (628m, 2060ft).

The groughs on Bleaklow are, if anything, worse than those on Kinder. Fortunately the Pennine Way avoids them for the most part by following a good track by the side of Torside Clough, an attractive little valley cutting into the moor from Longdendale.

Longdendale itself is far from attractive, but how could it be when it is one of the major cross-Pennine arteries? Road, rail, power—all pass this way between the two Roses, crammed into a fairly narrow valley, most of which is occupied by a string of reservoirs! Nevertheless, this is the end of the first stage of the Pennine Way, at Crowden Youth Hostel.

rests on a shelf above the deeper Vale of Calder. The path was built to provide employment during the Cotton Famine of the last century; for a hundred years it led nowhere. Now it leads Pennine wayfarers to a bed for the night!

Day 4: Mankinholes to Earby

I have always thought it regrettable that the next stage of the Pennine Way chooses to remain on the high moors instead of following the delightfully wooded valley of the Hebden Water. It misses so much of interest, including Hebden Bridge itself and particularly Heptonstall, which is one of the finest gritstone villages. But the Way keeps to the moors and beyond the reservoirs in Walshaw Dean it climbs over Withins Height to descend to the Ponden Reservoir. On the way down it passes Top Withins, the site of Emily Brontë's *Wuthering Heights,* now alas a sad ruin.

Haworth, the home town of the Brontë family, is close at hand and although it is only a dozen miles or so from Mankinholes, you might think it worth while to break your journey here. This would give you an opportunity to look at Heptonstall en route and, of course, Haworth itself with its Brontë museum and the famous Worth Valley Railway, where the film *The Railway Children* was made. Such diversions add another day to the journey—unless you are prepared to run two other stages into one!

Grim purists will doubtless treat these suggestions with disdain! Not for them momentary relief from the windswept moors, but relentlessly on over Ickornshaw Moor to Cowling and then to the delightful Lothersdale, a tiny idyll of a mill hamlet set in a secluded valley. Anyone who thinks that all mill villages are rather sombre places, will be pleasantly surprised by Lothersdale, with its trim little cottages and bright flowers.

The day ends at Earby Youth hostel, and a long day it has been unless you've taken a break at Haworth. More than that though, it sees the end of one distinctive section of the Pennine Way. Changes lie ahead: limestone is about to make its presence felt.

Days 5-8: Earby to Keld

It is pleasant, easy walking to Malham next day. Chief interest lies at the end of the journey where time out should be taken to see Gordale

Below left: **The famous Roman Road at Blackstone Edge is crossed on the third day of the walk.**

Below right: **Stoodley Pike stands on the moors above the Calder Valley and was built to commemorate the end of the Napoleonic Wars.**
(Photos: W.Unsworth.)

Scar and scramble into its inner recesses. It is one of the finest limestone gorges in Britain, with huge impending walls. The best known showplace of the area—Malham Cove—can be left to the next day because the Pennine Way goes past the Cove to Malham Tarn. The Cove, with its huge, sweeping, limestone walls, is indeed a magnificent sight.

The walking is now much easier than it was over the peat hags of the southern moors and the scenery more pastoral. There are trees, limestone outcrops and half hidden valleys. The climb up Fountains Fell (665m, 2191ft) is not too arduous and the summit gives marvellous views, including one of the next objectives, Penyghent (692m, 2273ft). The steep left-hand ridge, which has to be climbed, looks quite formidable, but it isn't difficult at all and this fine little mountain is one of the best on the tour. Across the Ribble Valley can be seen the two companion summits which make up the celebrated Yorkshire Three Peaks Walk—Ingleborough (723m, 2372ft) and Whernside (737m, 2419ft). Unfortunately, the Pennine Way veers away from these mountains to cross the Dodd Fell moors to Hawes in Wensleydale.

Hardraw Force is worth a slight diversion early next day. It is a spectacular waterfall, 30m (98ft) high, set in a little glen behind the Green Dragon Inn. The water has worn away some of the rock beneath the lip of the falls so that it drops completely free. With a little bit of balance it is possible to cross the rock ledge *behind* the pouring water!

Soon after Hardraw the climb begins up great Shunner Fell (713m, 2340ft): a steep pull up on a track which has been badly eroded, but the descent to Thwaite in Swaledale is easy enough and it is only a little further to Keld, the end of yet another day.

Day 9: Keld to Baldersdale

Opinions vary as to which is the most desolate section of the Pennine Way, but for my money the wild moors between Swaledale and Teesdale take some beating. True, there are a couple of roads and the walking is not as arduous as in the High Peak but the landscape is so bleak as to be almost unbelievable. In the middle of this desert, incredible though it may seem, there is a pub, the Tan Hill Inn, built for the miners who once worked the shallow seams of coal in the vicinity. It is probably the loneliest, and certainly the highest (528m, 1732ft) pub in the country.

The lonely 22km (15 miles) across these moors are dangerous in bad weather. Because of this there is a longer but lower alternative through the village of Bowes, famous as the scene of the notorious Dotheboy's Hall in *Nicholas Nickleby*. The building was up for sale the last time I passed through, so if you are thinking of starting a private school, with an established reputation . . .?

This tough day ends in Baldersdale and the next day could not be a greater contrast—an amble along the banks of the River Tees, past

the roaring falls of High Force to the Youth Hostel or inn at Langdon Beck. Perhaps more than any other stage of the walk Teesdale emphasises one of the charms of the Pennine Way: the continual contrast between high moor and deep valley, arid gritstone and lush limestone country.

Days 10 and 11 Baldersdale to Dufton

Leaving Teesdale the route, which has been travelling steadily north and slightly east, now switches abruptly westwards in one of the finest moorland crossings in the country. It follows the river into the narrow valley dominated by the black crags of Cronkley Scar and climbs up to the waterfall of Caldron Snout—a tumbling cascade some 60m (200ft) high, above which there is the dam of the Cow Green Reservoir. It is only a matter of minutes to scramble up by the falls to look at the vast reservoir. It was opened in 1971, after bitter disputes with conservationists about the unique flora which made its home in the valley, and nowhere else in Britain. Fortunately, many of the plants were removed to above flood level where they seem to thrive

Above: **Hardraw Force has a free fall of almost 30 m and a ledge can be followed behind the water.**

Far left, top left: **Malham Cove, an awe-inspiring limestone cliff.**

Far left, top right: **Walkers tackle Gordale Scar, an impressive gorge near Malham.**

Far left, bottom: **The Parsonage at Haworth, the home of the Brontë sisters, is now a museum.**

(All photos: W.Unsworth.)

Penyghent is one of Yorkshire's
Three Peaks (the only one crossed
by the Pennine Way) which climbs
the steep nose on the left. In the
foreground can be seen typical
limestone clints and grikes.
(Photo: W.R.Mitchell.)

well enough.

High fells rise on either hand as you meet the
Maize Beck, a large tributary of the Tees. You
seem to be walking towards the edge of the
world, for the valley ends in a sharp horizon
with nothing but blue sky above. Then, quite
suddenly, you come upon an amazing sight. You
are standing on the lip of a huge rocky
amphitheatre. The rock is basalt, columned into
towers and gullies, below which fans of black
scree run to the valley floor. It is known as High
Cup Nick, and is unquestionably one of the
scenic highlights of the Pennine Way.

The path down to Dufton is easy to follow.
Below lies the attractive Vale of Eden and on the
horizon, the blue hills of the Lake District.

Days 12 to 15: Dufton to Byrness

Next day, the climb is a long hard slog to the
Dufton Fells to meet the ridge line. Follow it
over a series of distinctive summits, Great Dun
Fell (847m, 2780ft), Little Dun Fell (841m,
2761ft) and finally, Cross Fell (893m, 2930ft).
The going is steady, if a little boggy at times, but
the panorama west over the Vale of Eden to
Lakeland, is superb. Cross Fell is really quite a

goal—it is the highest point on the whole walk,
and the highest summit in the Pennines.

From Cross Fell the route goes down across
moorland to the hamlet of Garrigill and the little
town of Alston, the highest market town in
England. Next day the walk follows the valley of
the South Tyne to Greenhead and the Roman
Wall.

The Roman Wall, or Hadrian's Wall, is one of
the largest and finest Roman monuments in
existence. It runs across England for 117km
(73.5 miles) from Wallsend on Tyne to Bowness-
on-Solway, though it is no longer continuous
because over the centuries its stone has been
used by other builders. The best part is traversed
by the Pennine Way for 14km (9 miles) from
Thirlwall Castle (itself built by medieval masons
with stones taken from the wall) to the great
Roman fort at Housesteads. It follows the
escarpment edge of the Whin Sill, a row of
basaltic crags which dominate the landscape. It
is easy to appreciate how the Whin Sill added to
the defensive possibilities of the wall. What
remains of the wall itself, though considerable, is
merely a shadow of its former glory. In Roman
times it was 6m (20ft) high to the parapet but

nowadays is only 2m (6–8ft), even in the best preserved parts.

Nevertheless, the walk is a rare combination of historical interest and beauty. To the north, dark forests blanket the skyline and small lakes, or loughs, sparkle in the sunshine. At Crag Lough, basaltic columns seem to rise from the water's edge, and the crag which once kept the wild northern tribes at bay now provides a playground for rock climbers.

The Pennine Way actually leaves the Wall a mile before Housesteads fort but the diversion is worthwhile because Housesteads is the best preserved of the forts and a site of great interest. Imagination stirs at Housesteads: what a bleak posting this must have been for a legionary—the Falkland Islands of the Roman Empire!

A walker who is particularly interested in the Roman Wall has got a logistics problem. The Wall and Housesteads can take up so much time that he might find it difficult to complete the day's walk of 32km (20 miles) from Thirlwall to Bellingham. Near the Wall itself there is a Youth Hostel at Once Brewed and an inn at Twice Brewed—delightfully evocative names!—but of course, it means adding another day to the itinerary.

After Housesteads, the Pennine Way trails northwards through the edge of the vast plantations of the Forestry Commission before entering the little town of Bellingham, set in a lovely valley. Forest walking is a novelty on this route so far, but the forests of conifers hereabouts are the largest in Britain and there's a lot more of it next day on the long walk to Byrness—a hamlet which owes its existence entirely to the Forestry Commission. Some people enjoy forest trails, but I'm not one of them. I've walked in the rain forests of East Africa and the jungle of the upper Amazon, and not really enjoyed either. Far too claustrophobic. At least in the Byrness forests you are not likely to be attacked by a wild animal or bitten by a snake!

Day 16: Byrness to Kirk Yetholm

Thankfully, the conifers are left behind shortly after leaving Byrness on what is the last stage of the Pennine Way. The walk ends on a high note—quite literally, for it traverses the splendidly wild hills of the Cheviots along a distinctive ridge line that ultimately leads to the summit of the Cheviot itself, at 815m (2676ft). Along the ridge, Windy Gyle (620m, 2036ft) is the best summit with superb views over the tumbled hills. The Cheviot itself is a disappointment: a boggy plateau best described as an elevated quagmire.

The Cheviot is out on a limb from the ridge so it involves a diversion of two miles there and back. Auchope Cairn (726m, 2382ft) is the next big hill, offering wide views to the north, but after that the path has only one more hill to traverse before it descends to the Halterburn and journey's end at Kirk Yetholm.

This last day is tough and inescapable—43km (27 miles) over some of the wildest Border country. You might even be too tired to celebrate!

On the moors above Teesdale the Pennine Way crosses the Maize Beck by this bridge. Here the beck is a meandering stream but often it is a raging torrent.
(Photo: G.V.Berry.)

Walk 6 GREECE: A Traverse of the Pindos Mountains by John Hunt (Lord Hunt of Llanfairwaterdine)

The First Crossing of Remotest Greece

The Pindos range has been well described as the back-bone of Greece; a continuous block of limestone mountains running the entire length of the Hellenic peninsular between the Gulf of Corinth in the South and the Albanian frontier in the North. Indeed, the range extends far beyond that point, forming another border between Albania and Yugoslavia.

In Greece, no mountain rises to 3000m (9800ft)—not even Olympus—but in the Pindos there are many peaks well over 2000m (6500ft). Parnassus (2547m, 8354ft), famous in Greek mythology, stands at the extreme south-eastern end of the chain, where it compels the eye of the traveller as he makes his way towards Athens along the northern shore of the Peloponnese.

Many parts of the Pindos are—or were when my group made the first traverse more than twenty years ago—known only to the mountain peasants who live in very simple conditions in remote hamlets, and eke out a living at the level of bare subsistence from the rocky land. Much will have changed since 1963, but even today I fancy that the Pindos retains its allure, as do all rugged landscapes; not least among its attractions is the opportunity to meet with people as yet untainted by 'civilization'.

The Greek mountaineers are a hardy race. Their menfolk still display those warrior-qualities which were so necessary to protect their homes and families during the long and troubled years of their country's history. Nowadays their more peaceful occupation remains, as it has since time immemorial, as that of shepherds and wood-cutters and tillers of the soil; their relaxation is taken outside the village *kafeneion*, talking politics over a glass of retzina or ouzo.

The women are no less stoical and perhaps more hard-working: sowing, hoeing and helping to harvest the crops; spinning the yarn and weaving the cloth for the family; cooking the meals and—not least—rearing the children of future patriots. For all that, the mountain people are a happy folk, who enjoy the festive occasions provided by the orthodox church. At such times the men put on the short Evzone tunics and long white stockings and the women bring out from the family wardrobe their wonderful and colourful embroidered costumes which are traditionally different in every village. We chanced to arrive in Metsovon at Easter-tide, long before it became a much favoured tourist attraction and a winter ski resort; we were the only visitors. The local people, gathered for the celebrations from far and wide, took us to their hearts; we shared the Pascal lamb, roasted on spits beside the road, cracked the coloured eggs and danced with them in wide circles upon the village green to the accompaniment of the zither.

I first became acquainted with the mountains of Greece towards the end of the war, when I was able to train my soldiers in mountain and snow warfare on the heights of Olympus and in the Vermion mountains. From the summits of Skala and Skolion, the long line of the Pindos, a ribbon of continuous snow, was clearly seen in springtime. Even in 1945 I entertained thoughts of travelling the whole length of those mountains. In 1961, during a British Council lecture tour in Greece, I made plans to realize this dream in discussions with members of the Hellenic Alpine Club. I was assured that no such integral journey had ever been undertaken; so the traverse in 1963 was probably a 'First'.

In the event it became a truly British-Hellenic expedition, consisting of British and Greek climbers, soldiers of the Greek Special Services Brigade and a large group of young people from both our countries. The general intention was to travel through and over the mountains by different, parallel routes, meeting at intervals to be replenished with supplies at agreed points accessible by road from the plains to the East.

Owing to limitations imposed by work and for other reasons, we had no choice but to undertake the journey during the first three weeks in April and had perforce to complete the whole distance within three weeks. After an exceptionally severe and prolonged winter, the

Ancient villages inhabit the Pindos – this is Papingo.
(Photo: Exodus Expeditions.)

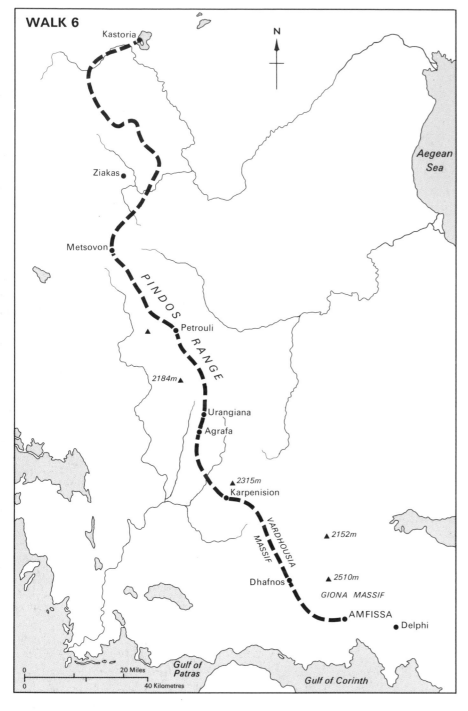

WALK 6

Kastoria

Aegean Sea

Ziakas

Metsovon

PINDOS RANGE

Petrouli

2184m

Urangiana

Agrafa

2315m
Karpenision

2152m

VARDHOUSIA MASSIF

2510m

Dhafnos

GIONA MASSIF

AMFISSA

Delphi

0   20 Miles

0   40 Kilometres

Gulf of Patras

Gulf of Corinth

Distance: Approx 270km (170 miles).
Time required: 15 days.
Type of Walk: Rugged. Good navigational skills and previous mountain experience recommended.
Start: Lidhorokion.
Best Time of Year: Early or late summer.
Maps: Those on the scale 1:50,000 are produced by the Army Cartography Service but are restricted. Commercial maps are on the scale 1:200,000 and are not therefore satisfactory for walking.
Guidebooks: *The Mountains of Greece* by T. Salmon (Cicerone Press).

mountains were deeply snow-covered above 1200m (4000ft) and the weather was atrocious for long spells: we had to wade, sometimes thigh-deep, in wet, soft snow for long periods in mist, rain, snowfall and strong winds. It was, in fact, a most arduous journey. In summer and autumn the conditions would be far less adverse.

There is doubtless a considerable choice of routes, especially when it is possible to find and follow tracks uncovered by the snow. For some, a traverse of most—or perhaps all—the high summits would present a splendid challenge; for others like ourselves, whether by inclination or because of the obstacles of wind and weather, a journey through rather than over the tops may have a greater appeal. In fact we enjoyed—or endured—both experiences in some degree. There are many tracks (some of which will have been converted into roads) and the hamlets (largely deserted in winter), are occupied for summer grazing and cultivation. So with a knowledge of Greek it is possible to ask the way; and also, as we did on one occasion, to obtain the services of a villager as a guide. But good navigation and a general competence in mountain travel are pre-requisites. The maps are misleading in places and not easy to read. As for distances, we estimated the journey from Amfissa to Kastoria to be at least 320km (200 miles), but such a measurement can only be approximate in mountainous terrain; it was probably more. We completed the journey, as a group, in nineteen days, but no single group within the total membership of the expedition covered the whole distance.

Apart from eggs and fresh vegetables, portable food can be obtained only at a few places such as Karpenesion, Agrafa and Metsovon, so load-carrying can present a problem. As for accommodation, we found overnight shelter on the floors of many schools along our way and occasionally we were offered the luxury of a house put at our disposal by generous local people. Water is no problem, save that the rivers and torrents, swollen in springtime, can present serious and dangerous obstacles.

I have divided the description of the journey into three main stages, based on our own experience.

Stage 1: Lidhorokion to Karpenesion

We started our journey at a river junction about 5km (3 miles) west of the village of Lidhorokion by following a river (unnamed on the map) north-westwards to a confluence of two valleys. Here we begin to make height by climbing the spur dividing them, attaining a ridge which led us over the summits of Makria Rakhi at 1176m (3857ft) and Ayios Pandeleimon at 1360m (4460ft). Our route was through a fir forest and gave us magnificent views of the Vardhousia massif towering above us, to the east. We descended along a good track— probably now a road—to the village of Dhafnos, a cluster of attractive houses, two-storied with stone roofs and wooden verandahs. The place was almost deserted at that time of year, but we received a warm welcome from the local schoolmaster and children brought us firewood and handfuls of eggs. We had travelled about 17km (11 miles) on that first day.

We continued on the following two days through the hamlets of Dhikhokhorion and Artotina and following a valley northwards, its river yellow with the bauxite soil over which we had travelled, we began climbing steeply to Grammeni Oxia, leaving the valley at the point where it is joined by the clear waters of a stream running from the limestone massif of Vardhousia. A short descent to the east of the village and a climb of about 300m (1000ft) led to a col. The highlight of that day was the traverse of a splendid ridge northwards during which, in a clear spell of weather, our spirits were cheered as we traversed the summits of Safaka Tambouria (1770m, 5805ft) and Arenda (1280m, 4198ft). We stayed overnight in the village of Stavia where, despite pouring rain, the priest and schoolmaster welcomed us at the end of a street lined with cheering children.

After following a valley downstream for a few kilometres we turned west and crossed a col leading to Gardhiki and onwards, in the same direction, to the villages of Paliokhori and Poungakia. A long pull uphill brought us to the summit of Ayios Konstandinos (1666m, 5464ft) from which, continuing westwards, we crossed a col between the summits of Rakhi and Plati to reach Miriki and another overnight stop. A spur to the north took us onto the summit of Kranies (1085m, 3558ft) and down to the motor road leading to Karpenesion, 2½km (1½ miles) away to the west, and perhaps 144km (90 miles) from our starting point. This first stage of our journey, undertaken for the most part in appalling weather and in deep snow on the high ground, made severe demands on the stamina of the party and some members had, on this account, to miss the next and finest part of the traverse to Metsovon. Route finding above 1200m (4000ft) was made difficult by the absence of tracks and poor visibility.

Stage 2: Karpenesion to Metsovon

In order to begin the second stage of about 144km (90 miles), through the highest part of the traverse, we again travelled some miles westwards by road, to the village of Vinion, passing through superb scenery which has justly earned it the title of 'Little Switzerland'. The village stands poised above the precipitous flanks of the Meghdova valley.

From the village, passing beneath the summit of Anemos on its west flank, we reached a col which provided a dramatic view of the Potomos Gavrinitis, some 700m (2300ft) below. A track descended north-eastwards and then swung to the north, still above the magnificent gorge on its eastern flank. A mile further on we had a choice of routes: to head for Marathos passing under the summit of Ouranos; or to follow the river to the village of Gavrina and continue along the high ridge of Fidhsakala northwards. With the latter alternative in view we spent the night in a small hamlet about one mile south of Gavrina. But local people advised us against the ridge route in the heavily snowed-up conditions, so we decided to regain the track to Marathos next day; it proved to be a most exacting undertaking.

Walking through an ancient land – an amphitheatre at Dodona.
(Photo: Exodus Expeditions.)

57

along the summit ridge until we found a gully which led us off that mountain on its western flank, where we were able to traverse across snow slopes and strike the track from the col, leading to the village.

Marathos is situated on a knoll above a confluence of rivers. Its eighth-century church contains some fine murals, which had been sadly defaced by Partisans during the war.

From Marathos we crossed a river to the north and climbed the slopes of Kaftra (1508m, 4946ft). We skirted beneath its summit to the east and arrived at a delightful herdsmen's hamlet, Paramerita, with wooden slatted huts. Descending to the river below (north) we climbed steeply to the little mountain township of Agrafa. We had travelled about 14km (9 miles) from Gavrina, climbed about 2300m (7,500ft) and descended about 800m (2600ft). In the conditions of that early April, it had been another strenuous day.

From the town we climbed another 300m (1000ft) or so northwards before traversing round a spur, heading first westwards and then north beneath the summit of Koukoventzas. There we plunged down some 300m (1000ft) to the Potomos Agrafiotis, following a spur which led us into the gorge. We followed the stream upwards, through impressive scenery, until it was possible to cross the turbulent river by an attractive stone bridge. A track led us onwards to Vrangiana.

A steep climb eastwards from the village leads to a col on which stands a shrine to Ayios Nikolas. To our astonishment, an old woman, clad in black and shouldering a heavy burden, passed us at this point as she plodded through the deep snow, unescorted, in the opposite direction. We descended northwards, crossed a valley and traversed towards the grazing alp of Elatos passing beneath the summit of Bourlerou. Down to Karitsa to conclude another demanding day, we met four stoical women from the village on their way to Bezoula, some 64km (40 miles) distant to the east, to fetch food for their village; the track not yet being passable for mules.

We chose an easier alternative for the following two days, in view of the difficulties we had encountered since leaving Karpenesion. Our route led us beneath Point 1254m (4113ft) into an undulating valley basin surrounded by high hills. Here were populated villages, country roads and cultivation. It was a softer, more relaxed landscape, in which we travelled northwards for several miles, crossing shallow valleys and through a number of villages, including Neo Khorian, Bezoula and Kerasia, before approaching the steeper mountains again. At Radhi we

Above: **The Vikos Gorge.**
(Photo: Exodus Expeditions.)

Far right, top: **On the ridge between Neraida and Metsovon.** (Photo: Andy Hosking.)

Far right, bottom: **On the ridge between Ayios Nikolas and Petrouli.** (Photo: Andy Hosking.)

We ascended by a steep gully to the west and continued with difficulty up wooded and snow-covered slopes, intending to reach a col to the north of Ouranos. Instead, in thick weather, we were forced to climb to its summit. Unable to descend directly to the col, we turned south

In the Aoos Gorge.
(Photo: Exodus Expeditions.)

received an especially warm welcome. We had travelled about 19km (12 miles) from Karitsa.

There was more easy walking through open country and the hamlets of Kiana and Dhodhapostoloi on the Potomos Patnisos, until we reached the head of that valley, climbed up a ridge and descended to the upper waters of the Paliopotomo. Passing through Rakhovoni we arrived at Zioli, another of our overnight stops. We were returning to the main line of the traverse, through two more villages, Xilokhori and Tirna, from where a track leads off to the north-west, climbing to a col between the summits of Kourouna and Manina. It leads down to the village of Petrouli on the Remma Petrouliotiko; the village is connected by a road to Kalabaka, a town on the fringe of the mountains and some 64km (20 miles) downstream.

From Petrouli we travelled westwards to the larger village of Neraidhokhori. Traversing across the lower, southern slopes of Paliomandri (1519m, 4982ft) and along the northern flank of the river Kamnaitikos, we arrived at Pirra for the night. We had travelled about 17km (11 miles) from Zioli.

A climb of about 800m (2600ft) from the village brought us to a high ridge at about 1900m (6200ft) just south of the summit of Sioula. We followed it northwards, plodding through deep snow in which we sank to our thighs, and over Paliosprag 1910m (6264ft). A wild panorama of snow-covered mountains

surrounded us on all sides. The only tracks were those of bears: they were a source of some excitement at the time. I have cause to be grateful to those bears for providing irrefutable evidence that the fabulous Yetı is not a bear!

We descended towards the north into the gorge of the Goutza Remma, steep and difficult to negotiate, especially in the prevailing conditions. Passing some houses at Konakia we arrived at Krania, a summer holiday resort, with a number of private chalets, looking singularly out of place in mid-April.

A road leads onwards to Stefani along the Remma Skilinastotiko. The village lies about 200m (650ft) above the head of this valley, at the junction of the river with that of the Remma Velitsenes, where we camped after walking about 22km (14 miles) since leaving Pirra.

Instead of climbing up to Stefani (but after taking the precaution of sending one of our members of the Special Services Brigade to the village to enquire about reputed war-time mines in the area), we made an improvised bridge of logs and climbed steeply up a hillside which, in April, was covered with wild pear trees in blossom and carpeted with primroses, cowslips, violets, blue scyllas, mauve and yellow crocuses and yellow daisies. This route leads the traveller to the ridge of Mesovouni, covered by deciduous forest; it involves a climb of about a mile from the river.

A ridge leads northwards to the summit of Tsouma Loupou (1735m, 5690ft). We descended its north-east ridge and climbed in succession Khioli East Peak (1799m, 5900ft) and its West Peak (1855m, 6084ft). We endured this section of the route in deep snow, minimum visibility and a Force 7 gale; bear tracks were our only source of comfort in this area.

So, thankfully down hill to the Remma Raltas flowing northwards to the large village of Malakasi. We followed this gorge with some difficulty (owing to the vertical limestone cliffs), downstream to a pleasant glade, amid giant pine trees. After fording the swollen waters on a number of occasions, we finally camped in this idyllic spot. Although we had only travelled some 11km (7 miles) since leaving Stefani, and despite the dreadful weather, my diary records: 'This has been a fabulous day'.

At first we found no tracks in the gorge until, forcing our way downstream, we came across one eventually. From that point we climbed about 600m (2000ft) in a north-westerly direction and then took a traversing line towards the north-west, across the spurs of Makrivouni (1726m, 5661ft) and Gö-zel-tepe (1872m, 6140ft), a name probably originating from the 400 years of Turkish occupation. We went further to a col, which is immediately to the south of Point 1501m (4923ft). There is a splendid and welcome view of Metsovon from this point. So onwards to that destination. From our bivouac in the Remma Raltas we had travelled a further 14km (9 miles) or so. The total distance since leaving Karpenesion was probably in the order of 144–160km (90–100 miles).

Stage 3: Metsovon to Kastoria

For some who decide to make the Pindos traverse, the obvious line to follow during the last stage of the journey would be that which I had planned for ourselves: namely over the highest ground through Vovousa and Dhistraton, over the summit of Smolikas (2637m, 8649ft) and possibly through the village of Aetomilitsa. From there it would be necessary to swing eastwards only a few miles short of the Albanian frontier. This would be possible only when the heights are snow-free; for ourselves, time and circumstances ruled it out.

My group stayed on the highest ground as far as the village of Ziakas so I will describe that journey in general terms. It proved to be the most remote and wild country we had encountered throughout the Pindos traverse: we passed through no villages and met not a soul during three of the four days of our journey.

Leaving the road north of Metsovon we travelled over continuously high, open uplands, traversing the summits of Katara, (1689m, 5539ft), Tasoumes Arvaniti, Koridi (1929m, 6327ft) and Mavrouni (2054m, 6737ft) the highest point attained during the whole journey. Bear tracks abounded, Golden Eagles and Griffon vultures were sighted and, on our first night we heard the call of a lynx. We spent it in a wild, forested glen, the Valla Kaida, after descending, soaked to the skin from many hours' plodding through deep snow, and restored our spirits in front of a huge blaze of dead tree trunks. That night we laid our sleeping bags on a thick carpet of pine needles, and were soothed to sleep by the roar of the last river we had forded.

The journey onwards led us north-east over Pirostia Babur (1967m, 6451ft) and, on the same compass bearing, along a ridge to Point 1803m (5913ft) until on the third day, after wading a river in dangerous spate by linking arms, we finally reached the escarpment of Orliakas Oros, just north-west of the village of Spiliaon, and climbed to the top of that mountain (1433m, 4700ft). Weary now that we were approaching the end of the long trek, we descended through pine forests to Ziakas.

The welcome we received was as warm as all the previous ones we had enjoyed along our way. It was the more touching for the fact that this was a Communist village, whose menfolk had fought the Germans as E.L.A.S. Partisans during the war. They had twice suffered the consequences by having their homes ransacked by the occupying forces. Some had fled to Bulgaria; others had remained hidden in the caves in the escarpment above the village. At the time of our visit the Greek Government was denying them the much-needed relief supplies because of their political affiliations and their part in the Civil War. The last entry in my diary for that day reads 'This was our last full day and it has been as good as any of the others'.

On our final lap now, we continued the journey eastwards for some miles towards the foothills, to a point where a motor road was reached leading to Kastoria. Here our support group picked us up to join the remainder of the party.

Kastoria made a fitting rendezvous at the end of the long walk. It is a beautifully situated town on the shores of its lake, rich in medieval history and boasting 74 eighth-century Byzantine churches; it is famed for its unique industry in making fur coats from scrap material imported from the United States. Here we were fêted by the Mayor and entertained by the Hellenic Alpine Club, before setting off in our minibuses, homeward bound through Yugoslavia.

Although we had not all walked the whole distance, one of our groups had completed this last stage on foot: from Metsovon they had continued their journey through Grevena, Tsotylion and Nestorian choosing a lower route on account of the injuries they had suffered to their feet during the first, gruelling stage of the traverse.

For all of us who experienced it, the first traverse of the Pindos was an unforgettable experience; for the boys it was an epic achievement. I rate the journey as highly as many other long walks which I have undertaken on higher and more prestigious mountains.

Walk 7 PERU: The Cordillera Blanca Trek
by Hamish Brown

View from the Quebrada Santa Cruz before dropping down into the valley. (Photo: H.M.Brown.)

A Trek over the Punta Union

The Cordillera Blanca runs parallel to the Pacific coast and only about 100km (62 miles) inland but is the continental watershed. The range is elongated and narrow, cluttered with majestic 6000m (1829ft) summits. Only in the Himalayas can you find a similar plethora of mighty mountains. Less than a dozen easy passes break through this chain and by combining two of these you can savour one of the world's greatest walks.

The mountains are relatively accessible from the west, for you can be in their midst just half a day's walk from the major road and, though

they are big, snowy mountains, long *quebradas* (deep glacial valleys) lead into them without any need for walkers to cross dangerous glaciers. The eastern side of the watershed is greener and very remote, its waters facing a 2500km (4,000 mile) journey to the sea! Most of the mountain range is part of the Huascarán National Park and visitors are asked to treat it as the treasure it is and respect the landscape. It has not been over-waymarked and indecently promoted, so the feeling of 'wild and wilderness' is real—something ever more rare these days. Tread gently in this 'wonderness'.

Those going into the Cordillera Blanca must register with the park authorities in Huarás or elsewhere. As the first couple of days are likely to be spent in Huarás anyway and knowing how conditions or regulations can change, it is probably easiest to call at the office there. They can help in many ways. Huarás is the only major town, so it is also the place to complete the trek's stocking-up. Some camping gear and equipment can be hired, primus stoves are on sale and fuel for the trip obtainable.

It is advisable to have at least one of the party who can speak Spanish as you may not meet anyone at all who speaks English. Delays in setting off can be expected but it is better to spend the time enjoying the local human contacts rather than raging at frustrations. Time is viewed very differently in the Rio Santa Valley!

Burros (mules) can be hired at set rates to do the load-carrying which makes for much greater enjoyment—and some minor excitements. The *arrieros* (muleteers) will make their own messing and camping arrangements. The use of burros also means that good tinned food, and fresh food, can be carried and the colourful market at Carás is an interesting source of fruit (oranges by the truckload), potatoes and other vegetables.

This circuit is a walk for the fit and acclimatised. It can be breathtaking in the sad context of above-normal risks of altitude sickness and pulmonary oedema and as medical assistance is not available and the remedy of losing altitude quickly is sometimes impossible, it is advisable to spend some time at altitude *before* trekking off (a good time to visit to Machu Picchu, etc). A few days in the Rio Santa Valley also helps (you may need them to organize the trip anyway) and the walking should not be forced. If you have time take two weeks instead of one.

The quality of the path varies considerably and at times may be almost non-existent. Only in the Q. Yanganuco, near the end of the trek, is there a road. Maps are of variable accuracy but basically the route follows major valleys and passes so the risk of being lost is slight, however often one may be temporarily confused. The circuit is described in a clockwise direction but it can be made in the opposite direction with less height to climb though it is not so aesthetically satisfying and burros are not so easily obtained locally at Yungay. Incidentally, the muleteers can help with route detail but you must state the day's objective.

There are few habitations once out of the Rio Santa Valley and the people are poor. Shops are few but hospitality is usually friendly and worth

accepting in order to meet people. It is worth taking lightweight items like packs of biros, sweets, aspirins, etc., to give in exchange in situations where an offer of money might be resented. They may be poor but they are still proud, however hard the times may be. A white 'flag' over a hut implies a place selling booze. At Huaripampa you may find everything from a shelf full of a well-known whisky brand to crates of the urine-coloured 'Inca Cola'—a pleasant change from the ubiquitous coke.

Nights in the Cordillera Blanca can be cold enough for a touch of frost. It becomes dark

Top: **In the Quebrada Santa Cruz we found a rock avalanche by one of the lakes.**

Above: **The fruit and vegetable market, Huarás.**

(Photos: H.M. Brown.)

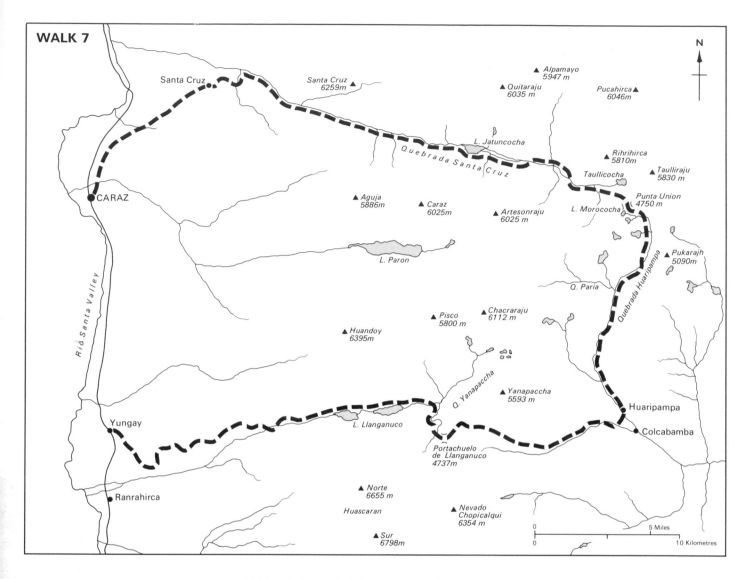

WALK 7

Santa Cruz

Alpamayo
5947 m

Santa Cruz
6259m

Quitaraju
6035 m

Pucahirca
6046m

L. Jatuncocha

Quebrada Santa Cruz

Rihrihirca
5810m

Taullicocha

Taulliraju
5830 m

CARAZ

Aguja
5886m

Caraz
6025m

Artesonraju
6025 m

L. Morococha

Punta Union
4750 m

Pukarajh
5090m

L. Paron

Q. Paria

Quebrada Huaripampa

Rio Santa Valley

Pisco
5800 m

Chacraraju
6112 m

Huandoy
6395m

Q. Yanapaccha

Yanapaccha
5593 m

Huaripampa

Yungay

L. Llanganuco

Colcabamba

Portachuelo
de Llanganuco
4737m

Ranrahirca

Norte
6655 m

Huascaran

Nevado
Chopicalqui
6354 m

Sur
6798m

0   5 Miles

0   10 Kilometres

N

Distance: 100km (62 miles).
Time required: 7 days.
Type of Walk: A walk only for the fit and ac-climatised.
Base: Huarás, 3050m (10,000ft).
Start: Carás (Caraz) 2255m (740ft).
Best Time of Year: Late May – mid-September.
Maps: The best made was the Sneider map of 1939 at 1:200,000 Cordillera Blanca (Peru), Inns-bruck. Worth finding or studying in a library. The kamkarte in Yuraq Janka *(see below)* would do if necessary and various maps are to be found in Lima and Huarás *(see Bartle book below)*. The Bartle book also has a good inset map. Ingemmet in Huarás produce 1:100,000 blueprints: 2 sheets for the C. Blanca.
Guidebooks: *Trails of the Cordilleras Blanca and Huayhuash* by Jim Bartle £4.95 (Cordee books) lists local maps, gives geographical terms and good names in Spanish and covers medical aspects. The definitive book is *Yuraq Janka, Guide to the Peru-vian Andes; Part 1, Cordilleras Blanca and Rosco* by John F. Ricker (Alpine Club of Canada/American Alpine Club). Though mainly for climbers, the photographs in this book make it a treasure.

quickly and day and night are nearly of equal length. A tent large enough for all the party to eat in (and to be sociable at night) is useful, as is a good tilley lamp. Early mornings are usually crisp and clear but clouds may build up and give rain or snow in the afternoon, so early starts pay dividends. Sunsets are often dramatic.

The majority of people fly to Lima to start their journey. It is a huge city with all the useful services and social stresses of any other. It is covered in a strange fog for several months each year, and apart from the museums of Inca treasures it has little to recommend it.

John Hemming's *The Conquest of the Incas* is essential reading before any visit to Peru and it is certainly worth seeing some of the Inca ruins. Machu Picchu should not be missed, because it surpasses all expectations, whilst railway fana-tics will want to make the trip to Huancayo, one of the most remarkable (and highest) journeys in the world. Other interesting travel books about

Peru are Dervla Murphy's *Eight Feet in the Andes* and Christopher Portway's *Journey Along the Spine of the Andes.*

Backpackers normally have no trouble with customs delays and should use all their weight allowance to save time and money in Lima or Huarás. Tents, sleeping bags and mountain clothing should be brought from home.

Trucks, buses and other forms of transport are cheaper but slower than the Peruvian speciality—the *colectivo*—which is a large American car which runs along set routes, or which can be hired in total. Any of these, however, will do the 300-km (187-mile) journey from Lima to Huarás in the day, with an early start. The Pan American highway is followed northwards and then the dry coastal plain is left for the climb into the Andes. The road reaches 4,100m (13,448ft) on the Conoccocha Pass, which gives the first view of the Cordillera Blanca, before plunging down to the Rio Santa

Valley (the Callejón de Huaylas) and Huarás. Huascarán, one of the highest summits in the Americas (6,768m, 22,199ft) looks near, but is still 50km (80 miles) away from Huarás, capital of this remote Province of Ancash. There are still signs of the huge earthquake of 1970 that killed half the population and destroyed ninety per cent of the town. The impact of reaching the Rio Santa Valley is one you will not easily forget. You will have busy days in Huarás, then in Carás, then the magical journey on foot begins. This is what you will remember most, and for ever.

Day 1: Leaving the Rio Santa Valley

The local knowledge of the *arrieros* is useful for navigating the fields and lanes of the valley cultivation. These fall below as the tracks steepen. The road is happily avoided as the burros stick to old paths which also halve the distance. Santa Cruz village, set on a shoulder, gives a welcome lunch break. The direct way up the gorge was abandoned after the 1970 earthquake (now re-opened)—and the alternative, more interesting track zigzags up further south, beside a landslip. After two hours of this a pleasant spot with clear mountain water gives a good camp site, with a view to the sun setting beyond the Cordillera Negra on the other side of the Rio Santa Valley. A truck can reach Santa Cruz but the walk is what you are here for and is helpful in acclimatisation.

Day 2: The Quebrada Santa Cruz

The day starts with another long haul up zig-zags, a landscape with a flora so different from Europe's, but then rewards with a spectacular view along the gun-barrel of the Santa Cruz valley. The path at once zig-zags brutally down to reach the *quebrada,* which is then walked up for the rest of the day. It has a touch of the Conan Doyle 'Lost World', a shut-in atmosphere, with strange plants and birds, and upwards views of mighty snow peaks: the Nevada Santa Cruz to the north, Artesonraju to the south. There are two small lakes and camp can be made either near them or further on (plenty of streams).

Day 3: To the head of the Quebrada Santa Cruz

A memorable day, walking through scrub or open pampas grasslands and dodging occasional marshes and streams to end camping at the head of the valley, a site of unbelievable beauty. On the way Alpamayo, often called 'the most beautiful peak in the world', spires up above a side valley, while Taulliraju closes off the valley head in a jagged crest of fluted snow and rock, Artesonraju rises over granite walls behind the camp and Quitaraju dominates the view back down the Q. Santa Cruz. Each of these peaks is a memorable sight, in circling conjunction they yield a surfeit of the spectacular.

Day 4: The Punta Union, 4750m (15,580ft).

This is an old route over a *pass* which is about the height of the highest *mountain* in Europe. The crossing is remarkably easy for the path zig-zags constantly and at times even breaks into steps or just wanders over bare slabs of rock. A small lake (Laguna Taullicocha) appears below, under Taulliraju's skirt of glacier, while the peak itself towers over the scene. Pucahirca, a sharp spur on its south-east ridge just above the pass, becomes a jagged peak in its own right. A dusting of snow may lie in the slot of the pass and, through it, Pucaraju, a more homely peak, sweeps up beyond a valley head sequined with a scattering of tarns (the Morococha lagunas). The descent starts down what feels like a spiral staircase and over more slabs to cross the plateau of tarns and descend into the valley itself: the Quebrada Huaripampa, whose waters eventually flow into the Atlantic as the mighty

Alpamayo rises above the Santa Cruz valley. This crenellated snow spire is regarded as one of the most beautiful mountains in the world. (Photo: H.M.Brown.)

Above: **Taulliraju from the path up to the Punta Union.**

Far right: **Chacraraju from high above the Huaripampa camp on Pucaraju.**

(Photos: H.M.Brown.)

River Amazon. Camp is made in the *ichu* tussock-grass by the river. A granite pinnacle looks down on the site and through a gap (Q. Paria), the 'Matterhorn' of Chacraraju appears––another mighty mountain guardian for a camp site of character. In August and September midges can be bothersome in this valley.

Day 5: The Quebrada Huaripampa

A day split between downhill and uphill walking. The former is enjoyed for the ever-changing, increasingly richer landscape: a succession of flats with wending streams, more birdlife and growing cultivation as one descends the spacious valley—so different from the Q. Santa Cruz. Even the village dogs are friendly! The descent ends at the main village, Huari-pampa, a pleasant spot. The route doubles back once through it to start the unrelenting uphill half of the day. (You can go on down to Colcabamba, the next village and the start of the main path up but this serves no real purpose.) Eventually the path twists out of the forest onto the open spaciousness of mountain country. It is time to camp. Nevada Yanapaccha is the pleasing peak overlooking the site this time.

With the pass not far ahead this is the highest site of the trip and, with a bit more walking, you can reach some tarns, an even better camp site. This is a day which could certainly be split into two, and Colcabamba makes a good overnight stop. You can eat out for once.

Day 6: The Portachuelo de Llanganuco, 4767m (15,635ft)

This pass, the highest point of the circuit, is reached by the path twisting up through the series of tarns. The jaws of the 'little door' hinge on Nevado Chopicalqui to the south. Double-headed Huascarán, highest summit in Peru, appears for the first time. It is a moving moment. Scaling a summit gives different, rather artificial feelings, but the successful crossing of a pass gives deep, shared, feelings, old- as the restless wanderings of man. The descent (you can take the road, but the mule track is more attractive) gives a series of zig-zags, contours a while and then zig-zags down again, to reach a more gentle country, a valley squeezed by 6000m (19,680ft) mountains: Chacaraju, Pisco, Huandoy to the north, Chopicalqui and Huascarán to the south. Rather than continue on the main

66

Quebrada Llanganuco, turn upstream (NE) on the Q. Yanapaccha and, after a bit of toil, camp on a shelf under Pisco, with a staggering view across to Huascarán.

Day 7: The Quebrada Llanganuco

This is a walk with no anti-climax. The last day is as amazing as any of the others. After the descent to the main valley it feels like a grand highway. The *quebrada* is a great U-shaped trench and two lagoons lie on the flat bottom of the glen. The path uses a causeway on the first, creeps below cliffs and crosses the rubble from huge rock avalanches to reach the second, which seems more friendly, with ducks on the water and red-barked *queñua* trees. Dramatically, the path zig-zags down again, shadowed by massive walls and prows of granite which soar for thousands of feet, while on the other side buttress after buttress hems in this last flourish of wildness. (A road reaches the pass—and walkers often use it—but the valley is too grand to waste by using transport. Walk, rather than travel in a cloud of dust.) After a final twist down the country opens out. There are fields of barley. The Cordillera Negra appears ahead. Trucks. People. It all suddenly feels over, but one deeply-moving place remains.

In 1970 the earthquake killed something like 70,000 people in the Callejón de Huaylas and left a million homeless. Huascarán Norte was so shaken that part of its 762-m (2500-ft) rock face collapsed. Millions of cubic feet of rock and ice fell, the pressure changing ice to water and pulverising the rock so it was a sludge that came down into the valley, travelling at over 200mph. It took just a few minutes to descend the 3963m (13,000ft) and 16km (10 miles) to Ranrahirca in the Rio Santa valley and the tongue of sludge continued another 16km (10 miles) to the edge of Carás. It took two days to 'set' and for two days dust filled the air so nobody could even see what damage had been done. The barren swathe is beginning to sprout grass and shrubs but you walk quietly, aware of the power of nature. Then you come to Yungay. It was usually safe from ordinary avalanches but this one of 1970 simply swept over the buffering 198-m (650-ft) hill of Cerro Aira and wiped out the town. 18,000 died, 241 survived. Ironically the cemetery was untouched. The figure of Christ with arms outstretched still marks the spot. It also marks the end of an unforgettable walk. A bus, truck or *colectivo* will all too soon bear you off to Huarás.

Above: **The twin summits of Huascarán seen from a camp below Pisco at dawn. On the right is Huascarán Norte and on the left Huascarán Sur.**

Far left, top: **Taulliraju and Pucahirca from the Punta Union.**

Far left, bottom: **Burros on the slabs near the top of the Punta Union.**

(Photos: H.M.Brown.)

Walk 8 FRANCE, ITALY, SWITZERLAND:
Tour du Mont Blanc by Walt Unsworth

Any of the vantage points around Courmayeur offers superb views of Mont Blanc's dramatic south face. This picture was taken from the Torino Hut.
(Photo: W.Unsworth.)

A Circular Walk around Europe's Highest Mountain

The Alps curve in a great white arc of over a thousand miles around the top of Italy from Yugoslavia to the Mediterranean near Nice. In this distance the mountains rise and fall to make up individual groups and the passes between them and one group, towards the western edge of the range, thrusts up a huge white cone which far exceeds in height any of the other Alpine peaks—Mont Blanc, at 4811m (14,664ft) is not only the highest mountain in the Alps, but in the whole of Europe, west of the Caucasus.

It is, by any standards, a beautiful mountain.

To the north it presents an almost benign aspect: snowy breasts pointing skywards, skirted by the blue-white glacier of Bossons, but to the south it is very different, for here the savage ramparts of the Brenva Face and the immense ridges of Peuterey and Brouillard created a wilderness of rock and ice unparalleled elsewhere in the Alps.

If Mont Blanc stood alone it would still be enough to attract the mountain enthusiast, but it doesn't. By divine chance it is linked by glaciers and ridges to its satellites, each of which is itself a superb mountain and lacking only the height of the monarch, though by no means small. Here

may be seen the famous rock obelisk of the Drus, the spiky pinnacles of the Chamonix Aiguilles, the huge rock walls of the Grandes Jorasses, and the curious challenging tower of the Géant. These, and others less well known, make up a diversity of peaks without compare anywhere else on this Continent. Small wonder that the Mont Blanc massif is the mountain climber's favourite playground.

The walker, however, can scarcely penetrate into the heart of all this magnificence. He may prod it in certain places, touch its skirts in others, and even, if he is wealthy enough, sail above its glaciers in Europe's highest cablecar, but he cannot enter into it as the climber can. He can, however, walk around it, marvelling at its beauty from every point of the compass.

Mont Blanc is surrounded by seven valleys, which define the limits of the group and separate it from its neighbours. The Tour of Mont Blanc, or TMB as it is usually called, links these valleys together and as it does so passes through France, Italy and Switzerland, for these three countries share the Mont Blanc group between them, their boundaries meeting on the summit of Mont Dolent.

Above: **Les Contamines in the Val Montjoie is a charming village still largely unspoilt by tourism.**

Left: **The TMB climbs out of the Val Montjoie by the Chemin Romain a route once followed by the Roman Legions.**

(Photos: W.Unsworth.)

Distance: 115km (72 miles).

Time required: 11 days.

Type of Walk: A high-altitude, well-signposted walk for the reasonably fit.

Base: Chamonix.

Start: Les Houches (or Col de Voza).

Best Time of Year: July – September.

Maps: IGN Massif du Mont Blanc 1:25,000 (two sheets).

Guidebook: *Walking Guide to the Tour of Mont Blanc* by Andrew Harper (Cicerone Press).

WALK 8

Taken in an anti-clockwise direction, starting in the north, the valleys are the Vallée de l' Arve (better known perhaps as the Chamonix Valley, after its famous town), the Val Montjoie, the Vallée des Glaciers, the Val Veni, the Italian Val Ferret, the Swiss Val Ferret and Val Trient. High passes—some over 2400m (8000ft) separate one valley from the next and the TMB crosses these on its way round the mountain. None of them are technically difficult and after mid-July in a normal season they may reasonably be expected to be clear of snow, but this is by no means a certainty. Snow on the passes adds another

dimension to the walk—but the wise traveller will be prepared and carry an ice axe.

Providing one is accustomed to crossing snowfields and knows how to use an ice axe as a brake in an emergency, there is much to be said for an early visit. The days are longer and there is not the same pressure on accommodation as there is during August, the main holiday season. More significantly, the flowers are better too: the Alpine flowers of August are only the pale remnants of the glorious profusion of July.

The seven valleys, with their lush meadows and rich *alpages* so suitable for rearing cattle,

have been inhabited for centuries. Villages, hamlets and individual chalets inhabit the landscape and even in the highest and most unlikely places there is often an old byre or cheesemaking hut. These were summer dwellings, and some still are, though increasingly few as modern farming methods and the easier living to be had from tourism take hold. Tourism has played an ever more important role in these valleys during the last hundred years or so and is a major factor—perhaps *the* major factor—in their obvious prosperity.

For the walker this means that there is plenty of choice of accommodation along his route so

The Col de Balme represents the frontier between Switzerland on the left and France on the right. In the distance is the huge bulk of Mont Blanc, whilst the nearer peaks are the rocky Dru and the Aiguille Verte. (Photo: W.Unsworth.)

73

From the cable car station on the Aiguille du Midi above Chamonix a wonderful panorama unfolds. The steep peaks on the right are the Grandes Jorasses. In the far distance is the Oberland (left) Grand Combin and Matterhorn (centre) and Monte Rosa (right). (Photo: A.Harper.)

that he can, within limits, make his day as long or as short as he wishes knowing he will find a bed for the night and food. For the backpacker the choice is even wider: camping places abound and he need never carry more than three days' supplies before the opportunity of re-stocking presents itself.

Compared with some of the routes in this book the TMB is not a wilderness walk because Man is seldom out of sight for long. Even parts of the Pennine Way in England are wilder, more desolate, but it can be tough going with a heavy pack: tougher perhaps than the Everest trek, and bad weather or deep snow on the passes would make a significant difference. How long it takes is a matter of individual choice, but ten to twelve days is usual, and it can comfortably be fitted in to a fortnight.

Day 1: Les Houches to Les Contamines

Les Houches is a straggling village set above the main road near the entrance to the Chamonix valley. It makes a good starting and finishing point for the TMB because it is easy of access, with good road and rail connections to Geneva or Paris. Traditionally, the TMB is done in an anticlockwise direction (I suspect it might be less arduous the other way round!) and Les Houches fits into this very nicely by offering a relatively easy first day. All one has to do is climb the wooded slopes above the village to the grassy Col de Voza—about two hours—then embark on a long, gradual descent to Les Contamines.

The route begins to the right of the Bellevue cablecar station and climbs steadily upwards through pastures and woods, past small chalets until it emerges onto the wide grassy shoulder that is the Col de Voza. On either hand the view is far reaching. The whole of the Chamonix Valley is laid out map-like, backed by the Brévent and the Aiguilles Rouges. On the other side of the Col, the eye is drawn to the Aiguille de Bionnassay and its glacier which completely dominates the view. The col itself is less attractive, there is a huge incongruous looking restaurant and, surprisingly, a railway track!

The track belongs to the Tramway du Mont Blanc, an electric cog-wheel railway that makes an incredible journey up the long spur of mountain called Le Prarion of which the Col de Voza is part. The Toy-Town cars, dwarfed by their immense environment, begin their journey at Le Fayet, crawl through the streets there, then haul themselves up through St. Gervais to the Col de Voza and beyond, ending at the Nid d'Aigle at the end of the stony wilderness of the Pierre Ronde, below the Aiguille du Gouter and overlooking the Bionnassay Glacier. It is a remarkable tram ride by any standards!

Beyond Voza the TMB follows an easy angled jeep track down to Le Crozat, where it divides into two. The right hand track leads to Bionnassay and the Val Montjoie but the TMB keeps to the hills by following the other branch which descends gradually to the deep and wooded valley of the Bionnassay stream, crossing it at the Pont des Places then following the other bank through woods to Le Champel, an uninspiring hamlet, but one with good views of the Val Montjoie.

After Le Champel it becomes fairly obvious that the TMB is straining to keep away from the main valley road for as long as possible but that circumstances are against it. The Gravac Gorge bars the way, forcing the walker to either climb up or descend to the valley floor—and the TMB chooses the latter, easier alternative. The road is joined at Tresse and there follow two boring rather uphill miles along the macadam to Les Contamines.

These last couple of miles are certainly an anticlimax to the day's walk but they can in fact be avoided by two 'unofficial' variations to the Tour. The easier of these involves no more than crossing the river at Tresse and following the

The view south-west from the Col du Bonhomme. (Photo. A.Harper.)

much pleasanter way on the western bank, which, apart from anything else, gives a splendid view of Contamines. The other variant is much tougher and starts way back at the Pont des Places where, instead of heading to Le Champel, a track can be taken to the start of the Bionnassay Glacier and a steep climb made over the Col de Tricot to the Chalets de Miage, then over the flank of Mont Truc to the Chalets du Truc from whence a good track leads down through the woods to enter Contamines at the Church.

There are several places on the TMB where variants like these—some recognised as 'official' variants—are possible, but it is worth bearing in mind that a TMB variant is *always* higher and tougher than the original path.

Les Contamines proves to be a pleasant Alpine village as yet hardly touched by tourism and looking much as Chamonix must have looked fifty years ago, before the developers got hold of it. On the Tour it is of particular importance to backpackers because it is the last village of any consequence before Courmayeur, which is three days further on, and consequently it is important to stock up with food and fuel. There are plenty of shops in the village.

Day 2: Les Contamines to Refuge de la Croix de Bonhomme

From Les Contamines the TMB continues along the Val Montjoie shortly quitting the detestable tarmac for a pleasant path by the River Bonnant which leads into a deep, steep-sided chasm where stands the ancient chapel of Notre Dame de la Gorge, its white walls and baroque splendour contrasting sharply with the dark forests which surround it.

From the chapel a curiously paved road climbs sharply uphill through the trees. It is too wide and too well made to be an ordinary Alpine track and then, of course, one recognizes the hand of those master road builders, the Romans. This was one of the principal routes by which the Legions came into Gaul—up the Aosta Valley then over the Col de la Seigne and Col du Bonhomme and down this well paved road into the Val Montjoie—the very route in fact, that the TMB follows in reverse.

At the Pont de la Tena all traces of Rome vanish, but the track is still a good one as it climbs quietly up past the Nant Borrant mountain hotel to the higher restaurant at La Balme. This is a good place to take refreshment for not only does it offer superb views back along the Val Montjoie and the great peaks of the Miage, but the way ahead looks fairly formidable. The next couple of hours or so are going to be tough,

especially if the snow is down.

A narrow but distinguishable track loops its way up towards the cliffs which form the head of the valley. Long before it reaches them however it swings away to the left, crosses a level and somewhat boggy patch of dull ground then, as if suddenly recollecting its purpose, shoots steeply uphill to a col. At least, it looks like a col from below, though it tempts only to deceive. A huge cairn comes in sight and beyond it a wide bowl in the mountains whose distant rim, a thousand feet higher, is the real col.

The cairn itself is no transient affair created by idle walkers with energy to spare but a thing of some antiquity, created nobody knows when. Some say it marks the place where once stood a temple to Mercury, others that it is a memorial to two women who perished in a storm at this lonely spot and as if to bear this out, the combe itself is known as the Plan des Dames. It is customary to cast a stone on the pile, perhaps to propitiate the ancient gods or reconcile the ghosts of the two ladies, who knows? How well your stone lands determines the good fortune or otherwise you will have in crossing the pass which lies ahead.

The track zig zags up the right-hand side of the combe and leads eventually to the Col du Bonhomme at 2329m (7641ft) where a valley falls away steeply to the Beaufortain. The TMB, however, ignores this obvious escape. Instead, it contours round the head of the valley, below the curious tower-like Roche du Bonhomme, then climbs almost imperceptibly over barren wastes to another and higher pass, the Col de la Croix du Bonhomme at 2476m (8123ft) marked by a stoutly constructed pillar of stones.

Unknown country opens up ahead: a long deep valley surrounded on all sides by minor but impressive peaks and away in the distance, dominating the horizon, the great snow cone of Mont Pourri 3781m (12,398ft). Below the col, almost within touching distance it seems, snuggles the comfortable Refuge de la Croix du Bonhomme, a reconstruction of the original hut destroyed during the war. Many travellers choose to spend the night at the hut, rather than push on into a land where the accommodation and food is likely to be inferior and harder come by.

From the hut there is a major variant of the Tour—a crossing of the Col des Fours at 2665m (8743ft) which, if taken, is the highest point attained on the entire walk. It has the virtue of keeping to the mountains (mountain walkers hate losing the height they have won with such labour) but it traverses some dreary scenery, and early in the season the snow may make a crossing difficult.

Day 3: Refuge de la Croix du Bonhomme to Rifugio Elisabetta

The original route descends from the hut in a swift swoop to the shepherds' huts at the Plan Vararo, then more gently to the Chalets de la Raja before joining the Vallée des Glaciers at les Chapieux, a hamlet of no consequence, but the only one in this long and lonely valley. There are a couple of inns, a few houses and some deserted military barracks complete with memorials to soldiers who died in the mountains in the early years of the century. It is like stepping back in time, and the people (such as there are) seem different too: isolated by high cols from the other valleys they have more in common with the men of Tarentaise than with the Savoyards of Chamonix or Courmayeur.

A long and tedious metalled road leads out of the hamlet towards the head of the valley. At first the defile is narrow but at La Ville des Glaciers—a pretentious name for a collection of mean looking huts—it opens up to reveal a corner of the Mont Blanc range. Straight ahead, and dominating all else are the Aiguilles des Glaciers, with their long sweeping skirt of ice, the Glacier des Glaciers. On the left, Mont Tondu rises in rocky eminence, but on the right the mountains fall away leaving only slopes of rough alpage and a high pass, the Col de la Seigne (2516m, 8254ft) which marks the frontier between France and Italy.

It is a wild and desolate place, this head of the Vallée des Glaciers but at its centre, strategically placed at the foot of the Col de la Seigne is a collection of stone huts which make up the café-cum-refuge of Les Mottets. One can spend the night here and tackle the Col de le Seigne refreshed the next day, or at least pause for sustenance—the next resting place lies a long way ahead.

The climb up to the pass is not particularly long or arduous and breasting the col, one is confronted with an astonishing mountain panorama. The long spiky ridges that march down the southern flanks of Mont Blanc are arrayed in their full, savage majesty, dominated by the spectacular Aiguille Noire de Peuterey, pointing to the sky like an immense spear. Nearer to hand the beautiful ice draped Aiguille de Tré la Tête rises from the Lex Blanche glacier.

Descent from the col is made into a combe which seems even more desolate than that just left behind. This is the Lex Blanche, the uppermost reaches of the long Val Veni, and separated from the rest of the valley by the overflowing snout of the Miage Glacier, whose huge moraines can easily be seen from the col.

As the path descends it passes below the Pyramides Calcaires, pure rock spikes which seem to spring from the valley floor and which effectively hide the next staging post of the TMB, the splendid Elisabetta hut, perched on a shelf above the valley.

The valley road almost reaches the Elisabetta

The dramatic Aiguille Noire de Peuterey dominates the Val Veni. (Photo: W.Unsworth.)

hut and at the week-end particularly, there is little pleasure to be had walking along it to Courmayeur. At Combal bridge, the parking place for tourists who wish to visit the glacial Lac du Miage, chaos reigns and the air is filled with petrol fumes and voluble Italian as drivers argue over rights of way on the narrow road. What a contrast to the previous two days! It is obvious that civilization—if that's the right word—is near at hand.

Day 4: Rifugio Elisabetta to Courmayeur

The TMB follows the road all the way, past the curious Lac de Combal, which is now no more than a marshy tissue of interlacing streams, under the edge of the Miage moraines and bursts out into a pleasant wooded valley which could hardly offer a greater contrast to the austere severity of the Lex Blanche. Lower down, yet another glacial tongue blocks the way—that of Brenva Glacier, and tucked in beside it is the delightful chapel of Notre Dame de la Guérison; the Italian counterpart to the chapel in the Montjoie gorge and representing the opposite end of the route over the two great passes of Seigne and Bonhomme. Beyond the chapel, as the road turns the foot of Mont Chétif on its way to Courmayeur the full splendour of the great peaks is revealed: the Géant, the Grandes Jorasses and the Brenva face of Mont Blanc. But whether one can enjoy them without actually being run over by a speeding car is another matter.

Fortunately there is an alternative, another TMB 'official' variant, which leaves the road at the Combal bridge and climbs up the hillside past the ruined chalets of L'Arp Vieille to a spur of Mont Favre. From this shoulder, which is at 2375m (7792ft), a wonderful panorama opens: the whole south side of the Mont Blanc range stretches across the horizon. The foreshortening effect of standing in the valley looking up at the mountains has gone, the nearer peaks which from below seemed so dominant are put into proper perspective. It is worth getting out the map and identifying them all, though some are so distinctive as to be easily recognizable—who could mistake the skywards pointing finger of the Géant, or the sombre black arrow tip of the Aiguille Noire?

From this high vantage point, too, Mont Blanc is seen in proper perspective for the first time. How it dominates with its great height and what imperial majesty is shown in its huge buttresses of rock and ice! No longer is it some half seen distant snow dome, but proud Queen over all, worthy of its place as the highest mountain in Europe.

The route traverses the mountain-side, past the Lac Chécrouit to the little col of the same name. Normally it is an easy walk, slightly downhill in fact, but snow can be a problem early in the season and some of the slopes which have to be crossed are quite steep and long. By some curious quirk of climate these north facing hills, and the Lex Blanche, are notorious for holding on to snow long after it has gone in other places. When the snow is down, the Lac Chécrouit, a favourite place with photographers who hope to catch the reflections of the surrounding mountains in its tiny surface, completely disappears.

Woods climb up to the Col Chécrouit and beyond, clothing the lower slopes of Mont Chétif, the cornerstone of the Aosta Valley and a favourite viewpoint with tourists from Courmayeur; duplicating the role that the Brevent plays above Chamonix on the opposite side of the range. There is a café at the col and a *télésiège* down to the lower *alpage* of Plan Chécrouit, but the TMB follows a broad track down and at the Plan (where the *télésiège* gives way to a giant cablecar) offers a superb bird's eye view of Courmayeur.

The cablecar spans the distance in no time, depositing the traveller in the heart of the town, but the track winds down gracefully to the ancient village of Dolonne, home of the famous Grivel ice axes, from where Courmayeur is only a few minutes' walk.

After the rigours of the past three days, Courmayeur comes as a relaxing and welcome contrast. It is a large, untidily arranged village with a main street that straggles on forever, an ever changing mixture of old and new architecture. People throng Courmayeur—there's no

Above: **In the lower reaches of the Swiss Val Ferret the harsh mountain scenery gives way to pastoral loveliness.** (Photo: W. Unsworth.)

Far right, top: **The Italian Val Ferret is followed throughout by the TMB.**

Far right, bottom left: **Climbing up to the Col du Grand Ferret which divides Italy from Switzerland. In the background is the Pré de Bar Glacier, squeezed between rock walls.**

Far right, bottom right: **The lush beauty of the Swiss Val Ferret. The Swiss valley is much lower than its Italian counterpart, and is consequently greener.**

(Photos: A. Harper.)

other word for it—but they are happy and good natured, giving the village an air of permanent fiesta. Enough of the nineteenth century still clings to Courmayeur to give an impression of old Savoy, but inevitably it is disappearing as the old buildings are tarted up or replaced by the modern instant plastic Alpine Architecture. The opening of the Mont Blanc tunnel in the 1960s accelerated the change; Courmayeur became a day trip by car or bus from Chamonix, and a link in the European motorway system. Heavy trucks from Milan roar past the village on their way to Hamburg or Manchester and vice versa. Before the drilling of the tunnel, Courmayeur was one of the most isolated and difficult to reach of all the Alpine villages.

So the change has been traumatic—and yet, it is still a pleasant place, absorbed and protected by the mountains, compared with which Man's scratchings are puny.

Days 5 and 6: Courmayeur to La Fouly

From Courmayeur the TMB follows the Italian Val Ferret to the Swiss frontier. It does this along a narrow tarmac road busy with tourist traffic, although there is a higher, more strenuous, path on the hillside above the valley. It is a savagely beautiful place. A towering mountain wall stretching from the Géant through the Grandes Jorasses and the Aiguilles of Leschaux and Triolet to Mont Dolent, sweeps down without interruption to the valley floor. Boulders litter the fields and the woods do little to soften the impression of menace created by the mountains.

The road ends a short distance before the Arnuva restaurant, the last habitation in the valley. From there a good path climbs the hillside to the alpage of Pré de Bar where there are a few stone huts. The view from here, back along the valley, is astonishing for the eye is carried far beyond, along the Val Veni all the way to the distant Col de la Seigne. Closer at hand, is the curiously ugly Pré de Bar Glacier, squeezed between its confining rock walls to emerge like some giant dollop of toothpaste.

From Pré de Bar the track swings away to the right, overlooking a gorge of black schist, then climbs steadily to the Grand Col Ferret 2537m (8323ft). This is the Swiss frontier, but the first view of Switzerland gives no impression of a Promised Land: a long sombre valley leads down to the upper reaches of the Swiss Val Ferret, which from this distance seems no better. Nor are the surrounding peaks of much consequence, particularly after the magnificence of the Italian valley. There aren't even any glaciers. The snows of Mont Dolent and the Grand Combin seem only to mock by their distance.

And yet the descent of the pass is pleasant enough: an easy jogging gradient, past the cowsheds at Le Peule and through the woods to meet the valley floor at Les Ars-dessous. Once again it is a tarmac road and one which will become very familiar in the course of time, but at least there isn't much traffic. The Swiss Val Ferret leads nowhere and is well off the regular tourist round.

About a mile down the road is the village of Ferret itself and if one had any doubts that this was indeed Switzerland, they vanish immediately. There is some indefinable hallmark about Swiss Alpine villages that is found nowhere else: they all look like full scale models, or film sets for *Heidi*. Every Swiss chalet is an *archetypal* Swiss chalet—and if that is an exaggeration, it's right enough as a generalisation.

Day 7: La Fouly to Champex

Ferret is no exception, a pretty little hamlet set just where the valley begins to show its beauty. A short distance lower down is the slightly larger village of La Fouly, favourite haunt of Alpine writers such as Emile Javelle and Charles Gos in former days and a climbing centre which became a quiet backwater as tastes swung towards Chamonix and Zermatt. On the walk between the two villages the peaks themselves can be seen to their best advantage—lower down the valley they disappear behind the foreground. A wide sweep of glacier, the Glacier de l'A Neuve, is backed by a ring of rocky peaks: Mont Dolent, Aiguilles Rouges du Dolent, Tour Noir, Aiguille de l'A Neuve, Grande Lui and the Grand and Petit Darrey. They are not as well known as the peaks in the centre of the range and sadly neglected by modern climbers, yet they form an impressive cirque.

As the mountains fall back more attention can be paid to the valley itself which justly deserves its reputation as one of the most idyllic in Switzerland. The meadows are alive with flowers of every hue, contrasting with the darker woodlands of larch and spruce. Chalets perch on rocky knolls, their window boxes a blaze of geraniums.

Before long the road winds down into the large village of Praz-de-Fort, the Les Arlaches and finally Issert, where the TMB leaves the valley to climb up to Champex. All three villages seem hardly touched by time: the old ways still carry weight, and it seems appropriate somehow that in this slightly unreal world the chief produce should be strawberries.

From the outskirts of Issert a path climbs gently up through the woods to the gorge of Darbellay where the torrent rushes down with

considerable force. If the water level is high, crossing the stream can be a bit of a problem for it is quite wide and there is no bridge. A fallen branch from the surrounding thickets can be used to make a steadying 'third leg' for the crossing but wet feet are more than likely. Not that this really matters—Champex is not far away, and the path to it holds no more terrors.

Champex is a brash little place, full of its own importance. A green lake occupies a wooded bowl in the hills. Along its north-eastern shore runs a road which acts as a promenade. Brightly coloured pedallos cluster at their moorings, trinket shops and tourist cafés line the street while the grand hotels hide discreetly amongst the trees. Once a noted climbing centre, then a favoured place for the wealthy in *la belle époque,* it now relies mainly on day trippers from the Rhône valley. It is all a little sad, really, but the setting has lost none of its magnificence: the water, the dark trees and far away, through gaps in the hills, the white crests of the Grand Combin and Dents du Midi.

Day 8: Champex to Trient

Beyond Champex the walker following the TMB is faced with a major decision. Ahead lies the most important variant to the official route, the climb over the Fenêtre d'Arpette 2665m (8743ft), which replaces the walk around the alp of Bovine. Unlike other variants this one alters the whole day's walk because although it eventually arrives at the same destination, Trient, it gets there by a completely different route. The Arpette route misses the beauty of the Bovine; the Bovine misses the grandeur of the Arpette.

Conditions may decide the issue. The Fenêtre d'Arpette is a high pass of somewhat greater difficulty than the others on the Tour and indeed, some maps mark it *Passage Dangereuse*. That's relative, of course, but if the snow is down it does mean that any attempt to cross the pass can be a tricky business.

The route goes through the woods to the attractive hamlet of Arpette then climbs steadily up into the wild and rocky valley of the same name, to reach a gap in the skyline which allows a crossing to be made into the Trient valley. It reaches into the heart of the mountains: the Fenêtre is close by the serrated ridge of the Ecandies, and there are superb views of the

During *la belle époque* Champex was a resort favoured by the wealthy. Now it is a popular tourist haunt for day trippers from the Rhône Valley. (Photo: W. Unsworth.)

Trient Glacier, the Aiguille du Tour and the Aiguilles Dorées. The descent to Trient (or Forclaz) is at first a little difficult but then eases rapidly into a wide path.

Day 9: Trient to Le Tour

The original way by the Bovine eschews all this. It follows the Champex valley to the bridge at Champex d'en Bas then climbs steadily up by the Plan de l'All and traverses the woods above the deep valley of the Durnand stream. Where the valley opens out at La Jure, the path swings across the cirque to cross the three streams which make up the headwaters. The going is rough, though the force of the streams doesn't seem to match that of the Darbellay. When the third stream is crossed the path plunges into a thick wood and zig-zags up one of the steepest slopes of the Tour to emerge amongst the cows on the great alp of Bovine. The place itself—a simple cowshed—lies around the next spur.

What an astonishing view Bovine offers! It stands on the very cornerstone of the Mont Blanc massif overlooking the dramatic bend of the Rhône, where that great trench comes down from Valais and turns on its way to Lake Geneva. The view extends right up the valley and only the heat haze prevents one from distinguishing all the towns and villages in its length. To the right are the beginnings of the Valais Alps—the Grand Combin group in all its massive majesty, whilst to the left lie the Bernese Alps, from Les Diablerets to beyond Wildstrubel. Further left still, across the trench as it makes its way to Lake Geneva, is the splendid group of the Dents du Midi.

Five thousand feet below, spread out like a map, lies Martigny, set amongst its vineyards and with the Forclaz road snaking up from it in horrific looking zig-zags. Down there is the heart of the Swiss wine country, the home of the deep red *Dole* and amber coloured *Fendant*—wines which nobody should visit this part of Switzerland and fail to sample. They are lusty, alcoholic beverages suited to a good mountain thirst but alas, they are no longer cheap as once they were. The Swiss, who are nobody's fools, drink most of it themselves.

The rock staircase at Les Grandes. This alternative to the descent into Trient offers superb views of the Trient Glacier. (Photo: W. Unsworth.)

83

The Aiguille Verte seen through the woods of the Flégère path. This section of the TMB offers outstanding views.
(Photo: A. Harper.)

The first couple of miles are possibly the most level of the entire Tour. Between the hotel at Forclaz and the Chalet du Glaciers the gain in height is less than 60m (200ft). The reason for this is that the path, which is wide and well made, follows the course of a *bisse* or water conduit which supplies Forclaz. Such *bisses* are a feature of the Swiss Valais, and though this one is a modest example of the craft, some are incredible feats of engineering on the part of the peasants who constructed them centuries ago.

The Swiss Alpine villages have for several centuries been organised into communes; closed societies where the villagers had to devote a part of their working year to communal projects in return for a share of the benefits. This way the *bisses* were made, and many of the paths too. There is a fine example of this as the TMB continues beyond the bridge at the Chalet du Glacier. The path, though now decaying, exhibits elaborate construction and must at one time have been of considerable importance. It climbs up a narrow valley to the ruined huts of les Grands, hemmed in by rock walls, and only escapes by means of a rock staircase, provided with iron handrails for safety.

Once on the upper alps, the whole of the Trient can be seen below. The route of the original TMB can be traced making its way into the dull side valley which lies below the rock peak known as Croix de Fer. It climbs up laboriously to meet the variant path at the Col de Balme 2191m (7188ft): the French frontier, and the last high pass of the Tour.

The Col de Balme is a broad grassy saddle which for centuries has been the summer grazing for cattle from the Chamonix valley. There is a stone built *refuge*-cum-restaurant which, since the frontier passes behind its back door is entirely in Switzerland; much to the chagrin of the Chamouniards, because it is a popular and profitable tourist haunt and most of the visitors come from the Chamonix valley by the cable car from Le Tour.

From the col the view is truly magnificent; one of the finest on the Tour. The Aiguille Verte dominates the middle foreground and beyond it, floating like a cloud, is Mont Blanc with the whole of the Bosses ridge leading across to the Aiguille du Goûter seen to perfection. Between these mountains and the rocky crest of the Aiguilles Rouges lies the long deep trench of the Chamonix valley.

A good track leads rapidly down to Le Tour, the highest village and the end of the valley road. From Le Tour in the north to Les Houches in the south, the valley of the Arve is crowded with villages and hamlets, almost every one of which is redolent of mountaineering history. Two

Beyond Bovine the path continues to contour round the hillsides on its way to La Forclaz. It dodges in and out of woods and at La Giete enters a truly sylvan hollow, where a stream sparkles and gentians carpet the ground. Then it enters the woods again and within a couple of mile reaches the huge motel complex at La Forclaz col 1526m (5007ft).

From La Forclaz the original TMB descends to the village of Trient before climbing once again to reach the Col de Balme, but this involves a loss of a thousand feet or so for no real purpose. A variant extends the walk, makes it more interesting and gives a closer view of the Trient Glacier.

centuries ago crystal hunters began to guide adventurous tourists amongst the glaciers and eventually up Mont Blanc and started a tradition of great guiding families which exists to this day. In the early years Chamonix came a poor third behind Zermatt and Grindelwald as one of the three great climbing centres of the Alps, but not any more. Today Chamonix reigns supreme: the valley is the haunt of climbers of every nationality from Poles to Americans, British to Japanese. It is the world's greatest mountaineering centre.

Day 10: Le Tour to La Flégère

The TMB resists the fleshpots. It touches the valley only at Le Tour and Les Houches, and between the two traverses the high rocky wall of the Aiguilles Rouges.

From Le Tour it descends the road to Montroc where, behind the railway station, a path leads off to the hamlet of Tre-le-Champ which stands astride the main highway to the Col des Montets, A well signposted track then climbs the lower slopes of the Aiguilles Rouges until it bursts out of the woods near a curious tall pinnacle or *aiguillette,* a favourite practice place for rock climbers. Just beyond the needle the TMB itself indulges in a little scrambling: the path leads to a chimney in the rock wall and for the next ten minutes hands as well as feet are necessary for progress. The holds are large and there is no real feeling of exposure—but a slip would have nasty consequences, so care is required. It is the only place on the Tour where simple walking is not enough.

The effort is well worth it. From the grassy slopes above the cliffs a vast panorama is displayed across the Arve valley. The whole range of Mont Blanc can be seen, from the Col de Balme to the Col de Voza: a veritable sea of peaks recalling Alexander Pope's well known line: 'And Alps upon Alps arise'. It is a panorama which remains a constant companion throughout the walk along the Aiguilles Rouges,

The Mont Blanc massif seen from the Brévent Path. The long Bossons Glacier is easily identified with the black cone of the Aiguille du Midi just to the left. The summit of Mont Blanc is the smooth dome in the centre of the picture. (Photo: A. Harper.)

A walker on the Flégère path looks across the splendid panorama of Mont Blanc and the Chamonix Aiguilles. (Photo: W. Unsworth.)

yet one which alters subtly the further south one travels. Here for example, on the balcony below Les Cheserys, the dominant peaks are the Verte, Chardonnet and Argentière; three noble mountains in the grand manner, all fluted rock and ice. From this vantage point the Dru seems some mere peculiar excrescence stuck on the side of the Verte, and doesn't assume its proper dramatic spear-shaped appearance until one has travelled to Le Brévent. The celebrated Chamonix Aiguilles don't assume *their* best aspect until one is well on the way to Les Houches—say, just above Merlet. So although the view is superficially constant it is actually changing slightly all the time.

In the valley below lies Chamonix, spread out like a map with all its modern developments from supermarkets to the imaginative new National Mountaineering School. The entrance to the Mont Blanc Tunnel can be seen too and it is satisfying to observe how quickly nature has covered the ugly scars which this vast undertaking once made.

Days 11: La Flégère to Les Houches

From the balcony the path descends steeply to the Flégère hotel and cable car station then climbs through a rocky combe up to the ridge again to the summit of Le Brévent, itself a cable car station and the most popular viewpoint for the Mont Blanc range. But the TMB walker who has been watching this scene unfold for some hours past may find more momentary interest in the starker country lying behind the Brévent, where a series of cliffs, the Rochers des Fiz, frown down on the dark recesses of the Diosaz gorge. Servoz, the most westerly village of the Chamonix commune, can be seen clearly.

From Brévent the route in fact keeps to this side of the ridge for a short way before climbing to the crest again at Bellachat, where it plunges down steeply towards the Chamonix valley, crossing the deep bed of a torrent en route. When the tree line is reached again the path eases off and leads to the small zoo at Merlet.

A little further and the path leads to the enormous and ugly statue of Christ the King which looks out from the trees over the valley. Already the sounds of busy traffic form a a constant background to the walk and Les Houches, where it all began, is only a few minutes away.

Walk 9 FRANCE, SPAIN: The Pyrenean High Route
by Kev Reynolds

A Challenging Trek Across Europe's Second Highest Mountains

The Pyrenean High Route is the mountain-trekker's dream of a route; always demanding, ever-varied, passing through some of Europe's most deserted and spectacularly scenic landscapes. At no time is it dull. At no stage does the interest wane; nor should it ever be treated lightly. It is a serious undertaking for anyone, and many of the stages should only be tackled by mountain trekkers of experience, and in settled weather conditions.

It's a long way, end to end of the Pyrenees. Some 400km (250 miles) separate the Atlantic from the Mediterranean; the blustery, Atlantic coast from the balmy scorched margins of the Mediterranean. Four hundred kilometres of great beauty found etched in the muddled contortions of complex massifs, in their 3000m (9840ft) summits and the deep fragrant valleys. And to trek across them demands fitness, stamina and, not least, an understanding of the problems that can arise among difficult and trackless terrain. Yet the rewards are there for the asking. Rewards like the vision of an unfolding panorama that becomes increasingly familiar day by day; like the insight into little-visited recesses of hanging valleys and a

Under the heights of Posets the Estós Valley gives easy access to the Maladeta, seen on the horizon. (Photo: Kev Reynolds.)

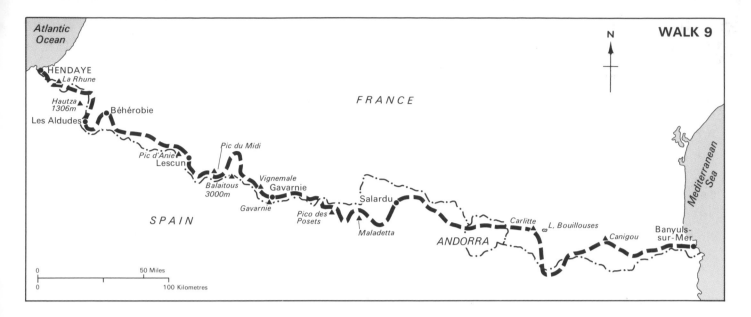

Distance: 400km (250 miles)

Time required: 44 days

Type of Walk: Demanding and varied, through deserted and spectacular landscape. For experienced trekkers only.

Start: Hendaye-Plage.

Best Time of Year: July – September.

Maps: IGN 1:50,000 as follows: Espelette, Iholdy, Saint-Jean-Pied-de-Port, Tardets-Sorholus, Larrau, Laruns-Somport, Argelès-Gazost, Gavarnie, Vieille-Aure, Vicdessos, Fontargente, Mont-Louis, Saillagouse, Prats-de-Mollo, Prades, Céret, Arles-sur-Tech, Argelès-sur-Mer, Cerbere. In addition for Spain, Editorial Alpina 1:25,000 Posets, Maladeta Aneto; at 1:40,000 La Vall d'Aran, Pica d'Estats Mont Roig and for Andorra, M.I. Consell General 1:50,000 Valle d'Andorra.

Guidebooks: *Pyrenees High Level Route* by Georges Véron (Gastons/West Col) for Hendaye-Banyuls, also *Walks and Climbs in the Pyrenees* by Kev Reynolds (Cicerone Press) for Lescun-Andorra sections.

close acquaintance with the unsung ridges and faces of mountains known only to a handful of enthusiasts. There's the richest mountain flora in Europe. There are tarns by the hundred to reflect in the clear, pure light. There are streams of liquid silver and cascades that pour from inaccessible cliffs. There are airy crests demanding sure footwork and a well-fitting rucksack. There are deep-shadowed gorges and high plateaux of dazzling limestone and tangled forests and grasslands alive with leaping insects.

It's a long way, end to end of the Pyrenees; but it's filled with the magic of the mountains.

There are two recognised routes across the range. One, the GR 10 *(Grande Randonnée)*, makes a low-level traverse over modest passes, skirting the higher peaks and sometimes taking to roads. It is waymarked throughout, remains at all times on French territory and presents no difficulties with overnight accommodation or availability of supplies. The other, the high route known as the HRP *Haute Randonnée Pyrénéenne)*, is the more challenging alternative. For most of the 44 or so days of this traverse it attempts to follow the line of the watershed, often hugging the Franco/Spanish frontier along ridges, sometimes crossing it where necessary to circle some of the highest Spanish massifs, and as a consequence samples the very best the range has to offer.

The HRP is not one single high route trail, but a main trail with numerous substitute sections, each with its own distinctive features. In its demands, in its severity, it is quite a different undertaking to that of the GR 10; stages there are where neither huts nor villages are on hand to supply accommodation, so either a lightweight tent should be carried or a beneath-the-

stars bivouac becomes the only option. Long periods are spent away from habitation, so for stages between manned *refuges* food supplies have to be carried. Where the route travels through France waymarking is mostly adequate, and in a number of cases, such as through the National Park, well used; but for stages in Spain, map, compass and an ability to read the country will be required. In the central region, the High Pyrenees, snowfields are frequently crossed and, depending upon the time of year it is tackled, ice-axes may well be needed.

It begins where the mountains begin, rising from the Atlantic in the Basque hills; green, wooded, mysterious. In from the Ocean roll the damp mists that are collected upon vegetated heights, and in the mists the walker struggles among gorse and bracken, confused by sounds that are distorted by the swirling vapours. On the coast Hendaye is a busy place of fishermen and tourists and a rucksack laden for the hills seems out of place, but the madness of town life is soon replaced by a more gentle pace, a more welcoming calm as lanes and the occasional path lead inland to the village of Biriatou. It's not far from Hendaye-Plage—a couple of hours or so—but the first night is usually spent here in readiness for the real journey that starts with seven hours of walking up into the hills.

Days 1 – 6: Hendaye-Plage to Les Aldudes

On the first day's trekking the summit of La Rhûne is reached; the first of countless summits, but one that does little for the mountain wanderer. There's a television mast on the top, and crowds of trippers brought by a rack-railway from Col de St Ignace. On a clear day the views are extensive; they stretch over the great Landes forest and the Atlantic, and inland across the confused hills of the Basque country that covers both sides of the frontier. However, the trekker will not be tempted to linger for south-eastwards there beckons a landscape of magnetic appeal. Out there will be found a solitude that is sorely wanting on this promontory.

For ten days the way crosses the Basque region, and in that period a deep impression is gained of this green, lush landscape. There are forests in the valleys which also clothe many of the hills right across their tops. There are grassy knolls and a few rock-shaven cliffs, but the feeling that is ever-present is of unseen movement. There are sheep trails to cause confusion; sheep in the mists, in the rain, streams dashing in a fury through meadows and forest glades. Basque villages emerge at nightfall, or sometimes not at all, and then a solitary shepherd's hut has to suffice. Otherwise, up with the tent. There are numerous roads crossing the range at this western end, and day after day a quiet path is suddenly traded for a stretch of tarmac or a forestry track climbing out of an unseen valley.

Sometimes the way strays through Spanish territory, but more often than not it is in France, or along the very border itself. Sometimes the waymarkings of GR 10 are followed for an hour or so, but again there are times when the actual route is lost among the regular trails made by generations of migrant sheep. Col follows col, often distinguished from the previous one only by a marker stone bearing a number. Now and then a sudden panorama unveils itself to catch the breath, revealing as it does the onward route. On day six a short diversion from the route to reach the summit of Hautza (1306m, 4283ft) gives such a panorama, an alluring collection of whale-backed hills rising to a hint of big mountains against the horizon, all blue with distance and spattered with snow.

Day 7: Les Aldudes to Béhérobie

The following day is a long one of ten hours' exercise, regardless of rests. It climbs out of the Vallée des Aldudes to find ridges and a series of cols that lead to the road pass of Col de Roncevaux where in 778 Charlemagne's troops, returning from their expedition against the Saracens in Spain, were ambushed by the Basques. The trekker has other reasons to curse this place for it means a wearisome uphill road walk of 5km (3 miles) before another path relieves the agony. There follow more cols, more confusion among meandering sheep trails, and

more forest paths before Béhérobie comes into sight.

Days 8 – 11: Béhérobie to Ansabère

Then comes the huge Iraty forest; the pride of the Basque country which spreads to both sides of the frontier with its lovely beeches. In the forest lie green pools. At their edges, green undergrowth, green shrubs, green leaves on the green-trunked trees. Even the air seems green. But the high route climbs through it to find space between the forest and the sky. Above Col d'Errozaté at 1076m (3529ft) the peak of the same name is crossed, a peak with an overriding view of trees forming a lush carpet around the hills. Another summit worth seeking out is that of Occabé, and another on the following day, Pic d'Orhy, on a day of many minor tops. But Pic d'Orhy is one of the classic Basque peaks with an immense panorama, and the stage that takes it in its stride is one of the classic walks at this western end of the Pyrenees. It's a day of about seven hours' trekking along a fine ridge with a short exposed section. At the end of the day, a shepherd's hut far from the madding crowd.

From forest to bleached limestone. From the solitude of pastureland to the bland commercialism of a ski resort. From greensward to the hard metalled spirals of a busy road. Such are the contrasts of the stage that leads to La Pierre-Saint-Martin. But it goes through a landscape of remarkable limestone formations, passes the Kakouéta gorges and skirts the famous Gouffre Lépineux, the cavers' paradise. Eastwards, the Basque country is at last traded for the region of Béarn and the first of the Hautes Pyrénées, marked by the bulk of Pic d'Anie across whose shoulder, all limestone contortions and guiding cairns, the high route goes. And then, welcoming in its pastures, in its temptation to linger, the smiling belvedere of Lescun.

Sadly, the official high route by-passes the village of Lescun in its determination to gaze upon the teetering pinnacles of the Aiguilles d'Ansabère. Sadly, for Lescun is one of those magical places too precious to miss, and it would so graciously repay the trekker to spend here a day of rest before moving on.

Day 12: Ansabère to Refuge d'Arlet

From the Aiguilles d'Ansabère to Pic du Midi d'Ossau will take at least three days, but better to make it four. It's a section of constant beauty and variety, gruelling at times, but with so much of interest that weariness is an acceptable form of payment. There is no accommodation to be had beneath the aiguilles; there is a shepherd's hut and sloping grass for a tent, but what a

The Acherito Cirque occupies an idyllic setting above remote Spanish valleys.
(Photo: Kev Reynolds.)

backcloth to dreams! Leading away from this enchanted cirque the route goes steeply up to the frontier ridge, then descends sharply to a Spanish tarn trapped in a rocky bowl of mountain with huge vistas of empty valleys and sun-dusted sierras stretching away to the far ends of the earth. After some hours of wandering along a smooth green hillside the frontier is regained for a late-afternoon walk in the sky, a walk far above the valleys where streams in the distance murmur, while far ahead rears Pic du Midi, beckoning from its solitary perch. Refuge d'Arlet, built by the National Park authorities, sits above its little lake and offers an evening's comfort after the rigours of a magical day.

Days 13 and 14: Refuge d'Arlet to Refuge d'Ayous

Downhill, through pudding-stone littered pasture, across minor ridges and through patches of forest, a short day's walk leads into the lovely Cirque d'Aspe and the Somport road, but this is soon left behind as the way climbs once more, this time above the eastern slopes of the Aspe valley in a region of fragrant shrubs and masses of wild flowers. Birds fill the air with their song and *isard*, the Pyrenean chamois, may be seen grazing on the higher slopes. Over a brace of high passes the waymarked path leads directly to the steep-roofed Refuge d'Ayous in full, glorious view of Pic du Midi d'Ossau, the symbol of the Pyrenees.

Day 15: Refuge d'Ayous to Refuge de Pombie

The high route guide suggests continuing across Pic du Midi's shoulder as far as the Pombie hut, but to do so is to miss the possibility of one of the loveliest sights of these mountains, one of the great pleasures of the end to end traverse; sunrise over the mountain, dazzling in the calm waters of Lac Gentau immediately in front of the hut.

From Refuge d'Ayous to Refuge de Pombie makes a fine outing in its own right. It links several varied cols, collects a number of tarns on its switch-back journey, and constantly offers changing views of Pic du Midi from hour to hour. There are great herds of *isard* around the mountain. There are swamps of flowers early in the season and at all times the gaunt cliffs of the peak echo to the piton hammers of climbers, for whom this is the most popular climbing arena of the whole range. It is a day to remember, to savour in the years that follow.

Days 16 – 21: Refuge de Pombie to Refuge de Barroude

With Pic du Midi now behind, the next milestone is the huge, stark bulk of Balaitous, first of the 3000m (9840ft) massifs to be met. Trees and soft-turf valleys are traded for an uncompromising landscape of huge boulders, screes, blackened tarns and slender glaciers. But for all that it holds a peculiar fascination all of its own. This is country that creates no false illusion. It's a hard world, a haunted world, a charismatic world. There will be difficulties here for the inexperienced, with one or two scrambling pitches to contend with over the highest passes so far, and if the weather turns nasty here then problems will be compounded. But there is an alternative way that goes south below Balaitous itself, avoiding the major difficulties and rejoining the high route proper in the Marcadau's pastures. The true route goes over the high, craggy north-west ridge of Balaitous at Port du Lavedan (2615m, 8577ft) and drops steeply down to the black depths of Batcrabere. Then it works a long traverse around the northern slopes of the mountain before finally escaping its clutches across another high pass, Col de Cambales (2706m, 8875ft). This is a pass to be avoided in bad weather, but on a fine sunny day the greeting given by a string of smiling tarns banked by white granite mouldings is but a foretaste of the good things in store lower down, in the bright, light pastures of the Marcadau Valley.

The Marcadau is one of the loveliest of all Pyrenean valleys, and consequently, because of

its ease of access from Cauterets, one of the busiest. The hut there is always in demand and a peaceful night should not be expected, however much it may be craved.

Rising to the south-east the gentle slopes of the Arratille lead the trekker beside a stream of many pleasures that here bursts through a mini-gorge, there spreads itself over a broad, flattened platform; that gushes in foaming spouts over the lips of grey cliffs, and elsewhere gurgles with delight along a flower-speckled channel of turf. Higher stretches a deep-blue lake, but then a slog up a treadmill of scree brings a discovery of a haunted tarn set just below the towering crags that guard Col d'Arratille on the edges of unknown Spain. Here is an enclave, where the calm upper reaches of the Ara Valley are surrounded on three sides by French mountains. Directly opposite rises the highest of all the frontier mountains, the Vignemale (3289m, 10,827ft), and around its northern slopes, across its craggy shoulders, goes the high route.

Down among the littered boulders of Spain waymarking splashes lead before one climbs steeply out of the Ara to emerge breathless and weary upon Col des Mulets (2591m, 8498ft). Then down again, this time in France with Vignemale's huge north face growing with each succeeding minute as the glaciated levels at its feet are fast approached. It's a face to set a climber's fingers itching, and at the hut, Refuge des Oulettes de Gaube, eyes are forever turning towards it in expectation. Over the next col a new facet of the mountain becomes evident, that of its great eastern glacier, the largest in the Pyrenees. Even so it is insignificant when matched with those of the Alps, but it has a charm all its own, and on its former moraine bank the path wanders past the caves of Henry Russell, the eccentric pioneer who, a century ago, fell so in love with the Vignemale that he lived for weeks at a time in the grottoes he constructed in its walls.

Nearby sits Gavarnie, the most-visited place in the range, but the true high route makes a careful diversion to avoid its busy street. It goes up towards the frontier again to reach the hut so carefully placed beneath the strange cleft in the Cirque de Gavarnie's walls, the Brèche de Roland. In the morning the route plunges dramatically into the hollow depths of the

One of the few relaxing stages on the high route leads from Refuge d'Arlet into the Aspe Valley. For much of the descent a good trail leads through bright landscape. (Photo: Kev Reynolds.)

cirque, with cascades pouring over neighbouring cliffs in feathery ribbons. Then over green hillsides and through a neat pass in the eastern wall of Gavarnie's valley to find quiet walking in the Estaubé valley.

Héas is a small hamlet beside the torrent that comes surging from the snows of the vast Cirque de Troumouse. It is a quiet place of cowbells and gushing water, a good place to spend the night before setting off to find Barroude, a high, enchanted place hidden behind the walls of Troumouse. Up there, found beyond a pair of harsh cols, a lake gleams beneath the long Barroude wall to one side and a grassy mound to the other. On the grassy mound sits a little refuge, cut off from the world, lost in the solitary peace of the mountains and the stars. Up there, in the surrounding tranquillity, the lover of mountains will bare his soul before plunging into the reality of his journey once more. That reality here must be carefully weighed, for beyond Barroude is a stage of full commitment, only to be tackled in settled weather for it follows the crest of the mountains all day with scarcely one decent escape route in the event of bad weather or injury. There's no water along the route either, so bottles should be topped up at the start, and then you may go with faith.

Day 22: Refuge de Barroude to Rioumajou

Along the ridges to Rioumajou is a demand-ing, yet satisfying, stretch of at least nine hours' travel, excluding halts. High above the valleys, sometimes on grassy patches, often on crumbling rock, sometimes over lofty peaks, sometimes skirting their summits, the way pushes ever forward. Then a narrow gash of a pass is reached, with no more than a hint of Rioumajou's meadows far, far below, and one of the most tiring descents to be experienced in these mountains. It goes on forever. Even after the clattering screes are traded for steep turf there is no respite for the route demands total concentration until the very valley floor is finally reached. And then there's no accommodation to be had.

Days 23 – 28: Rioumajou to Salardu

Spain, the next day, gives of its best. A long, long haul starts the day, but then the descent from Port de Caouarère in full view of the glorious west face of Pico des Posets elevates this as one of those special days to store in memory for all time. A day of great beauty, of fragrance, of empty valleys and crystal streams and high vistas. There are hillsides clutching acres and acres of alpenroses. There are crickets by the million buzzing like fury and leaping away from the threat of vibram-soled boots. And there are those views, lovely beyond words.

Posets is second highest of all Pyrenean mountains and around its considerable flanks flow grand valleys. From a western approach another high pass (2580m, 8462ft) grants access to the Estós Valley which moats it to the north in fine pastures, gnarled pines, dashing streams and herds of *isard*. The official high route denies itself these pleasures and returns to France to savour other joys. But my preference is for this Spanish interlude to be extended, even though the Estós hut has been burned down and either bivouac or stream-side tent will be have to be acceptable. By going down through the Estós to the Esera, then up-valley heading north, the true high route will be regained in the shadow of the loftiest of all these massifs, the Maladeta.

Crossing the Mulleres ridge beyond the Maladeta is a long, hard stage to be avoided by those of limited trekking experience. It is the highest pass of the whole route, 2900m (9280ft) high, difficult to find in misty conditions and with an awkward descent on the eastern side that works a tortuous way among desolate boulders and great crags that would be mur-derous in poor visibility. But beyond this, beyond the shaft of Noguera Ribagorzana, there lies a high granite landscape littered with tarns, cradled by encircling ridges in an attitude of loving protection. It's a region of surprising beauty. On a bright day there is a rich, clear light

The little Refuge de Barroude is a National Park hut two days' walk from the Cirque de Gavarnie, superbly situated on a grassy knoll in full view of the huge Barroude Wall. (Photo: Kev Reynolds.)

and the nearest thing to silence. Few birds come here, there is little vegetation, and the only sounds to break the awesome quiet are those of tinkling water or the distant clatter of a stone falling in a gully, or the plop of a frog leaping into a pool. Cairns guide the route across white granite shapes like sleeping whales, while above rise the big peaks of Besiberri.

This is a Spain totally unknown to the crowds of the Costa del Whatnot, totally divorced from the posters and travel agents' brochures. It's an empty, trackless wilderness. A magnificent wilderness, and those who work their way through it gain riches with every stride. Over lofty passes, around deep lakes, along shafted valleys in the shadow of peaks that never receive the adulation of crag-scramblers the high route goes on its ambitious way. Eventually it leads to the outside world in the form of Vall d'Aran and the little old-world village of Salardú.

Days 29 – 32: Salardú to Vall Ferrera

The Rio Noguera Pallaresa rises in the marshy Pla de Beret, a high plateau cupped by the green mountains east of Salardú. Although the river's aim is to flow south and then east to find the Mediterranean, it first makes a curious detour of a loop going north towards the frontier before bearing round the mountains and scurrying along its true course at last. The high route follows the river for several hours through soft pastures and lush woodlands with the frontier peaks rising high above. Again the high route proper, like a well-trained dog, seeks its home territory by climbing to a high pass and picking up its earlier intentions on the northern side. However, these Spanish vistas have a definite appeal, and so this alternative is offered. It has its difficulties and once more there comes a stage that is only recommended for experienced mountain trekkers to tackle in settled weather conditions.

It heads up out of the Noguera Pallaresa a little north of the hamlet of Alós de Isil to find a series of wearisome passes that lead around the south and eastern shoulders of Mont Rouch. It's a big country up there. Tarns lie trapped in idyllic hollows and immense panoramas show a confusion of blue valleys lost in time. A long, long day it takes to get around this mountain, and it is almost nightfall before the safety and relief of meadowland are at last regained. Two days later the compass bring you into the Vall Ferrera; still Spanish, still fragrant, still rich in its vistas, in its tranquillity. But on climbing out of this valley France is seen as a narrow projection caught between Spain's mountains and those that mark the beginnings of the little State of Andorra.

Days 33 – 44: Vall Ferrera to Banyuls-sur-Mer

Andorra is all noise and ambitions to swamp itself in concrete; or so it would seem upon emerging from the Port de Rat, but on the loop around its northern boundary wall the peace

Top: **Estany Tort de Rius lies trapped in a landscape of granite.**

Above: **With the high passes of the Maladeta now behind, a high Spanish hillside near Port de Rius gives views back over a hard day's journey.** (Photos: Kev Reynolds.)

Above left: **The North Face of Vignemale, the highest peak on the France/Spanish border. The high route crosses the grassy plain before climbing over craggy Hourquette d'Ossoue.**

Above right: **Estany de Monges is just one of several bright tarns near the Aiguilles de Travessani.**

(Photos: Kev Reynolds.)

and tranquillity of highland landscapes restores once more a touch of sanity and sense of purpose. A couple of days are spent traversing Andorra, then the Carlitte massif comes into focus, the next major obstacle between this tiny bustling state and the sea.

The Carlitte is all in France; a granite battleground coloured by lakes in its interior and flowers and shrubs on its margins. The high route goes right over the summit of its highest peak and drops down on the other side to wander among a ribbon of tarns to reach the long dammed lake of Bouillouses where there is no shortage of accommodation. Beyond there it goes southwards into the broad level pastures of the Cerdagne, the only such valley in the Pyrenees and a delightful change after spending so long on the heights. There's the valley of Eyne, the flower garden of the Pyrenees, then pass upon pass leading along the broad-backed hills of the frontier to the long-cherished peak of Canigou from whose summit generations of Frenchmen have gazed in wonder at the vast panorama, while in spring the blossoms of the orchards that cluster on its flanks make it a place almost of pilgrimage.

Four days later the mountains subside into the warm waters of the Mediterranean, and with them the weary trekker. He has earned their calming influence.

Walk 10 JAPAN: A Traverse of the North Alps
by Christopher C. McCooey

From Renge Onsen to Kamikochi in the footsteps of the Reverend Walter Weston

The Reverend Walter Weston climbed Shirouma from Renge Onsen in the summer of 1894. It was his last summer in Japan at the end of his first tour of duty (he was to return twice more) and he had already climbed and hiked extensively enough to write his popular book *Mountaineering and Exploration in the Japanese Alps,* when he went back to England. Although he did not coin the phrase 'the Japan Alps', the good reverend did more to popularize the region and

introduce the Japanese to their own mountains than anybody else. Today all the Japanese hikers and climbers, and many of the day trippers, who go into the mountains of Japan (a record 3.68 million for July and August 1984) refer to Walter Weston as the 'Father of Mountaineering', and as most of the 15,000 who visit Kamikochi *each day* in the peak summer season make a pilgrimage to his memorial, it seems fitting to both start and end this walk in places strongly associated with him.

The Reverend Weston has at least fifteen Japanese mountain 'firsts' to his credit, was

The view south-west from Echizawa. The peak on the right is Yakushidake and the trail can be seen leading up to the Sugo hut. (Photo: C.McCooey.)

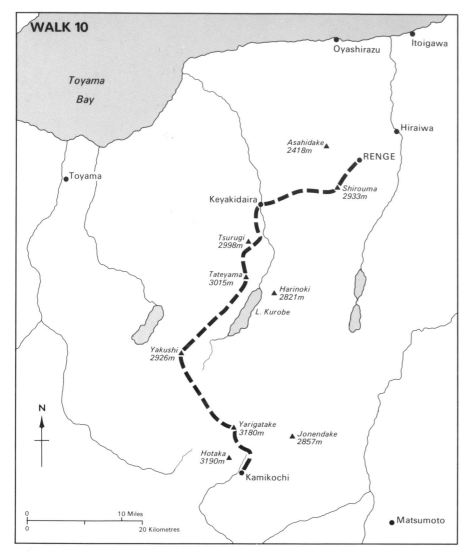

WALK 10

Toyama Bay

Oyashirazu • Itoigawa

Asahidake 2418m ▲ • RENGE

• Toyama

Keyakidaira • *Shirouma 2933m* ▲

• Hiraiwa

Tsurugi 2998m ▲

Tateyama 3015m ▲

▲ *Harinoki 2821m*

L. Kurobe

Yakushi 2926m ▲

N

Yarigatake 3180m ▲ • ▲ *Jonendake 2857m*

Hotaka 3190m ▲

• Kamikochi

• Matsumoto

0   10 Miles
0   20 Kilometres

Distance: 80 Km (50 miles)
Time required: 11 days
Type of Walk: Strenuous
Base: Boigawa (5 hours by train from Tokyo).
Start: Itoigawa – Renge Onsen (train 35 mins, bus 2 hours.)
Best Time of Year: Last week July, first in August.
Map: Shobunsha Area Map: *Mountain and High Places, Number 0.*
Guidebooks: *Mountaineering and Exploration in the Japanese Alps* by the Reverend Walter Weston (John Murray 1896), remains a very interesting background read. There is nothing more up to date published in English unfortunately. *The National parks of Japan* by Sutherland and Britton has a section on the North Alps as does the JNTO *Japan Official Guide* but both are general descriptions and not detailed walking guides. The Japan National Tourist Organisation (6-6 Yurakucho 1-chome, Tokyo) also has 3 useful pamphlets *Japan Alps* (MG-24) *Matsumoto and Kamikochi* (MG-15) and *Camping in Japan* (MG-084) available free on request, but send the cost of the postage. If you read Japanese there is a plethora of guides, maps and booklets available in every bookstore.

co-founder with Usui Kojima of the Japan Alpine Club in 1906 and for all of his long life (he died in 1940 at the age of 79) worked and lectured to introduce others not only to God's love but also to God's creations previously known to only a few ascetics and hunters. He opened people's eyes to the beauties of mountains; a fine and lasting achievement for a man who had been blind in one eye from birth.

The road stops just before the group of wooden huts and cabins of Renge Onsen (*onsen* means a spa or a place where naturally hot mineral springs may be enjoyed and they are very common throughout Japan). There is a large communal wooden bath in an annexe attached to the main building, which is constantly fed by piped water that bubbles up from the ground. If you prefer you can take an outside bath *(a rotenburo)* as the steam rising from fissures and sulphur-stained vents on the hillside just above the huts is where the hot water

actually breaks surface. There are a number of natural baths and wooden tubs dotting the hillside; some are very hot and are only for those who enjoy being par-boiled, others are at a more inviting temperature. The secret of enjoying an *onsen* is to enter slowly and not to move once you are totally immersed. There is nothing quite so delicious, after hiking all day in the hot sun, as to slip into a hot bath and soak those aches and strains away, with a cool tin of lager in one hand and the insect repellent—for the repugnant *abu* is no respecter of weariness and invariably appears when you are at your most vulnerable—in the other.

The evening *onsen* should have you in fine fettle for the early start the next morning. Breakfasts in the huts are from 5am and most hikers are away at 6. Fill up your water bottle with green tea *(o-cha)*, brown tea *(ban-cha)* or at the taps on the grass area in front of the huts and then head off into the undergrowth: the trail starts immediately at this point. Another trail follows a valley further to the west and it was this route that Weston took. It goes past an old silver mine that was still working in Weston's day but the more popular route is the one which leaves from the huts.

Day 1: Renge Onsen to Shirouma

The first hour is a very steep climb but steps have been made and the trail winds its way up the shoulder of the mountain through mixed woods. As the forest thins, more and more pines appear and soon you reach Tengu no Niwa, the mountain Goblin's Garden at 2000m (6500ft)—pines whose thick trunks and branches have been twisted by the wind and snow into fantastic shapes. Above the tree line there are fine views to the north-west of the mountain that stands sentinel at the head of the North Alps chain—Asahidake (2418m, 7931ft). Behind it to the north the Alps plunge into the Japan sea at Oyashirazu, with steep, heavily vegetated slopes, not cliffs, right down to the pebbles on the beach. The two rounded peaks in front of Asahidake are aptly named Akaotoko, the 'Red Man', as the exposed rock is of a reddish hue and Yukikura, the Snow Store House, as the exposed summit rock has changed within a distance of two kilometres to white.

The geology of the Alps is highly complex. Formed by tectonic plates pushing up against each other the mountains form a crumpled chain running broadly north–south from Oyashirazu on the Japan Sea to Ontake, an active volcano 100km (62 miles) north-east of Nagoya—in all some 120km (75 miles). The sedimentary rocks have been highly metamorphosed and the geology is further complicated by volcanic intrusions of tuffs, andesitic lavas and granites. The absence of any large-scale glaciation has meant that running water has been the main weathering agent, cutting deep gorge-like valleys, especially in the spring thaw when the metres of snow that cover the region in winter, melt and run off. Japan's record snow accumulation of 8.18m (27ft) in February 1927 occurred in the North Alps, where dry Siberian air masses pick up moisture crossing the Japan Sea and dump it—to the delight of Japan's 10 million skiers—on the mountains of Hokkaido and Honshu.

There is a very thick and luxuriant vegetation cover up to about 2000m (6560ft). Where this has been disturbed, by hikers cutting trails or by forest fires, then the processes of erosion or an unsettling earthquake or tremor, may account for a whole lot of the scenery slumping down in to the valleys. Evidence of landslips and slides are common all along the trails. Only above 2500m (8000ft) does bare rock show through and this tends to be broken into slabs and chunks by freeze-thaw action and the results of chemical weathering.

Shirouma Lake lies in a depression on the shoulder of the mountain at about 2300m (7500ft). Surrounding it are some fine alpine flower meadows which have been roped off to prevent hikers from trampling them. Volunteers, usually university students, and some full-time mountain rangers, are very zealous on matters of conservation. In alpine flower meadows (designated by red shading on the map) you wander from the path at your peril, even if your intentions are honourably photographic. From the lake it is a fine undulating ridge walk to Korenge (2769m, 9082ft). Just below the summit of Shirouma, where Weston's trail joins from the north, is the precise point where the boundaries of Nagano, Niigata and Toyama prefectures meet, so if you have a stick to lean on you can straddle all three.

Then on to the summit of Shirouma. You will meet numerous other climbers in the peak season as this mountain is very accessible from Hakuba, one of the most popular ski resorts in Japan. Everyone will offer you at least a 'konichiwa' (hello), most a 'ganbatte' (keep going) and some a 'fighto' (Japanese-English for fight). To the Japanese it symbolises the necessary guts to continue against all adversities until you succeed in your goal.

At the top of Shirouma there is a brass plate showing a panorama of the mountains all around. To the north Asahidake, to the east Mount Myoko (2446m, 8022ft), an extinct volcano in the Joshin-Etsu Kogen National Park, to the south-west Tsurugi (the Sword

Peak, but in fact more like a Saw Peak with its jagged teeth, the highest one being 2998m (9833ft), and directly south a long string of peaks towards the Spear Peak that Weston dubbed the Matterhorn of Japan—Yarigatake.

Because it is very unusual to see foreigners in this part of Japan you will be in great demand to join 'memorial' photos, groups of snap-happy Japanese who will urge you to say 'cheezu'——their approximation of what every one says to unzip a grin in front of a camera—and to pozu (pose). To the Japanese who must cram their summer mountain refreshment into three or four short days, every occasion for fun and 'memory' is important. They are happy to share their green tea, their miso soup, their beer and brandy with a henna gaijin—an affectionate term which means something like 'crazy outsider'. Smile, enjoy, share and laugh as there is no language barrier in the mountains of Japan—the welcome and warmth is genuine and if you can remember nothing else, just remember the Japanese for 'domo arigato gozaimashita': thank you very much indeed.

Most of the huts have camping facilities adjacent for those who want to camp. Water is available where indicated by the kanji 水 on the map and toilet facilities have been constructed, often with the exterior walls made of the surrounding rock so that they blend in. The standard camping charge in 1984 was 500 yen per person (about £1.60) The site at Shirouma is in a well-sheltered gully, unfortunately next to a rubbish disposal area which can be smelly. If

A typical Japanese mountain hut encountered on the walk: Babadani Onsen.
(Photo: C.McCooey.)

you can afford to stay in the huts with all meals bought then your pack is correspondingly lighter. Once on the trail only tins of fruit and packets of biscuits are readily available at the huts for the camper, so all provisions have to be carried. When I made this hike in the summer of 1984 for half the time I was self-sufficient and camped, but for the latter half of the hike I used the mountain huts, sometimes just taking meals in them. I was very grateful for the shelter and drying facilities of the huts when a typhoon swept up from the South China Sea, curved around the Noto Peninsula and passed along the Japan Sea bringing winds that made walking on exposed ridges impossible and lashing rain that convinced me of one fact that all mountain walkers know—that there is no such thing as a 'water proof' garment even if it is the product of years of research and made of some hi-tech, breathable wonder fabric.

Day 2: Shirouma to Babadani

The trail from Shirouma via Shozudake to Babadani Onsen is the hardest day's hike on the whole trip. You drop more than 2000m (6560ft) from the exposed Alpine peaks into a narrow valley verdant with maple, oak, beech, willow, and birch, and all manner of grasses, shrubs, plants and flowers. The valley reverberates with the most evocative sound of a Japanese summer—the cicadas; in fact the whole valley hums and buzzes with insect life in contrast to the shattering silence of the peaks above. Your reward for nine hours of joint and muscle-aching toil is some of the finest views in the whole Alps, an uncrowded trail through alpine flower meadows and the prospect of luxuriating in a river *onsen* to savour and replay the day's hike.

From the Shirouma huts you hike westwards dropping down into a snow-filled col. All away to the south are panoramic views with the grey and jagged peaks of Tsurugi and Tateyama the most dramatic. Having crossed the snow field the trail undulates along a ridge to Shozudake (which means 'clean water' in Japanese). Bottles may be filled from a melt-water stream that drains an open, snow field plateau, before tumbling off into the valley below. There is a stunning meadow of buttercups here, thousands upon thousands of rich gold heads smiling at the hot sun, the colour of butter when it was made by a maid in a wooden churn in a dairy. Still on the ridge the trail then passes through another meadow of grass, spiked here and there by the stately Yellow Trumpet Lily.

You lose height gently as the trail turns south and follows the shoulder from Kaerazudake. From here you can look east to the ridge across the valley; this is the more popular trail and

another way to descend into the same valley. In places there are chains and fixed ropes to help descend short vertical sections. Once the end of the shoulder is reached there is a very steep section which is very tiring. Boulders, and trunks of trees slain by the wind hamper progress, and it's here that you plunge into thick forest and lose sight of the ridge to the east. Woodpeckers hammer away in staccato bursts of activity, the liquid trill ('hoo-hokekiyo') of the bush warbler is frequently heard as it sulks about in the dwarf bamboo underbrush, and above, busily picking through the canopy of leaves are bands of willow, coal and long-tailed tits. If you are lucky you may see a nutcracker, a piebald jackdaw-size bird that eats pine cones, or be startled by the raucous raspings of that bold bully, the Japanese jungle crow, which has a larger, more vicious-looking beak than its European cousin. The insect life hums and flits, bustles and rustles all around you: lurid metallic-pink or bottle-green beetles; huge dusky blue butterflies with ragged wings; loose packs of dragonflies like miniature helicopters; the cicadas from time to time peaking out into a crescendo and falling strangely silent before winding up again—and just when you are enjoying this natural superabundance, as you pause to wipe the sweat and rest your tremulous knees (a condition the Japanese call 'laughing knees'), the irritating whine of a mosquito is detected, or a menacing green-and-bug-eyed horsefly materialises and forces you to press on downwards.

Eventually the trail breaks out of the forest when the valley floor is reached; the last kilometre is a much appreciated forest workers' track alongside the swift flowing river to the Babadani Onsen hut. Next to the hut are two rather uninviting concrete tanks reminiscent of those used for sheep dipping. These are filled with hot spring water. If you are not too weary it is better to walk back up the valley for ten minutes to the place where steam rises from the river bank. Strip off and feel your way into the river, finding just the right place so that your buttocks are not boiled, nor your toes tortured by the eddies of melt water. The boiling water bubbles up into the river bed here and once you have located the ideal spot lie back against a boulder and watch God enjoying Himself in that part of a subsiding day as the sun creeps up to highlight the peaks from which you have just descended and the first stars begin to peep through a darkening, deepening sky. White-rumped swifts and house martins swoosh for one last snack before roost time and your bath attendants, the dipper and the grey wagtail, follow the Japanese custom of bowing, by bobbing their tails before retiring. You are

Far right: **From Keyakidaira to Asohara Onsen the trail follows a miner's track cut from the rock of the Kurobe Gorge.**
(Photo: C.McCooey.)

sitting in a river deep in the mountain fastness of Japan; Toyotas that talk and *Makodonarudo* 'dead-cow-bun' shops and similar emporiums purveying fast food are far, far away.

Day 3: Babadani Onsen to Asohara Onsen

The narrowness and steepness of the valley may be best appreciated the next day as you walk down it to join the main Kurobegawa valley at Keyakidaira. Even in August at a height of just a few hundred metres above sea level there are snow bridges across the river—the sun only directly attacking them when passing overhead around midday. At Keyakidaira there is a train station disgorging a lot of day trippers so it is something of a relief to get above them and back on the mountain trail. From the station it climbs very steeply up, almost vertically so, until about 1000m (3200ft) where it turns south and follows the contour alongside the valley for most of the day's walk to Asohara Onsen. It is a spectacular trail, unusually even, because it follows a mining track hewn out of the sheer rock on the side of the gorge that has been cut by the Kurobe river. In places there are vertical drops of several hundred metres, but fixed chains and metal bridges reassure the faint-hearted. Many sections are in the form of a three-sided tunnel cut for the average Japanese mine worker to walk comfortably—but as you are possibly taller and will have a high pack with a tent sticking out at either side, these sections need special care. Your pack snagging a rock can critically unbalance you as you trudge along, bowed if not bent, in a parody of drudgery and serfdom.

Along the gorge are huge vertical rock faces which contrast with parts of the valley where even a thin soil enables the vegetation to take root. Tributary valleys are crossed for the most part by following the contour line into the valley, but two larger valleys are snow filled and ladders assist the drop down onto the snow and ice and the climb back out onto the rock ledge path. One valley has had a concrete barrier built across the river valley floor to arrest the eroding river tumbling huge boulders into the main valley during the spring thaw; a tunnel has been incorporated into this so you walk under the river. Three hours along the trail, a tree falling river that charges over a 25m (80ft) cliff above you, is a popular place to rest and take lunch.

Just before Asohara Onsen a recent landslip has obliterated the miners' track and a detour through the bamboo undergrowth is made; care should be taken here not to join the scenery that has slid down into the gorge.

The *onsen* is the site of a former mine and the

The volcanic nature of the land is shown by the number of thermal springs. Hot water bubbles out of the river at Babadani Onsen.
(Photo: C.McCooey.)

hot water is piped out of the horizontal mine shaft, suggesting that it was discovered by accident during routine mine tunnelling. Nonetheless it is most welcome after a day's hike, even though the bath is of the sheep-dip-tank variety. It is located on a ledge below the hut and is reserved for the exclusive use of ladies between the hours of 7 and 8 every evening. A special feature of this *onsen* is that the toilets are of the water closet variety and not over-poweringly redolent of disinfectant as in most of the other huts.

Day 4: Asohara Onsen to Sennin

From Asohara the next day's hike is all upward following a valley that runs west then turns south. At least an hour should be spent at the *onsen* of Senninyu, which means the Hermit's Hot Water and is about half way up. In my ten tears of living and travelling in Japan this outside bath is *ichiban*, the best, in my opinion. The master of the hut here is helped by his two sons every summer, one of whom attends Tokyo university and speaks good English, although this was the first time this season he had had a chance to use it. For 300 yen you can take a bath in front of the mountain hut; the master has constructed a rock-lined tub capable of taking ten at a time with the most spectacular view imaginable—out across the valley of the Kurobegawa eastwards to the chain of mountains that runs from Asahidake and Shirouma through Mountain Goblin Head (Tengu no

Atama 2812m, 9223ft) and the Five Dragons Peak (Goryudake 2,814m, 9229ft) to Kashimayarigatake (2889m, 9475ft). Sennin means 'mountain ascetic' or 'wizard' and is named after the hermit who lived in a cave just below the *onsen* 500 years ago. The ascetic could not have chosen a more aesthetically pleasing place—all that mountain fastness and beautiful solitude, and hot water all day and every day to contemplate it from!

Much of the next section to the ridge at the head of the valley is up a snow field which is steep enough in places to warrant kicking steps. Just as the snow began I encountered a film extra on location for an Edo period drama. He wore a traditional bamboo strip hat, a kimono of black cotton, with a wickerwork basket containing a spare kimono, a samurai's sword stuck in his belt, and on his feet were *tabi* (socks with the toes split into two parts, between the big toe and the other toes) and straw sandals called *waraji*. The only non-Edo era item was a startlingly red pair of Y-front underpants visible because he had hitched up his kimono to facilitate walking. Of course he was really a salary man in disguise and he told me that every summer he hiked in the Alps like this to 'refresh his Japanese spirit and Japanese heart'. I was delighted to have met him, particularly as he was wearing one item favoured by Walter Weston––when clambering over wet and slippery rocks he always tied his *waraji* under his hob-nailed boots as the grip was so much improved. His hunter guides wore them all the time and discarded them as they wore out. Kobo Daishi, the ninth-century Buddhist priest who founded the Shingon sect and invented the writing system called *hiragana* as well as the 47-syllable poem, is said to have worn out 6000 *waraji* in his unsuccessful attempt to climb Tateyama.

At the top of the valley, Sennin mountain (2211m, 7252ft) is a few minutes hike to the north and is a fine vantage point to watch the sun set behind Tsurugi and Ikenodaira (2505m, 8216ft). There are two huts to choose from here and they are about thirty minutes apart––Ikenodaira goya (*goya* means 'mountain cabin') or Senninike Hut (pronounced *hyuute*).

Day 5: Sennin to Tsurugizawa

The next day you follow a ridge that runs directly south down into the valley between Sennin and Tsurugi. The trail here has been badly eroded by countless boots over the years, cutting deep ruts made worse by rain run-off. Attempts have been made to arrest the erosion with steps to shore up the path and wooden ladders in places, but this section was the most badly eroded of the whole hike. In the floor of the valley, where two rivers meet are two huge rocks, one of which has been cleft in two and is known as the 'Rock Split by Lightning'. This place is known as Futamata, which means a cross-roads, a bifurcation, in Japanese.

On top of one of the rocks is a simple brass plaque, held in place by four climbing pegs. It is to the memory of Kenichiro Fukushima who lost his life in Showa 47 (1972) at the age of 21 while climbing on the mountain that dominates this whole area—the grey, craggy Tsurugi. The mountains claim lives every year (35 were killed in July and August 1984) and in this area and the other popular climbing centre of Kamikocki there are numerous memorials to those who die in the places that they love. In the past 30 years more than 500 have died on Yarigatake and Hotaka, the two most popular peaks that overlook Kamikochi.

An iron suspension bridge affords an easy crossing of the swift flowing river that tumbles down from the ridge known as Sannomado, and then the trail follows along by the Tsurugizawa river. In places it is difficult to follow as the ubiquitous paint splasher seems to have been getting low on paint around here, but by keeping the river to your left, you head up the valley in the direction of Tsurugi. Much of this hike is on snow with one tributary valley half way up joining from the north, again full of snow, which leads right up to the summit of Tsurugi. With crampons this is the easiest route to the top. Other routes have bolts and fixed ropes on vertical pitches described by Smoke Blanchard as 'a bit hairy'. Smoke is a veteran climber who has spent 15 years in the North Alps guiding small groups.

Tsurugizawa is a plateau area which is used as a base for rock climbers who want to climb the numerous pitches and faces of Tsurugi. There is a very big campsite and four huts to choose from. It is less than four hours up Tsurugi from here and if you have an extra day the climb is well worth it.

Day 6: Tsurugizawa to Goshiki

From Tsurugizawa the trail heads due south up to the pass just below Wakareyama (2874m, 9426ft). With fine weather the views from here are superb—north-east back to Shirouma, north to Tsurugi, south-west to the interesting lava plateau of Murodo and south to the three peaks known collectively as Tateyama, the Standing Mountain. The trail undulates along to the highest of the three peaks Onanjiyama (3015m, 9889ft). There are comparatively few people here resting on the shattered boulders of granodiorite gneiss. Not so for the next peak Oyama (2992m, 9813ft)—suddenly it seems that

you have come upon all of Japan atop one of the country's most sacred peaks (along with Fuji, Ontake and Hakusan). In the peak season you will encounter hordes of day trippers—from toddlers to grandmothers—and all ill-equipped for serious mountain climbing compared with those you meet elsewhere along the trail who tend to be over-equipped. The trippers will have done well to reach the top since it is about a two-hour ascent, the last hour of which is up a very steep and loose-rocked slope that must turn countless ankles. No less than 10,000 people visit the shrine on Oyama *daily* in July and August. For the payment of a small fee you can be blessed by the resident priests who recite a prayer and wave a sacred wand over you. The shrine must do, if not a roaring, then a mighty jangling trade, for it seems that every one of those 10,000 descends to the bus terminal with a charm that has a bell attached to it. It is like being caught in a gigantic herd of mountain goats.

In the mid-seventh century a kind of mountain asceticism came to be established made up of elements of Buddhism, Confucianism, Shinto and Taoism. The village folk who lived in the valleys believed that the mountains were where the *Yamanokami* (mountain god) lived and it was also the place where the spirits of people went after they died. The mountain god was essentially amoral and ambivalent by nature, neither good nor bad, but manifested himself as benign or destructive to the villagers' interests according to the treatment received. Treat him correctly with proper worship and the right offerings and the *kami* would bless the

Oyama is a sacred mountain with a Shinto shrine and is popular with day trippers. (Photo: C.McCooey.)

people with good health, protect them from fire and earthquake and ensure that their rice grew strongly. Offend him, by neglect or exposure to pollutions of blood or death, and his benevolence would turn to rage; sickness would strike, fires would burn down a home or barn and the rains would not come, so the rice withered and died. Of paramount importance was the ceremonial purity of the worshippers. Until late Meiji, women were prohibited from climbing to the top of sacred mountains because of the fear of 'the red pollution' (menstrual blood). Weston mentions in one of his four books that when he climbed Tateyama his guide showed him a rock which was reputedly the petrified remains of a woman who had dared to go beyond the accepted limit.

Today very few Japanese truly believe in the old asceticism—but if the great majority are not particularly religious then they certainly are superstitious, with mountain shrines such as Oyama remaining popular places to visit. The Japanese still yearn for the mountains; no longer are they a kind of sacred 'no-man's land', stronghold of mystery, a place where only spirits dwell. The thousands who flock to Oyama may not love the mountains in the same way that the hikers and climbers do, but the fact that they are there is testimony to the irresistible force and power that mountains still exert on the national psyche.

Looking down from Tateyama, to the east in the valley of the Kurobegawa river which flows from the slopes of Yarigatake 85km (53 miles) to the Japan Sea, can be seen Kurobe dam. It is the largest of its kind in the Far East and the fifth largest in the world. For those that like statistics it was completed in 1963 at a cost, in human terms, of 171 lives; it has a lake of 3.5 square km; the arch-type dam wall is 186m (610ft) high and 492m (1613ft) long with a storage capacity of 149 million cubic metres. Naturally, it is very popular with tourists.

From Oyama the trail is very steep and very crowded down to the pass between Murodo and the Kurobe valley. Trails lead off to the east (to the Kurobe dam), and to the west where a made-up path leads down to the Murodo bus terminal that most of the day trippers take. It goes past the oldest mountain hut still in existence, first constructed in 1617 for pilgrims who visited the Oyama shrine. The priests of the shrine used to consider the mountain so sacred that none of them stayed the night on the summit—they descended to Murodo (2450m, 8036ft) to overnight. But in 1927 a shrine office was built on the peak itself and since then people have slept the night on the mountain.

A third trail heads directly south and this is the one to take, climbing up to Ryuodake, (2872km, 9420ft), the 'Dragon King Mountain'. Then the trail undulates along a ridge which overlooks the lava flow that makes up the Murodo plateau and a dramatic volcanic caldera, both to the east. There is a steep zig-zag climb down to the lip of the extinct volcano before a steep pull up to the first of two huts at Goshiki, that are run by a couple with the family name of Saeki, a common name in the North Alps area. Most of the huts in the mountains are run by couples who take the franchise for the summer season, often working in the ski resorts in winter. They take pride in their huts and keep them spotlessly clean; the Saeki hut at Goshiki even has a fine wooden bathtub which is the next best thing to an *onsen*. The food varies in the huts but most, especially the smaller family run ones, try to serve a variety of tasty dishes with fresh fruits and vegetables not uncommon, as most are regularly supplied by helicopter. Some are also supplied by backpackers who bring mail as well as other provisions and items that do not warrant the use of the helicopter.

The master of Goshiki, Saeki san, has been running the hut for 22 years and before him his father did the same. It is characteristic of the smaller, family-run huts, which are preferable to stay in rather than the larger more impersonal ones on the more popular mountains. His son gives slide shows of the alpine flowers to be seen around the hut on the lava flow that has a very rich peaty topsoil that makes it very verdant. The master is very friendly and likes to drink whisky and yarn in the evening looking out at the great towers of cumulus rising above the mountain peaks all around. If the conditions are right there is another show prior to the alpine flower slide one. The billowy clouds shift and change in shape and colour, enhancing the magnificence of the peaks.

Day 7: Goshiki to Sugo

From Goshiki the trail heads south-west over the lava flow where hikers' boots have cut through the peat to the underlying rock, and you walk with the alpine flowers—the primulas, the anemones, the daisies, the lilies—which are all at chest height, making photographing them easy. The route skirts Washidake, (2617m, 8583ft) (Eagle peak) and then goes over Tobidake, (2616m, 8580ft) (Black-eared Kite peak) and through a curious forest of stunted pines whose branches are interlocked overhead. From Echuzawa (2591m, 8489ft) the trail is very steep down to a col before a correspondingly steep pull up to the hut at Sugo, which nestles in amongst the pine trees and is constructed of the same, making it look very like a North American

Far right: **In the Kurobe Gorge, tributary valleys filled with snow need to be crossed with care.** (Photo: C.McCooey.)

Tsurugizawa and Tsurugi mountains. (Photo: C.McCooey.)

pioneer's cabin.

Day 8: Sugo to Taro

From Sugo you climb up a ridge trail that undulates across slabs of quartz porphyry to the summit of Yakushidake at 2926m (9597ft). This ridge is very exposed and the wind can buffet and jostle you here. An approaching typhoon hurried my progress, but if the very boisterous wind made things tricky it also accounted for the superb views to the west—to Toyama Bay and the Noto Peninsula.

Anywhere above the tree line you can come across the delightfully, even naively tame, symbol of the North Alps—the ptarmigan. Called *raicho* in Japanese, it is otherwise known as the 'thunder bird' because of its feeding activity in the not infrequent electric storms that tend to build up in the hot afternoons. In Weston's day it was not a protected species and his hunter guides would often augment the Reverend's Japanese army biscuits (made of flour and potato and flavoured with sugar and sesame seed), his cocoa and his marmalade, by adding a thunder bird to the pot or even, on one occasion, a Giant Salamander, now a very rare beast and only occurring in Wakayama prefecture. *Iwana,* a kind of trout, were also commonly eaten by him in the mountains and sometimes his guide might shoot a *kamoshika,* a kind of chamois, whose heart was the most prized delicacy.

The summit of Yakushidake has a Shinto shrine and a golden Buddha image sheltering amongst the jumbled, shattered slabs of quartz. The approaching typhoon prevented a lengthy inspection but it would be a fine vantage point in good weather from which to photograph or sketch Toyama Bay to the north-west or the mountains leading to Yarigatake to the south-west. Dropping down to the hut at Goya the trail follows a stream bed which has interesting conglomerate rocks. Sections are very steep and it is hard going but the prospect of a roof over my head was incentive enough as the already lowering sky was beginning to turn a livid purple (perhaps I should have insured myself with divine protection by purchasing a bell at Oyama shrine).

Day 9: Taro to Kumanodaira

From Taro there is a choice of routes in the approach to Yarigatake. Follow the ridge that arcs around to the south and east, or approach more directly cutting across the valley of the Kurobegawa headwaters. Most hikers choose the latter course. From the hut the trail drops quickly to the valley floor and then follows along beside the river through a mature forest of pines. At Yakushizawa hut, where the tributary river joins the Kurobegawa, a suspension bridge crosses the river. The climb up from the river is very steep and hard going; the tall pines keep all sunlight out with a consequence that the boulders are mossy green and very slippery. Once having climbed out of the steep gorge-like valley the forest opens out and you are on the 'plateau of the Clouds', Kumonodaira; it is renowned for its rock and flower areas with such diverse names as the Alaska Garden, the Swiss Garden, the Alps Garden and the Greek Garden. The hut at Kumonodaira is set back off the trail a few hundred metres up and to the south and can be easily missed in thick cloud or mist. The plateau is well named; but if the weather is good it is a fine place for the botanist, sketcher and photographer to wander. An early start from the previous night's hut at Taro would mean that you could be at Kumonodaira by lunchtime with the afternoon to enjoy the plateau's forest, rock formations and flowers.

Day 10: Kumanodaira to Yarigatake

The trail continues across the plateau, soon crossing an area of exposed rocks that look like weathered clay bricks—a very distinctive rock with, presumably, a high iron content. There is a steep section coming off the plateau which drops down into a narrow valley—this is very slippery if the rocks are wet—before a steady climb takes you up to Mitsumata in a col just below Washibadake (2924m, 9590ft) 'Eagle Feather Peak'. From there you look down into a deep

valley and across to the ragged ridge that runs up to Yarigatake. Skirting round the head of the valley and without losing height it is an easy walk to the next hut at Sugoroku. The master here, Koike san, is proud of his warm and comfortable hut built in Showa 10 (1935). Over a cup of freshly brewed and excellent coffee, he will tell you the best places nearby to see bears (shy but not uncommon), chamois, martens, badgers, weasels, foxes, squirrels, mountain rabbits and monkeys. I have seen all but the Japanese bear (which is black but with a distinctive white crescent patch on its chest) in my time in the mountains. Bears have been known to attack people, but very rarely; they usually do their best to keep out of a human's way. Some mountain hikers take a bright coloured umbrella with them with the three-fold possibility of using it as rain protection, a

distress signal in case of accident, and, if opened and closed rapidly, to frighten away bears.

From Sugoroku the trail climbs steeply then undulates south-eastwards at about 2600m (8500ft). To the north you look down into a valley that has evidence of recent geo-thermal activity with a large area of exposed solfatara white rock (the whiffs of rotten eggs as you hike along suggest subterranean passing of wind from the earth's bowels). The last stretch to the hut at Yarigatake is very steep and rocky. Progress is slow as the altitude begins to tell. Yari is a fine, majestic mountain worthy of the greatest respect and to be savoured. From the hut it is another twenty minutes to scramble to the summit point, the apex of the Spear, with fixed ladders to help. The day after the passing of a typhoon could not have been better for watching the sun's descent and its rise eleven

Above left: **A typical day on the trail with the peak of Tsurugi in the background to the left.**

Above right: **A walker pauses just below the summit of Yarigatake, Japan's fourth highest mountain.**

(Photos: C.McCooey.)

105

hours later. The shadow of the mountain was projected onto the clouds below, with a translucent, trembling halo of light around the Spear's point. If the conditions are right Yari should be, quite literally, the high spot of your hike.

Day 11:Yarigatake to Kamikochi

The descent into Kamikochi valley is very steep at the beginning, across a huge field of shattered rocks. Once the tree line is reached the trail follows along by the side of the Azusagawa and becomes easier by degree as you descend. The valley is a classic V-shape and quickly becomes heavily wooded with a dense and uniform undergrowth of dwarf bamboo which seems incongruous below pines of great girth. The dappled sunlight, the dancing butterflies, the clear turquoise waters of the boulder-strewn river growing in strength and noise all the time, make it a satisfying last day. The valley floor begins to open out and the river finds channels in a wide and rocky bottom, only spreading out to its limits during the time of the spring thaw.

The trail becomes more even with pine-trunk platform bridges affording a smooth traverse around rocky abutments where the river itself meanders to the valley side. And then you see it—the first since Renge Onsen, a device that makes legs redundant—a car! (owned by one of the hut masters). Only taxis and buses and residents' cars are allowed in the valley in an attempt to reduce pollution of the air from exhaust fumes. Before long you have left the real world for the other world—no longer are you greeted with a *konichiwa,* you are back amongst the Holly Hobbit straw hats, the Wiggy and Eagle Sam T-shirts, the Mickey Mouse handbags and pretty-pink canvas slip-on shoes. There are compensations: the price of beer has come down with the altitude, and the chocolate and icecream taste good.

All that remains is to make your way to the Weston Memorial—a shady rock by the river where the dog-collared Englishman looks out with a kindly expression.

Pilgrims have left a small pile of 5-yen coins, called *go-en* in Japanese, a word that also means 'bond' or 'close relationship', implying that those who leave the offering will remember the place (and the person), and be remembered by it (and him). I am sure the Reverend is smiling in his grave to know that so many have a bond, a close relationship with the mountains, and that so many are refreshed in body and soul by time spent amongst his beloved Alps.

Additional notes

Mountain huts

All mountain huts are open at the beginning of July until about the first week of October with the more popular ones open from May to the end of October. The less accessible ones however have a shorter season. Reservations are not required and in 1984 the average cost for sleeping (bedding is provided but you might like to bring your own sheet sleeping bag) with supper and breakfast was 5000 yen (£16).

Food

The food is typically Japanese so if pickles, raw egg, dried seaweed, rice and fermented soy bean soup is not your idea of a hearty hiking breakfast then you will have to bring a stove for preparing your porridge and instant coffee. Huts prepare box lunches, called *bento,* for a few hundred yen or you can consult the map and time your midday meal to your arrival at another hut where you can buy a bowl of noodles. It's a good idea to take hiking snacks with you and to prepare a nibbling bag for each day. As well as the usual provisions of nuts and raisins (bought in large bags from one of Tokyo's wholesale markets such as Ameyoko or Tsukiji) try such Japanese specialities as dried persimmon *(kaki),* pickled plums *(umeboshi*—a refreshingly sour fruit with the added bonus of a stone to suck on), and fried and dried banana to go with your boiled sweets, oranges, biscuits, salami etc. It is virtually impossible to keep butter, margarine and chocolate from melting if you hike in July and August.

The Walter Weston Memorial in Kamikochi. This bespectacled vicar is honoured as one of the founders of Japanese mountaineering.
(Photo: C.McCooey.)

Trails and Equipment

The trails are very uneven and a stick is a great aid to balancing and when it comes to goat-like hopping from boulder to boulder; one of the collapsible sticks is best for it can be stowed in your pack on the few sections where you need two hands for scrambling. An efficient insect repellent is also highly recommended to ward off not only mosquitoes but a far more painful winged curse, the *abu*, a kind of horsefly. If you intend to hike at the beginning or end of the summer season then an ice axe is useful for cutting steps in the gullies where snow lies all summer. If you hike in August then an ice axe is not necessary as it is easy to kick steps in the soft surface snow melted by the hot sun. Good rain-gear is essential and take a torch with spare batteries as the generators wind down and the lights go off early in the mountain huts.

Weather, Best Time

It is very hot in the day time in the height of summer and you will sweat a great deal (I lost 5 kilos on this hike and I was not over weight when I set out). Salt tablets, a good skin protection suncream, sunglasses, a wide-brimmed hat, a towel to protect the neck and soak up some of the sweat, and a large water bottle to fill with tea are essential. There is a rainy season in Japan (not quite a monsoon but with weeks of high humidity when it rains often); this is usually declared at an end around the middle of July when high pressure extends over much of Japan bringing sunny and hot days through August. Typhoons can occur in August (and did on my trip) but are more likely in September when the weather becomes more unstable. Around O-Bon time (a kind of extended summer Bank Holiday when festivals are held to welcome the return of departed spirits) most businesses close down for a few days. At this time, the middle of July or the middle of August depending on the part of Japan you come from, the huts and peaks are very crowded. As far as one can predict mountain weather, and to avoid the peak seasons, the two-week walk would be best undertaken the last week in July and first week in August (although schools will be on holiday at this time) or the last week of August and the first week of September (schools are back but universities are still on holiday). If you take a chance with the weather and want to enjoy the stunning riot of colour on the heavily vegetated slopes in autumn then the last week in September and the first in October would be best, but check that the huts you want to stay in are open as some close promptly on October 1st while others remain open until well into October and even November where access is easy.

Maps

Several publishing companies produce excellent hiking maps printed on water-resistant paper. I recommend those published by Shobunsha in the series Area Map: Mountain and High Places at 500 yen each including a guide booklet. Number 0 covers all the route as described and the whole of the North Alps (except Ontake at the southern end of the range) at a scale of 1:120,000. More detailed in the same series are No. 1 covering Tateyama, No.2 covering Shirouma and No. 4 covering Yariga-take and Kamikochi. These maps are continuous and all three at a scale of 1:40,000. However they are all in Japanese. But do not despair! . . . you will quickly get accustomed to reading Japanese maps; instead of letters and words there are little stylized pictures called *kanji*, Chinese characters, which tell you where you are or where you are going. Before setting off it is a good idea to go over your route with somebody who can read Japanese and write in the names of the mountains and the huts in *romaji*, Roman letters. You should make a point of being able to recognise the *kanji* for drinking water, dangerous place, fixed chains, unstable rocks, falling rocks, hours and minutes (all trails have approximate hiking times which tend to be fairly accurate assuming a steady plod and regular rests). The main drawback to the maps is the absence of grid lines to enable quick and accurate orienteering of the map with a compass, but as the trails are usually very well marked by red, blue or white splashes of paint (the next one being visible even in thick mist and cloud) this is not so much of a drawback.

Walk 11 CORSICA: The Corsican High Level Route
by Duncan Unsworth

Above: **The Refuge de Pétra Piana is surrounded by wire fence, not to keep campers in but to keep pigs out! The pigs forage in the surrounding alder thickets. In the distance is Monte d'Oro.**

Far right, top: **The snowy peak of Monte Rotondo looks down on the picturesque Bergerie de Tolla.**

Far right, bottom: **Walking through the tall pine woods of the Manganello valley.**

(Photos: Duncan Unsworth.)

A Tough Walk in an Island Paradise

The idea of trekking on a Mediterranean island seems a little incongruous at first. Holiday brochures suggest nothing more than hotels, beaches and a few villages off the beaten track for sampling the atavistic pleasures of the 'genuine' locals. A week-long backpacking trek amongst fully fledged mountains doesn't quite fit the image somehow, and boarding the flight to Ajaccio does little to allay any fears that such walking may be non-existent as the passengers are laden with beach mats rather than Karri-mats. However, the first sight of Corsica from the air is a revelation, for the island rises out of

the water in a series of increasingly rocky ridges resembling an exaggerated relief model.

Corsica, lying some 80km (50 miles) off the coast of Italy and north of Sardinia, forms a province of France. Although best known in history as the birthplace of Napoleon, the island has had quite a chequered past, being repeatedly conquered and ruled by different peoples––including the British from 1794-6 (Nelson lost his eye during a seige on Calvi). Today, despite the occasional bombing by Corsican nation-alists, things are a little more peaceful. Suffering the economic problems of many islands, Corsica has turned to tourism as a major source of

income. Most of this is based on the coast with the mountains only a secondary attraction, and those going solely for the mountains are very much in a minority. However, the mountains are by no means second-rate and although perhaps not possessing grandeur on the same scale as the Alps, they are certainly very spectacular and possess their own charisma. The main chain forms the backbone of the island, running from north-west to south-east, the subsidiary ribs running off at right angles. Formed entirely from granite these youthful mountains rise to 2706m (8875ft) in the north, which, for perspective, is over twice the height of Ben Nevis on an island measuring only 180km (112 miles) by 80km (50 miles).

Traversing the chain of mountains is the Corsican High Level Route, now modified and designated as *Grande Randonnée* 20, between Calenzana in the north-west and Conca in the south-east. The GR 20 is divided neatly into two halves by the major east–west valley through the mountains at the village of Vizzavona creating the option of two shorter walks to the whole length. Despite the attractions of the Bavella Towers and the views from the summit of Mount Incudine some of the walking in the southern section is relatively tame and by contrast the northern half is much more glamorous. Although the track itself doesn't ascend any of the major summits there is a greater sense of being amongst spectacular mountains and consequently the northern section is deservedly the more popular walk, and the one I have chosen to describe.

The guidebooks to the GR 20 describe the route from north to south starting at Calenzana. However, I personally feel this to be a mistake. If only to maintain a sense of drama, with each day's mountains being superior to the last I consider the walk better in the opposite direction, from Vizzavona to Calenzana, even if it is against the flow of most French walkers following the guidebook!

Involving about 90km (60 miles) in distance and 6300m (20,600ft) of ascent and descent, the usual time taken for the walk is eight days, although it could be done in less—or even more, depending upon any deviations taken. The combination of covering some very rough terrain with the lack of villages along the route for provisioning has earned It a reputation of being one of Europe's harder walks. To add to the difficulties the heat in the valleys can be quite exhausting. However, despite the usual prevailing Mediterranean weather it *is* a mountain region and as such subject to the vagaries of mountain weather. In particular: it can be quite cold at night at altitude; subject to rain often

Distance: 90km (62 miles).
Time required: 8 days.
Type of Walk: Strenuous, over rough terrain, backpacking essential as little accommodation and few places for buying provisions are available.
Base: Ajaccio.
Start: Vizzavona.
Best Time of Year: June–September inclusive.
Guidebook: *Sentier de la Corse* (GR 20) Cordee.
Maps: IGN Carte Touristique No. 73 (1:100,000), Didier et Richard No. 20 Corse Nord (1:50,000).

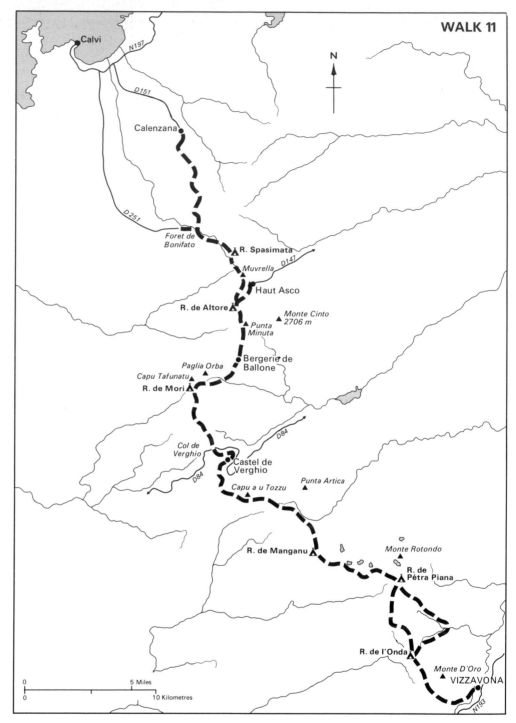

WALK 11

associated with thunderstorms; and before July snow can be a problem requiring extra equipment to be carried.

Along the route there are two hotels and a number of *refuges* (or huts) offering accommodation for between 15 to 30 people. However, the majority of people prefer to either camp or bivvy. Apart from the space provided at the *refuges* for camping there is no shortage of potential sites along the route, although there are now notices forbidding camping in a number of places. To stop the spread of these restrictions it is important not to create damage or litter and in particular not to cause fires which, due to the dry vegetation, are a very serious problem.

Vizzavona, the starting point of the route, is a small railway village nestling below the solid pyramid of Monte d'Oro. Travel on the Corsi-

110

can railway can be quite an adventure by itself. Diesel railcars connect Ajaccio, Bastia and Calvi, rattling their way across the mountains, and reaching speeds of 30mph—unless delayed or cancelled due to forest fires! The village is also on the major road of the island, the N193, which has a good coach service along it.

Apart from the station the village consists of a couple of hotels and bars, a small shop, and a few houses, all gaining their charm from an air of rustic dilapidation. Indeed, the village is largely distinguished from the others suffering endemic backwardness and decline along the railway by the number of rucksacks around the place. No doubt the influx of walkers will eventually alter the character of the village, but as yet it is delightfully like stepping into a past era.

Day 1: Vizzavona to Refuge de l'Onda

A few hundred metres to the south of the village there is an extensive, if basic, camp-site amongst the woods run by the 'Maison Forestière'. The route starts from the rear exit of the camp site crossing a concrete bridge into a new forestry plantation. Following the red and white flashes that mark the entire route it begins as little more than a gentle amble through beech woods, belying the tasks ahead. Entering the L'Agnone valley, dividing Monte d'Oro from Punta Migliarello, the deception is soon ended as the track crosses the stream and ascends by the left-hand side of the Cascades des Anglais. This first encounter with the Corsican mountain stream is quite a classic. The water races across the rocks to plunge into deep crystal-clear pools against the backdrop of the rocky mass of

Above left: **The first ascent on the walk climbs by the side of the Cascades des Anglais through delightful pine woods. In the background is Monte d'Oro.**

Above right: **Crossing the Manganello river by a log bridge en route for Monte Rotondo.**

(Photos: Duncan Unsworth.)

On the eastern ridge of Punta alle Porte, part of the traverse from the Col de Rinoso to the Brêche de Capitello. (Photo: Duncan Unsworth.)

a ford the track leads past the ruins of an old C.A.F. hut before the relatively easy going of the valley becomes a steeper climb up the headwall. Climbing the increasingly rocky terrain a col is reached and the track leads across to Punta Muratello and for the first time distant views to the north.

Although the GR 20 itself never reaches any of the major summits it leads to within such a close striking distance of a number of them that short subsidiary walks to the summits can almost be regarded as part of the walk. Monte d'Oro is no exception, and before Punta Muratello is reached a marked track leads off initially in the direction of Bocca di Porco and then along the ridge to a final summit scramble. The views from the top are magnificent with the next day's walk and the rocky jumble of Monte Rotondo to the north, whilst lying to the south is the deep wooded valley with Vizzavona and, beyond, the distant white peak of Monte Renoso.

From Punta Muratello the route descends the obvious ridge to the north with no great difficulty to the Refuge de l'Onda.

Day 2: Refuge de l'Onda to Refuge de Pétra Piana

There are two alternative routes between the Refuges de l'Onda and Petra Piana, one via valleys and the other the ridges.

The valley route descends through the woods of the Grottaccia Valley to the confluence with the Manganello Valley. Leaving the wide track that leads on down to Canaglia it crosses the Passerelle de Tolla, a bridge of planks on two fallen tree trunks over the cascades and pools of the Manganello river. From the bridge a short climb through open pinewoods offers good views back to Monte d'Oro's more amiable north face before reaching the Bergerie de Tolla. This is one of the more picturesque *bergeries* (farms) posing as it does in the foreground of the day's first view of Monte Rotondo. Like many of the other *bergeries* it also sells its produce of goat's cheese to any passing epicurean walkers.

Beyond the Bergerie de Tolla the route passes through a very tall pinewood with glimpses and roaring noises of cascades off to the left. One of the delights of the GR 20 is the opportunity to escape the warmth and grime of several hours' walking by short invigorating swims in the glassy clear pools of the streams. However, as the water started as snow not far away, the temperatures are even more bracing than Skegness.

The full extent of the temperature extremes involved in the walk becomes evident as the trees providing shade end to leave the upper section of

Monte d'Oro framed either side by pine trees on the banks.

As altitude is gained the forest recedes to give way to the *maquis* (tough scrub, from which the French Resistance took their nickname in the last war) as an upper valley is entered. Crossing the Manganello Valley as a suntrap. There were once trees here, but all that remains now are the dead trunks and branches refusing to rot in the dry atmosphere and bleached white by the sun to form macabre skeletons. The living vegetation is now scattered juniper bushes, hellebores, thyme and other herbs creating a distinctive heady aroma, frequently encountered on the walk. As if to highlight this arid aura the place is festooned with bluish-green lizards. These disconcertingly dart to and fro as if in a ritual dance around your feet whilst walking. Quite a few of them have part of their tails missing for some reason—perhaps through getting too close to walkers' boots?

To add to the heat the route also becomes steeper again, at one point ascending by the side of a ravine with a series of steps made from the rock. Continuing up the flank of Monte Rotondo through the alder bushes and past a ruined *bergerie,* the Refuge de Pétra Piana is reached over a small crest. After such toil it's a rather depressing sight: a couple of buildings and a large wire-fenced compound with numerous people milling around inside, rather like some exotically located gulag. The fence is apparently to keep the wild pigs out rather than the people in, but even the panoramic views of Monte d'Oro can't make up for the initial disappointment.

The alternative route from L'Onda to Pétra Piana follows the smooth ridge between the two. Although shorter in distance than the valley route it isn't an easy option.

Day 3: Refuge de Pétra Piana to Refuge de Manganu

From the back gate of Refuge de Pétra Piana the route ascends steeply, initially through alder bushes, to a ridge running down from Monte Rotondo. This barren ridge can be climbed to reach the summit of a Maniccia and closer views of Monte Rotondo and the mountains to the north, but the GR 20 takes a more gentle path to the Col de la Haute-Route between a Maniccia and Punta Mozzello. The col is a looking glass into another world, a world of granite towers and faces, snow and icy lakes. A small snow patch leads to the Col de Rinosa, the edge of a vast, awesome, amphitheatre. The view is dominated by Capitello opposite, a clean face of granite reminiscent in shape to the Dru, which forms the centrepiece of the northern ridge of Punta alle Porte, a ridge surmounted by pinnacles like crocodile teeth. Making the scene more awesome is the diagonal thin grey line crossing the snow on the precipitous slopes of the ridge, the route ahead.

Leaving the Col de Rinoso the route descends steeply amongst the alder bushes before cutting off sharply to the left, to leave the unwary continuing to descend towards Lac de Mélo. Traversing around the amphitheatre, through the alders, over scree and around the contorted

Top: **From the Col de la Haute-Route the pinnacled northern ridge of Punta alle Porte can be seen.**

Above: **The bergerie de Vaccaghia sells cheese to hungry wayfarers.**

(Photos: Duncan Unsworth.)

113

Descending into the Cirque de la Solitude, at one of the fixed chain sections. The scrambling is relatively easy but very exposed and is regarded as the crux of the walk. (Photo: Duncan Unsworth.)

castellations of the ridge at its head, finally leads onto the face opposite the Col de Rinoso. Despite its earlier appearance it is actually quite benign and a well graded track leads over the rocks and snow to a gap in the teeth, the Brèche de Capitello, and back through the looking glass.

From the Brèche de Capitello a steep descent down scree leads into the Manganu Valley and a pleasant green bowl popular as a bivvy site. A little further on down by the side of cascades is the Refuge de Manganu.

Day 4: Refuge de Manganu to Castel de Verghio

The Manganu valley soon opens out onto a large high-level grassy triangular plain, the Pianu di Campotile. On the opposite side the route leads past the Bergerie de Vaccaghia and over a small ridge into the Tavignano Valley and the remains of the Refuge de Campiglione. Destroyed by fire in 1975 it now sports notices prohibiting camping and bivvying.

As the valley ascends it adopts an uncharacteristic topology for Corsica, a wide gentle valley covered in a mat of short green vegetation. Reflecting the name of the adjacent peak, Punta Artica, it has the appearance of windswept tundra in complete contrast to the previous day's showy scenery. With seemingly scant regard for geomorphology, virtually on the col into the Golo Valley is Lac de Nino, a diamond-shaped mirror for the gods. This is the largest and warmest lake on the route.

Rather than take the direct route into the Golo Valley the GR 20 climbs from the lake to the Bocca â Reta by the side of Capu a u Tozzu whose delicately shaded pink and green northeast face is glimpsed from Lac Nino. A short deviation to the summit of Capu a u Tozzu is well worth the effort for the first views of the striking Paglia Orba and Monte Cinto massif to the north as well as territory already covered.

From Bocca â Reta the route drops into the pinewoods and along a ridge to Col de St. Pierre. This is honoured by a rather shabby shrine surrounded by spent gun cartridges; a sign of the Corsican low esteem for anything that flies, as evidenced by the local delicacy of blackbird pâté. The route then drops back into the woods and along to Castel de Verghio, a hotel on the road next to a winter ski run.

Day 5: Col de Verghio to Bergerie de Ballone

The GR 20 leaves the road at a hairpin to enter the valley to the north flanked by Punta Licciola. This valley soon becomes a barren rock-strewn environment all but camouflaging the building of Bergerie de Radule. A romantic imagination could easily see this as bandit country which probably isn't too far from the truth, if not now at least in the past. Seemingly now the only life in the valley is the stream as it tumbles down the Cascades de Radule.

Gradually the purple peaks of Capu Tafunatu and Paglia Orba begin to dominate the valley. Paglia Orba, which means 'curved straw', is easily the most striking mountain along the walk. Its appearance varies between a half dome and a tooth from different angles, but despite being only the second highest mountain on the island, it remains the focal point of any view during the northern section of the route.

Climbing the ridge to the left of the valley the route traverses round to the Refuge Ciottulu di l'Mor: just below the Col de Maures between the two peaks. Built in 1974 this hut has the unusual feature of solar panels on the front of the terrace. The route continues beneath Paglia Orba to the Col di Foggiale; a viewpoint for the unique hole through Capu Tafunatu, as well as into the Valley de Foce Ghialla and the towers of the Cinque Frati, although one of the friars at first appears to be missing as only four are immediately evident.

A steep descent leads round below the rock sculpture of Paglia Orba into the Vira Valley and a large number of charcoal trees giving ample evidence of the fire hazards. Set amongst the living trees are the ruins of Bergerie de Ballone, now rings of low walls half full of empty gas cylinders and other rubbish. Despite the litter this is still a pleasant bivvy spot and consequently quite popular.

Day 6: Bergerie de Ballone to Refuge de Altore

Bergerie de Ballone is the start of the longest unbroken climb on the GR 20. Fortunately, the track up the desolate Ravin de Stranciacone remains in the shadow of Cupu Falu during the early morning, giving relief from the worst excesses of the heat, and the climb is not without its recompense, for it leads to Bocca Minuta and the edge of the Cirque de la Solitude.

Despite the number of walkers, the seemingly bottomless chasm of the Cirque de la Solitude is well named. It maintains an almost reverential sense of austere wilderness. Rock impinges on the void from all directions: the mass of Punta Minuta at the head of the Cirque, the sombre deep maroon face of Pic von Cube opposite, and the vertical towers by Bocca Minuta itself, all adding to a feeling of claustrophobia, despite the drop.

The route becomes a technical scramble as it plunges into the void, first down a loose track and then with the aid of fixed chains and ladders down the steeper, more exposed, rock faces. The fixed chain sections are partly responsible for the reputation of the walk and the cirque is generally

A short traverse with the aid of a fixed chain in the grandeur of the Spasimata valley which leads down to the edge of the mountains.
(Photo: Duncan Unsworth.)

**Looking back from the Col Perdu
to the Cirque de la Solitude. The
Paglia Orba is the dominating
peak; the smaller one being Capu
Tafunata.** (Photo: Duncan Unsworth.)

regarded as the crux. More than 200m (650ft)
lower a short path across the scree leads to the
way back up the other side. This starts in the
broken rock of a fault line below Pic von Cube
before moving out onto the more solid rock in a
game of join the flashes. Although the scramble
up is easy, it is also exposed with the steepest
part, just below Col de Perdu, having the aid of
fixed chains.

From the col the route descends rapidly over
snow and scree beneath the massive north face
of Pic von Cube (the peak is named after the
German Dr Felix von Cube who led several
expeditions to the area around the turn of the
last century) to the Refuge d'Altore. Below the
hut, off the GR 20, is Haut Asco in the valley.
Although possibly the major ski and mountain
resort on the island it is not a Chamonix or
Zermatt, consisting as it does of one hotel and a
few chalets. This relative lack of development is
indeed one of the charms of the route. In
summer Haut Asco forms the main base for
ascending Monte Cinto, the island's highest
mountain at 2706m (8875ft). Compared to the
GR 20 the walk to the summit is consistently
arduous and at times less than inspiring,
involving a lot of ascent up scree. However, it is
not without merit, particularly the views and
makes a good day off the GR 20.

Day 7: Refuge de Altore to Refuge de Spasimata

From the Refuge d'Altore the GR 20 leads
across the head of the valley and behind the
rocks of Punta Stranciacone and Punta Culagh-
ia to a col just south of Muvrella. The direct
ascent from Haut Asco meets the main route at
this point and it is also the start of a short easy
deviation to the summit of Muvrella. As often
the summit gives an early view of terrain yet to
be covered, but in this case no more big
mountains rather a classic deep valley leading to
the edge of the coastal plain and the Bay of Calvi
in the haze.

The main route itself crosses the western
slopes of Muvrella to another rocky col and the
entry into the Spasimata valley. Dropping
steeply down, the head of the valley leads to the
small Lac de Muvrella surrounded by alder
bushes. Alder bushes are one of the major banes
of the walk. At best they are dense green foliage
hiding tough woody branches designed to
scratch any passing legs; at worst they can cause
skin rashes for some people.

Descending into the valley from the lake the
route follows a rocky spur with fixed ropes on
one short steep step, before following the
left-hand side of the valley. Once again, the GR

20 shows another facet as the full grandeur of
Spasimata Valley becomes evident. Although
the whole walk is in granite landscape this valley
displays the rock at its most glorious. The river
gully, the easy angled peeling slabs, the gothic
decorated buttresses and faces of the valley
walls, and the impossible ridges are all sculpted
out of pink rock as if caught in a perpetual
dawn. Together with the deep blue Mediterranean sky and the green of a few scattered pine
trees clinging to the rocks for their frugal
existence, the pink gives an explosion of colour
upon the canvas surpassing any of the previous
sights of the walk.

The route follows the rocky valley down
another fixed rope section to a dubious-looking
suspension bridge across the stream. Those for
whom the sight of the missing planks from the
bridge (piled up on the bank) is too much can,
during the dry summer months, climb down to
the stream and out the other side to the Refuge
de Spasimata.

Day 8: Refuge de Spasimata to Calvi

Once below the bridge the route is within the
range of day trippers out for a day's rest from
the beach. Fortunately, apart from the number
of sandalled families and one small area of
picnic tables, this detracts little from the walk.
Yet again, the character of the walk changes as
with the descent towards the coastal plains the
temperature rises and the vegetation becomes
increasingly luxuriant with species new to the
walk growing amongst the tall pines isolating
the route from the mountains around.

Eventually the track arrives at a 'T' junction.
A short distance to the left is a small settlement
at the head of a road which is the source of
daytrippers and frequently used as an end to the
walk. Alternatively, the GR 20 turns right and
back into the forest again. Unfortunately, the
Forêt de Bonifato was damaged by a bad fire in
1982 which killed four walkers. A final climb out
of the valley to Punta Pinzalone leads to the long
descent to Calenzana and the official end to the
walk.

The real end to the walk, though, is a short
bus journey to the hedonistic delights of Calvi.
Despite being a tourist centre, Calvi still retains
its historic walled citadel which is worth visiting
but the greatest pleasure it offers is to lie self
satisfied in the warm sea water easing away the
aches of walking and reflecting upon the
wonderful scenery all the other bathers missed.

Walk 12 AFRICA: The Ascent of Kilimanjaro by Walt Unsworth

A Walk to the Top of Africa's Highest Mountain

'As wide as all the world, great, high and unbelievably white in the sun, was the square top of Kilimanjaro'. So wrote Ernest Hemingway in his famous story *The Snows of Kilimanjaro,* and if the description lacks precision it certainly catches the spirit of this vast African mountain. Kilimanjaro *is* wide, *is* high. It is one of the highest volcanoes in the world, and measures some 80km (50 miles) by 48km (30 miles) in area. In this great upland massif there are a number of smaller volcanic craters and three main ones. From west to east these are Shira 4006m (13,140ft), Kibo 5896m (19,340ft) and Mawenzi 5149m (16,890ft).

Shira is the remains of a collapsed caldera now forming an attractive moorland plateau whose general height is between 3300–3700m (11,000–12,000ft) accessible by a rough forestry road. Mawenzi, on the other hand, is a huge rocky crest with four separate tops guarded by steep ridges and gullies, attainable only by skilled mountaineers. It is the middle and highest peak—Kibo—that is the goal of the trekker.

Kibo is a huge dormant volcano rising like an ill-made plum pudding from the high plateau of the Kilimanjaro massif. The western side has eroded into steep cliffs, seamed with ice gullies and on all sides glaciers guard the rim, with but one exception—to the east, where a wide, desert-like saddle stretches between Kibo and Mawenzi. This is the way of the walker; the only breach in Kibo's massive defences.

The whole of the Kilimanjaro massif is a National Park lying just within Tanzania on the border with Kenya. This border has been closed for some years now and though there are constant rumours of its reopening, nothing seems to happen and the only sure way of attempting the mountain is from Merangu in Tanzania. Fortunately access is easy because the large Kilimanjaro International airport lies just a few miles south-west of the mountain, and aircraft coming in to land circle very close to the peak so that passengers get a bird's eye view of it. From up there, sitting in a comfortable Boeing, it seems as though you could stroll up Kilimanjaro in a few hours, given the right weather. In fact, it takes five days.

An airport bus runs to the little town of Moshi and from there another bus travels to Merangu and Park Gate where the trek actually starts. There is good accommodation in all these places and accommodation is necessary for at least one night, in order to organise the trek.

This is darkest Africa, and by long tradition treks are known as safaris; a term itself reminiscent of the days of Hemingway, when the only reason for going out into the bush was to shoot wild animals. The only shooting allowed today is with a camera. The National Park is strictly controlled and everyone who enters must check in at the Park Gate and pay the appropriate fee.

How much it costs you to climb Kilimanjaro depends on how you go about it. The easiest way is to let one of the hotels, or the Park Gate authorities, organise the whole thing at an inclusive fee. They will provide a guide and a cook/porter, all the food and utensils; everything, in fact, except a sleeping-bag and

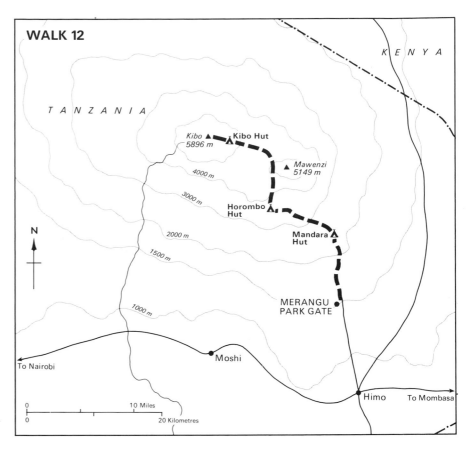

WALK 12

Distance: 67km (42 miles).
Time required: 5 days.
Type of Walk: A high level walk, exhausting in its upper reaches.
Base: Moshi, Tanzania, 22km (14 miles) from Kilimanjaro International Airport.
Start: Merangu Park Gate.
Best Time of Year: August – October inclusive.
Guidebooks: There is a climbers' guidebook to Mt. Kenya and Kilimanjaro published by the Mountain Club of Kenya, but it is not necessary for this trek. Good maps are hard to come by, but again, not really necessary.

personal walking gear—though even these can be hired at Park Gate if necessary. Hardier souls, however, may prefer to backpack up the mountain (provisions are available at the Park Gate shop) but though that is cheaper it has serious disadvantages in the higher reaches of the walk where the altitude begins to take a heavy toll on stamina. Not only that, but the final ascent of the peak is done in the dark of the night and Kibo is a confusing mountain for anyone not sure of the way.

Day 1: Merangu to Mandara Hut

Park Gate is a cluster of modern wooden buildings, Scandinavian style, set above the coffee and banana *shambas* of Merangu. A few tall, spare-looking trees reach up into the sky; the forerunners of the mountain forest. From the Gate a broad path leads into the forest, climbing gently. On either hand the trees and undergrowth crowd in, the home of elephant and rhino, though both seem to keep away from the popular trail.

It hardly seems like Africa; the forest is not jungle in the sense of a South American jungle, but more like an overgrown woods in Surrey and the walking is nothing if not pleasant. Some four hours from the Gate, and 914m (3000ft) higher, the Mandara Hut appears in a forest clearing.

The simple little stone hut which once marked Mandara as a staging post up the mountain is shuttered and semi derelict. Beyond it, the National Park authorities, with the help of Norway (of all places) has built a series of triangular wooden cabins arranged throughout the clearing like sections of a giant Toblerone bar. A larger building acts as a dining hall, and there is a row of porters' accommodation, equipped with huge cooking stoves. Each of the huts is divided into two rooms, with four comfortable bunks apiece.

Mandara is an idyllic place—until night falls. Then the forest becomes alive with the sounds of animals. Screechings, roarings, the occasional trumpeting of elephant, all combine to remind you that this is indeed Africa. The dark outline of the forest takes on an altogether different meaning!

Day 2: Mandara to Horombu Hut

From Mandara next morning the trail, narrower and greasy in places, climbs steeply for a few minutes and then eases off. Before long the edge of the forest is reached. The transformation is abrupt. At one moment the trees are crowding in and then, almost at a step, they are gone, replaced by open skies and rolling savannah. Volcanic hillocks fill the foreground and beyond

them, far away, the tops of Kibo and Mawenzi.

The path winds around the hillocks. Away to the south a tremendous vista opens. The lower forested slopes and *shambas* sweep away like a mottled green carpet to lose all identity in the vast Masai Steppe which stretches across to a blue horizon. Lake Manyara lies in the distance, in a shimmering blend with the sky. In between, conical hills, volcanic remnants such as Kibo is, stand ridiculously stark. Nearest, and biggest, is Meru, a peak almost 4600m (15,000ft) high which is sometimes taken as an alternative trek to Kilimanjaro. Away in the distance are the blue peaks around the Ngorongoro crater. As the day advances the scene shimmers in the hot sun.

For the first time on the walk the sun becomes a problem. Out of the shade of the forest the rays strike the unwary with a fierce intensity. It is easy to be caught out. The walking is at a leisurely pace and there may even be a gentle breeze blowing so that one doesn't feel hot or sticky and therefore tends to ignore the sunshine. But at these altitudes—you are climbing towards 3700m (12,000ft) now—the effect of the undiluted rays on bare flesh can be dramatic. Without an adequate high-altitude barrier cream, the skin will eventually blister and peel. In severe cases it can be an acute medical problem and will certainly prevent an ascent of the mountain.

Here too, altitude makes itself felt for the first time, especially for those with no previous experience of high mountains. The Horombo Hut, which is the day's destination, stands at 3721m (12,200ft) which is higher than many famous peaks in the Alps.

Fortunately there is sufficient of interest to allow for a leisurely ascent. The grassland soon gives way to a landscape which can only be compared with a gigantic rock garden. Volcanic outcrops spring from a crumpled carpet of heathers, helicrysums and other exotic plants. Streams come gurgling down, the water crystal clear, and where they have cut back into the hillside, forming sheltered gorges, there are giant lobelia and groundsel, weird plants from another age.

The hut at Horombo is similar to that at Mandara. It is perched on a shoulder of the hill with spectacular views over the Masai Steppe. A fiery red sunset over Meru is a bonus before turning in for the night.

Day 3: Horombu to Kibo Hut

The walk next morning begins with a brutal pull up a spur of hillside behind the hut. A spring is reached, marked by a signpost warning that this is the last water you will meet; every drop used at the Kibo hut has to be carried up from here. It will be 36 hours before you pass this way again, so quite a lot of water needs to be carried—extra weight, just as the walk starts to get arduous!

The track climbs up to a ridge overlooking the Saddle; a broad desert of laval dust and rocks stretching between Kibo and Mawenzi. For the first time in days the full height of Kibo can be

Above: **From Merangu Park Gate the track plunges into lichen-draped tropical rain forest.**

Far left, top: **The snow-capped summit of Kibo.** (Photos: G.E. Donnan.)

Far left, middle: **The first night is spent at the chalets of Mandara.**

Far left, bottom: **The barren wilderness of The Saddle.** (Photos: W. Unsworth.)

Trekkers crossing the heathland towards Kibo. (Photo: Ulf Prytz.)

Day 4: Kibo to Gillman's Point to Horombu

At the Kibo Hut most trekkers try to snatch a few hours' sleep before tackling the mountain. The start is made at 2am. It is dark and bitterly cold outside the hut. Kibo looms as a vague shadowy mass of rocks and scree. Almost at once the walking becomes extremely arduous what with the altitude and the scree. Will power is stretched to the utmost to put one foot in front of another: time is a void without beginning or end.

'... all identifying features are lost,' wrote one trekker, 'and we have become impersonal zombies trudging upwards step by weary step. No-one even has breath to speak ... the silence is awesome.

'Now that I have stopped I can hear my heart thudding against my ribs and the creak of my frozen anorak as my chest heaves like an overworked bellows.'

The route zig-zags up the mountain. With dawn the rim is near and there is the glorious sight of the sun rising behind Mawenzi as a great orange disc. The top is reached at Gillman's Point (5682m, 18,640ft) which is two hours and a further 213m (700ft) of climbing away from Uhuru Peak (5896m, 19,340ft) the highest part of the rim.

The caldera is impressive, a deep bowl 2½km (1½ miles) in diameter in the centre of which there is another, smaller, crater, emitting sulphurous fumes which tell that Kibo is dormant, not dead. It comes as a shock to realise what one should have known all along—that the highest point of Africa is hollow!

There is a book to sign and then it is down, down, zig-zagging easily across the slopes which were such a labour in the dark. Down to the Kibo Hut for a drink, then on across the Saddle and down again to the Horombo Hut for a good night's sleep.

Day 5: Horombu to Merangu

Next day is a long one—all the way back to Merangu. But nothing seems hard now after the struggle with cold and altitude on the heights of Kibo. Back at Park Gate they will give you a certificate of achievement.

appreciated as it rears its huge volcanic ramparts into the blue sky. The Kibo Hut looks near enough to touch, but it is in fact still two hours' distant.

Across the desert of the Saddle the walking is wearisome; a dusty trail climbing to 4695m (15,400ft) where the stone-built hut lodges between some enormous volcanic boulders.

Few people enjoy the Kibo Hut, for though the hut itself is comfortable enough the altitude brings headaches and nausea to many walkers, and lack of appetite to most. It is seldom more serious than this, but the hut carries emergency oxygen just in case. A lot of people find that Kibo Hut is far enough and high enough; ambition wilts in direct proportion to altitude, and what seemed like a pleasant jaunt down at the Park Gate, now assumes sterner proportions.

The weather too, can make a difference, for though Kibo can be climbed at any time, the best months are August to October. At other times 'the rains', which make very little difference to the walker lower down the mountain, can blanket Kibo in soft snow. I can well remember once arriving at the Kibo Hut in a blizzard as ferocious as anything I'd ever met in the Alps.

Walk 13 NEPAL: The Everest Trek
by Walt Unsworth

Through the Sherpa Heartland to the World's Highest Mountain

Of all the walks described in this book none has risen so rapidly in popularity over the last two decades as that through the Kumbu Valley of Nepal to the foot of Mount Everest. A little over 30 years ago the area was quite unexplored by travellers: a mysterious land known only as the home of the indomitable, cheerful Sherpas who journeyed out of their remote mountain fastness to act as porters on Himalayan expeditions. The Sherpa 'capital' Namche Bazar, was as little known to the outside world as Lhasa in Tibet; possibly less so.

After the successful Everest expedition of 1953, when Edmund Hillary and Sherpa Tenzing reached the roof of the world for the first time, all that changed—slowly at first, but then more quickly as word spread that the 'walk-in' to Everest Base Camp encompassed some of the finest mountain scenery on earth. The opening of an airport at Kathmandu and the whole-hearted embracing of tourism by the Nepalese Government, completed the change.

For a long time it was the custom to start this walk at Lomosangu, a village which lies some 3-5 hours' bus journey from the capital along the Kodari road, and from there trek eastwards

Looking back down the Khumbu Glacier from near Pheriche, the trekker sees a wonderful display of peaks. (Photo: W. Unsworth.)

WALK 13

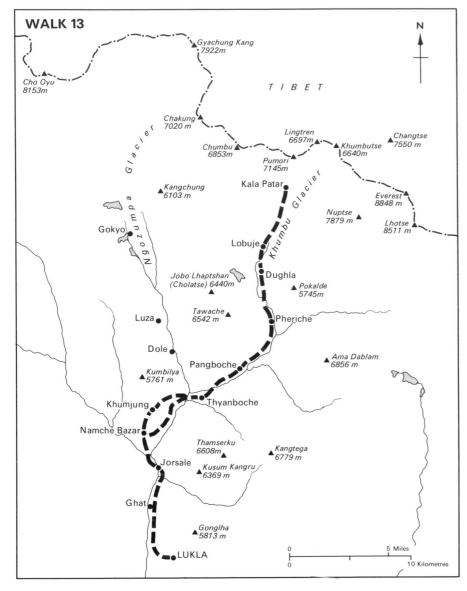

Distance: 80km (50 miles).
Time required: 13 days.
Type of Walk: A fairly tough walk at high altitude.
Base: Kathmandu.
Start: Lukla.
Best Time of Year: Spring – autumn.
Map: 1:50,000 Khumbu Himal.
Guidebooks: *A Guide to Trekking in Nepal* by Stepehn Bezruchka (Cordee).

across the grain of the country for ten or twelve days to Namche Bazar. This is still a good way of acclimatising, and you see some interesting country, but it has the disadvantage of taking more time than many people can afford. It is also tough going—up and down across five major ridges and numerous rivers.

Nowadays it is more usual to fly into Lukla, a STOL airstrip perched on a mountain shelf above the gorge of the Dudh Kosi, two easy days from Namche. Lukla lies at 2827m (9275ft), so there should be no immediate problem with altitude, though the ascent up the valley from there gains height fairly rapidly, which is why progress should be made in short stages, with suitable rest days in which to acclimatise.

If the weather is bad, there are problems at

Lukla. Too much cloud cover and all flights are cancelled. ('In Nepal the clouds sometimes have rocks inside 'em', an American pilot once told me, as we dodged our way through seemingly innocent fluffy vapour to Lukla.) This not only prevents people from flying in, but prevents others from flying out—and a log-jam of would-be passengers builds up. So it is necessary to be prepared for such an eventuality: *you simply cannot guarantee that you will be able to fly out of Lukla on any given day.* Of course, Lukla is not alone in this—similar delays can occur at places like Leh, Skardu, or even Cuzco. Anywhere high mountains make their own weather!

Day 1: Lukla to Phakding

From the airstrip a path leads north, descending into the Khumbu valley to join the main track along the valley floor. It takes about three-quarters of an hour to descend—a happy start to the walk which, as the days go by, climbs into the rarified atmosphere in the manner of a snakes and ladders board. Up and down to cross and recross the river or overcome some spur of hillside—but there's more up than down, and so height is quickly gained.

For the first two days the altitude is hardly noticeable. The walking is in the deep gorge of the Dudh Kosi, whose name, which means 'Milk River' is aptly demonstrated, especially if it is in spate. Rushing rapids, white with glacial dust from the foot of Everest, give the river an angry appearance. It seems incredible that anyone could actually have canoed down such a torrent, yet a British party did just that a few years ago and made a spectacular TV film of it.

At Phakding you are down to 2652m (8700ft) and it may be as well to rest here for the first night. Whether you camp on this trek, as the commercial treks do, or stay at Sherpa 'hotels' as many individual trekkers do, will no doubt depend on circumstance. Not all the camp sites are savoury, but then some of the 'hotels' would give an RAC hotel inspector nightmares, too!

Day 2: Phakding to Namche Bazar

Next day the trek continues along the narrow gorge. Rhododendron bushes flourish and in autumn the flame coloured berberis gives an orange glow amidst the darker green. Cross the river, and cross again—how many times? The teashops come as welcome relief and you soon pick up the drinking habits of the country.

They offer hot, sweet, milky tea poured (preferably into your own mug) direct from the kettle in which it was brewed. The Sherpas, who have learned their tea-making from expeditions, have dispensed with any refinements the process may have acquired in western kitchens and come up with a basic brew which is more than welcome on the dusty trail. Sugar is essential, for Sherpas love sugar, and they simply do not comprehend tea without sugar. In any case, with the amount of energy you are expending each day the sugar won't come amiss!

This tea has nothing in common with their own traditional Tibetan tea which is served with butter and salt. You are unlikely to come across it in a teashop along the trail, though if you have the good fortune to visit a Sherpa home you will probably be served it. To say that it is an acquired taste is putting it politely!

But tea is not the only drink obtainable at these road-side bistros. Equally popular is the local beer called *chang* and there is also the more potent *rakshi;* a rough spirit which is reminiscent of turpentine. *Chang* is brewed from fermented grain—millet, barley or rice—and is a white liquid not unlike alcoholic milk. It varies enormously, in quality and potency. Robert Schultheis, in an essay on the subject, summed it up perfectly: '...*chang* is wonderful stuff at its best, the Pol Roger, the Château Rothschild of beers. At its worst, it is a dirty, thick, sour yellow gruel, with not enough alcohol in it to stone the bugs that swim merrily through it.' A drink to savour.

It is certainly worth having a drink and a rest at Jorsale on the second day for there's a stiff climb ahead—just over 610m (2000ft) up the spur between the Dudh Kosi and its tributary, the Bhote Kosi, to Namche Bazar. It takes just over two hours. It is said that from a point on this climb, about a quarter of the way up, you can just see Everest for the first time, peeping over the Lhotse-Nuptse wall, but I doubt if many do. It's a heads-down sort of climb, just as the altitude is beginning to take effect.

Namche Bazar is a remarkable village in a wonderful setting. The white houses with their brightly coloured paintwork are arranged like a crescent in a bowl of the hills. There are 'hotels' and shops, and the streets bustle with activity, especially on market days. All sorts of goods can be bought here—at a price—from tinned food and expedition equipment to articles of local craftwork and antiques of dubious antiquity. It was once a great trading centre for caravans travelling over the Khumbu La into Tibet, taking food north and bringing back borax. The trade hasn't entirely died out—I once stayed with some Sherpas where the head of the family was about to make the journey. It wasn't food he was carrying, however, but plastic buckets, tied to his yaks in multi coloured bundles!

From the junction of the Dudh and Bhote Kosi to the Tibet border at Everest, the area has been declared the Sagamartha National Park, Sagamartha being the Nepalese name for Mount Everest, (but not the local name, which is Chomolungma). Namche is the Park's administrative centre and it is necessary to check in here, pay for a park permit, and ensure that you have enough fuel for the onward journey. It is now forbidden for trekkers to gather wood for fires because of the serious depletion of the forests.

Day 3: Rest Day at Namche Bazar

Namche Bazar lies at 3445m (11,300ft) and it could well be your first rest day, on the principle of slowly ascending in order to acclimatise. The day is not wasted, however, because there is plenty to see. I recommend a walk over the intervening saddle to Khumjung, a large village tucked away in a little valley a short distance north. The path leads up for some 500m (1500ft) past the airstrip at Shyangboche to a *chorten,* then descends through a pleasantly wooded gap to the Khumjung schoolhouse built by Sir Edmund Hillary for the villagers. Over to the left, beyond the potato fields is a *gompa,* or monastery, where for a small charge the monks will show you the scalp of a yeti. Make of it what you will!

A short distance beyond the monastery lies the 'twin' village of Khunde, where there is a hospital, again built by the Himalayan Trust founded by Hillary.

Great crags seem to threaten Khumjung on its northern side, but opposite the hills are less steep. Here amidst the woods is the Everest View Hotel, a Japanese venture which aims to provide western-style comfort for those who cannot withstand the rigours of the trail. Tourists fly into Shyangboche airstrip then walk the half hour or so to the hotel, where the bedrooms are all equipped with oxygen cylinders and there is a doctor in attendance. It is not a happy scheme. The sudden transposition from Kathmandu to the heights of Khumjung is enough to knock some people flat on their backs with altitude sickness. I have witnessed a very fat Japanese lady being carried by a diminutive Sherpa down to the airstrip in a rapid evacuation. Good job the planes were flying that day!

The shortest way back to Namche is to return along the same path by which you approached, but if time and energy allow, it is possible to make a circular walk out of the trip. The way leads out of the eastern end of the village then descends rather steeply by a rocky path to meet the main Everest path which can be followed back to Namche Bazar. The round trip probably takes about four hours, plus any diversions for sightseeing.

Day 4: Namche Bazar to Thyangboche

On the following morning this same section of path is followed for the next leg of the journey. In two hours it leads fairly steeply down to the river at Phunki, crosses a bridge, then climbs up even more steeply for another two hours to the monastery at Thyangboche at 3867m (12,687ft).

Here indeed is Shangri La! A small, level meadow stretches like a grassy parade ground between some huts on the right and the white monastery building on the left. The latter is not a particularly impressive building—there are far more impressive monasteries in Ladakh, for example—but it is an important centre of lamaic Buddhism, which once had connections with the famous monastery at Rongbuk, on the other side of Everest, now sadly destroyed. Its situation is little short of idyllic. It lies in the very heart of the spectacular mountains for which the Khumbu is renowned.

Immediately overhead the twin peaks of Kangtega and Tramserku rise like two ice-coated shark's fins, to almost 6700m (22,000ft). They are savagely beautiful, the Gemini of the

Khumbu, and have made their presence felt all the way from Namche. In the opposite direction, across the valley, Taweche rises to 6542m (21,463ft), though its best form is seen from further up the valley on the morrow. Pride of place is taken by Ama Dablam (6857m, 22,493ft), whose lovely white spire dominates the scene as befits a peak recognized as one of the most beautiful in the world.

And in the far distance is the Lhotse-Nuptse wall, with the tip of Mount Everest just peeping over.

Day 5: Thyangboche to Pheriche

Thyangboche rests on a forested spur overlooking another junction in the river, so on the next stage of the walk you descend again through acres of rhododendron, past the little nunnery at Deboche, to the valley floor. Once across the bridge you soon come to the extensive village of Pangboche, which seems to be a maze of low-walled enclosures where you need to keep your wits about you if you are not to take a wrong turning. Once, through being over enthusiastic about photography and not looking

where I was going, I became inextricably mixed up in all these stone walls and it took me some time to find the way out!

It takes about one and a half hours to Pangboche from Thyangboche. Beyond the village the trees thin out as the track climbs steadily towards the next staging post, which is Pheriche, two or three hours further. This is the stage at which altitude first begins to have real effect: legs feel more tired than usual, trail and distance seem to stretch.

Pheriche itself turns out to be little more than a first aid post and a couple of 'hotels' built out of turves, jerrycans and plastic sheeting. The first aid post was established by the Himalayan Rescue Association in 1973 with the dual function of providing emergency medical treatment for trekkers and carrying out research into altitude sickness. The altitude here is 4253m (13,950ft) and even if you have disdained rest days lower down the trail you should certainly take one here.

Day 6: Rest Day at Pheriche

Perhaps 'rest day' is the wrong term. There is no need to rest as such. It is more beneficial to

Top: **Many experienced travellers regard Ama Dablam as one of the most beautiful mountains of the world.**

Above: **The Everest group seen from Kala Pattar. The snowy West Shoulder is on the left, then the great peak itself to 29,028 ft. The right-hand skyline is roughly the route of the first ascent in 1953; the left-hand skyline the scene of many pre-war attempts. In the foreground is Nuptse.**

(Photos: W. Unsworth.)

the valley—is the immense obelisk of Taweche, 6542m (21,463ft); a stark savage block of rock and ice. Behind it, rising to a similar height though with not the same ferocious aspect, is Jobo Lhaptshan.

Day 7: Pheriche to Lobuche

These mountains dominate the next morning's walk which is through an open, treeless valley towards the foot of the Khumbu Glacier. At Duglha, glacial streams are crossed and the path traverses moraine landscape to climb up to a low line of teashops and 'hotels' at Lobuche (4931m, 16,175ft). The walk takes three or four hours.

Lobuche is the highest habitation in the Khumbu; the last link with civilization, so to speak, though to tell the truth it is a grotty place which makes severing the link easier to bear. Beyond it lie the moraines of the huge Khumbu Glacier and the immense icy wall of the frontier ridge, bristling with some of the world's highest mountains.

Nowadays, few trekkers make for the site of the Everest Base Camp, which is just a rubbish dump in the middle of the glacier. Instead they climb the little peak of Kala Pattar on the south ridge of Pumori, which gives superb views of the great mountains. However, opinion is divided on how this should be done. One school of thought advocates climbing Kala Pattar direct from Lobuche. This has the advantage in so far as you need not acclimatise any further, since you return to the same height that you started from. The disadvantage is that it means a climb of 600m (2000ft) at altitude, and an equal descent, on some very rough terrain. It is a very long, hard day.

Day 8: Lobuche to Gorak Shep

If you have acclimatised sensibly on the way up the valley then putting in an extra night at a higher altitude than Lobuche should be perfectly all right. The place chosen is usually the moraine lake at Gorak Shep (5183m, 17,000ft) where there are two rough stone huts, unoccupied. They should not be relied upon for accommodation because they are no longer maintained: camping is the only alternative here. Gorak Shep is reached by a track through the moraines in about three hours from Lobuche.

Day 9: Ascent of Kala Pattar and return to Lobuche

Above the lake the stony slopes of Kala Pattar rise up to a height of 5625m (18,450ft). The climb takes about two hours: two hours of breathless struggle from block to block until the

cross the shoulder of hill to the east of the hamlet and visit the large village of Dingboche, which lies all unsuspected up the lateral valley of the Imja. The point about a rest day is to spend a second night at the same altitude.

Above the hamlet is the rocky crest of Pokalde, which at 5793m (19,000ft) is as high as Kilimanjaro, the highest peak in Africa, and far higher than anything in Europe, and yet looks insignificant compared with the other mountains round about. Nearest of these—just across broad ridge line is reached. It isn't the top, of course, but happily the top is not too far away. A sense of relief mingles with a sense of achievement at having reached the ultimate goal of the Everest trek.

The view is astonishing, awe inspiring. Curiously, the first thing to strike you is the nearness of Pumori (7146m, 23,441ft). Climbing to your vantage point is technically no more difficult than climbing a hill in the Lake District, yet at the top you find yourself on a ridge of one of the world's great mountains! A little further and you would need ice axe, crampons and ropes to tackle the first icy gendarme!

In a wide panorama, peak piles on peak. The mountain shapes passed days before can be recognized in the distance, like old friends. Ama Dablam is particularly easy to pick out, though some of the others are lost in the jumble.

But dominating everything is the Everest cirque. Nuptse's icy ridges rise to a superb spire of fluted ice. Nuptse is 7881m (25,851ft), and though what you see is not the actual summit, which lies some way back, it is no matter. Everest itself is massively bulky, the great south-west face showing to perfection. The world's highest hill is not handsome, it is just *there,* as George Mallory said many years ago.

Days 10 – 13: Return to Lukla

Most trekkers return from Everest by the same route. On the way back, naturally, there is no concern about altitude acclimatisation, so there is no need for rest days. A fit party could probably combine two stages of the journey into one. There are alternatives: over the Kongma La to Bibre and Dingboche, or over the Chola La to Gokyo, for example, but these diversions are

longer and tougher than the original. A modicum of mountaineering skill is desirable.

Finally, a word of caution. The popularity of this trek should not blind you to the fact that it is a fairly tough undertaking. There is no reason why a fit person, given the help of porters, should not make it to Kala Pattar—yet quite a few fail. Some get no further than Thyangboche. Altitude is the chief culprit—it cannot be emphasised too strongly that there must be a constant watch for symptoms of altitude sickness. Sadly, too many have died through pressing on regardless.

Pumori from Kala Pattar. One of the many superb peaks at the head of the Khumbu Valley.
(Photo: W. Unsworth.)

Walk 14 NEPAL: The Circuit of Annapurna by Dennis Kemp

Above: **Trekkers spin prayer wheels in the the mani wall outside Manang village. In the background is Annapurna II.**

Far right, top: **Dhaulagiri I with, on the right, Tukuche Peak, seen across the arid landscape around Muktinath. In the foreground are three** *chortens.*

Far right, bottom: **The view down the deep Kali Gandaki valley near Marpha.**

(Photos: John Cleare.)

128

From Dumre to Pokhara across the Thorong La

The Annapurna massif is a magnificent block of Nepal's central Himalaya roughly 80km (50 miles) across and 50km (30 miles) deep. To the west is the natural boundary of the deep Kali Gandaki valley, and to the east, the Marsyandi valley. Beyond the Manang valley to the north lies Tibet, and to the south is the valley and city of Pokhara, with road and air communications to Kathmandu and India.

The Kali Gandaki valley, that has long been a major trade route and a pilgrim trail for Hindus and Buddhists, has only over the last three decades become accessible to Western tourists. The route to Manang has been open to trekkers only since 1977, and together they now make possible a magnificent trek right round the Annapurna massif, provided conditions are right for a crossing of the high Thorong La pass, a Himalayan pass of about 5400m (17,650ft). Add to this a sortie into the Annapurna Sanctuary in the centre of the massif, and you have a trek of over 350km (218 miles) which takes you through spectacular mountain scenery, villages of great ethnic diversity, and through climatic zones from sub tropical to the bitter cold of the high mountains. It is a trek to be classed among the world's best.

Preliminaries

The two usual ways of undertaking this walk are either to organise it through a trekking agency where everything can be arranged before you leave home and you travel accompanied by the traditional Sherpas and porters (all luxury, no hassles), or to do-it-yourself as a live-off-the-land trek, which will probably involve hard work, discomfort, restricted food and language problems. But there is a third way which is a compromise between the two, and which is perhaps the best combination for the adventurous. This is to trek with two or three friends, stay in local accommodation, and to hire a Sirdar to accompany you who would arrange a porter or two on a day-to-day basis to take some of the weight off your back.

Accommodation is not a problem as there are so many lodges and places to stay all along the route—though you could take some bivouac gear for the Thorong La pass or for any impromptu side trips. If there is no teahouse or commercial lodge you can ask at a farmstead for food and accommodation and share with the family, paying the same as you would at a lodge.

But whatever you do, read the Bezruchka and Armington books before you go and heed their plea for travelling as sensitive tourists, with maximum regard for the environment.

Stage 1: Dumre to Manang

The bus pulls up at Dumre, 450m (1400ft) above sea level and rather shaken, you get your luggage down from the roof and stagger into one of the many fast-food cafés serving tea, rice and vegetables, the standard diet for the next month. Dumre is a shanty town, the roadhead for the vast catchment area of the Marsyandi river to the north, which is set in the Himalayan foothills amongst rice fields, banana plantations and some forest. The heat and humidity can be quite ferocious in the lowlands and you can expect little relief until you begin to gain height.

From Dumre you head north, and wade across a small river to a wide and stony earth track on the opposite side. In the first village of Bhansar an engine running a mill makes strange noises—the last infernal combustion engine (apart from aircraft) you will hear for the next month. Here the trail forks. I took the left, the wrong one, but was alerted because the smooth, shiny surface polished by porters' bare feet was no longer there. I asked at a house—'Tuture janne? (Tuture: going to?) –and was smilingly given a child as a guide to cut across fields to the right trail.

Distance: 350km (200 miles).

Time required: 25 – 32 days.

Type of Walk: High altitude, through spectacular mountain scenery; from sub tropical to bitterly cold temperatures.

Base: Either Kathmandu or Pokhara.

Start: Dumre, on the road between Kathmandu and Pokhara.

Best Time of Year: September – November; May – June.

Maps: A trekking map by Nepal Police Mountaineering and Adventure Foundation, Naxal, Kathmandu is readily available at bookshops, roadside stalls and Immigration offices.

Trekking Permits: Must be obtained from the Immigration Office in Kathmandu or Pokhara. Two passport photographs needed. Cost (1983) Rs 60 a week.

Guidebooks: *A Guide to Trekking in Nepal* by Stephen Bezruchka (Cordee). *Trekking in the Himalayas.* Stan Armington (Lonely Planet).

Far right: The Pilgrim trail from Muktinath to Kagbeni descends arid hillsides below Jharkot village. In the background is Dhaulagiri. (Photo: John Cleare.)

Beyond the village of Barabise the trail follows a ridge that is reminiscent of a forested South Downs with a Vale of Clwyd beyond and a forested Snowdon beyond that. Afternoon clouds pile high on the horizon with the two peaks of Himalchuli and Baudha visible to the south-east. The trail here is busy with people: families walking to Dumre, porters carrying mysterious loads, trekkers in twos and threes or in groups with porters.

After passing through Chambas, the trail leads on to Tuture, where there is a choice of lodges, before descending to the Marsyandi river. Crossing a tributary on the west bank you walk on through farmland to a point opposite Tarkughat, a fair sized bazaar on the opposite bank. Here the old Kathmandu to Pokhara trail that was the regular means of communication between the two cities before the present motor road was built, crosses the Marsyandi on a suspension bridge. Unless you decide to visit the bazaar don't cross the river here but continue on the west bank.

Half an hour later a suspension bridge takes you over a tributary coming in from the west, the Paundi Khola. The heat and humidity here were so great I feared dissolving in my own sweat; and was glad of the shade of my umbrella which at that moment was worth its weight in gold plated rupees. Black storm clouds and rumbling thunder gave enough excuse to stop early at Udipuk.

Udipuk is half an hour short of Phalesangu (670m, (2197ft). At Udipuk there is a suspension bridge over to the east side.

The main trail however continues on the west side through Nadiwal and Bakunde, to Bensisahar, the city of the Lamjung District. It has a wide main street, stone buildings, many shops, a post office, government offices, lodges and two photo studios. Strange two-metre-wide stone walls are being constructed at the entrance and exit to the town, though for what purpose is not clear.

Bensisahar is on a shelf above the main river from which you descend to cross a tributary, before starting to climb steeply. Here the trail becomes a footpath and the valley a deep river gorge. There's subtropical forest: you are now at an altitude where the air is cooler and there's excitement at leaving the low country behind. A tributary is crossed on a suspension bridge, then there's a major tributary, the Khudi Khola, to cross by another suspension bridge. Directly over this one, nestling in the anchoring arms of the suspension cables, the small town of Khudi is perched on the hillside. It is a place of stone houses with a flagged main square and many stone steps. There are shops, lodges and teahouses—all accompanied by the constant roar of water from the two rivers joining just below. It is a Gurung village where the Buddhist influences from the north mix with the Hindu from the south. Many Gurkhas are Gurungs, and several ex-soldiers talked to us of their service in Hong Kong, Malaya and Borneo, while sharing glasses of raksi distilled locally from home-grown grain.

From Khudi the trail climbs past the school to the main Marsyandi Khola valley. Soon there's a suspension bridge just below on the right, but the trail seems to continue straight on, along a broad and inviting path. As we started along this, however, small boys in a farmstead we'd just passed whistled and gestured that we were to take the bridge; tourists are watched over and cared for in this country. The bridge was a smart new one with many side wires—a man-made cobweb to cross to the east bank, to the town of Bhulbhul.

The route now continues northwards through extensive terracing and small villages to a beautiful thin waterfall—the first of many—with views of Manaslu and Peak 29. At the hamlet of Ngadi where at least three out of the ten stone-built houses are 'hotels', you can shelter from the heat and take tea at the Himalaya Restaurant and Lodge, with wall chinks plastered with pages from Chinese colour supplements. As we sat there a train of porters passed through carrying masses of crates of Coca Cola.

Despite what the map says, the trail now goes up a major tributary valley to the east, the Musi Khola, to cross by another suspension bridge. Then it is back into the main valley for steady climbing through more terraces and forest to Lampata and, higher, to the village of Bahundanda ('Hill of Brahmins') which is set on a saddle. Here, there is a large, stone-built Hindu temple with a huge pair of scales outside and a police check post.

The views are most spectacular as the trail descends from the saddle in a big arc, an arch of misty cloud bridging one side of the terraced valley to the other. Then the trail becomes carved out of the rock-wall of the valley. On Himalayan treks there is a real danger of falling off a path like this—I've actually seen it happen on another trek, to a companion who, without thinking, stepped back to take a photograph and was only saved by a small tree ten metres down. A girl in another party was not so lucky; she vanished into the river 100m (328ft) below and lost her life.

It was raining heavily at the next hamlet; two little farmsteads set above the main river which runs below in a deep gorge. One of the farmsteads is a lodge with a small dormitory of five beds which are reached by stepping over the goats and chickens—that live in the downstairs rooms—and up some steep, open stairs. Although it was only midday, the heavy rain encouraged us to stay overnight here, and we spent the rest of the afternoon drinking tea and watching the waterfall opposite, now in full spate, turn to a deep chocolate colour as mud

and debris cascaded over the edge.

It was still raining hard the next morning and as the family pressed us to stay, we spent the morning learning Nepali from them and the afternoon when the rain had eased we made our way to the stone village of Syange, built into the wall of the ravine.

Beyond Syange the trail is spectacular––narrow and blasted out of the side of a steep jungle-clad gorge––as it passes many waterfalls. At the village of Jagat, in a saddle in the forest, you can buy provisions before climbing through forest and past more waterfalls to Chamje where there's a suspension bridge back to the east bank. A tributary valley comes down this side. The trail is rough and climbs steeply high above the Marsyandi river, an impressive situation. You come across some huge boulders hiding the river and you are suddenly edged onto a plateau, a silted up lakebed, and the small settlement of Tal. The hamlet comprises just a line of wooden built houses by the trail, with big piles of firewood in Austrian-farmhouse style, and vegetable gardens. A couple of big waterfalls sit at the head of the 'lake'.

This is the Manang district, and the air is as sharp and clear as in the high Alps with the same characteristics of clear starlit nights with hard frosts, and hot sun by day.

Tal wasn't marked on our police trekking map, but seemed to be a finger's width before Dharapani. North of Tal the cold stream from the waterfall is crossed on a wooden bridge. The trail here is in a gorge, blasted out and stonewalled, with stone steps that have collapsed in places through landslides and water erosion. Climb to a ridge and then down to the river and you reach the new suspension bridge (carrying all the cables and steelwork for this from Dumre must have been a major contract for the porters). Cross over to the west bank of the Marsyandi and in five minutes you reach Dharapani—marked on the map as on the east side of the river, though your eyes tell you it's on the west. An unpainted stone archway (a *khani*) welcomes you at the entrance to the village and another stands at the exit. A long wooden covered bridge over the Marsyandi is not for our route. Continue northwards instead on the west of the river through splendid forests. Trekkers on the trail returning from the Thorong La pass told tales of the pass being blocked by snow with plenty of it in Manang too.

Bagarchap looks Tibetan with its flat-roofed houses piled with firewood but some shingle roofs indicate you're not quite in the rain shadow of the Annapurnas yet. The trail now swings round to travel north-west to Manang about three days further on. The peaks of Lamjung and Annapurna II are to the west, and Manaslu is the big mountain behind and to the east. Now on the south side of the river and in fine forests, we made our way to Thangja as it was called on the map (or Lata Marang on the spot) where we sheltered for the night.

We were away in the gloom at five, the first on the trail. Walking through very pleasant forest, the main river—not as big as I expected for one draining such a large area—foamed over boulders below on our right hand. A carved-out trail with steps and a waterfall led us to a land slip that had carried away the trail during the night. While discussing how best to scramble across, a large pine tree, 30m (100ft) above, detached itself from the hillside and dropped past us into the river, followed by a mass of mud and rocks. They say Nepal's main export is soil to India by way of the rivers.

We walked on ignoring the wooden bridges over the main river, to cross a largish tributary to the village of Kuparkodo (spelt Qubar at the police check post) where there were shops, lodges, an old lady weaving on a rather basic loom, and a magnificent, enticing gorge splitting the mountain mass north of the village of Nar Khola (out of bounds to foreigners).

Thirty minutes further on is Chame, a major town, compact and very picturesque, which is the headquarters of the Manang district. Views of Annapurna IV, two banks, a medical post and a wireless station join the more usual mixture of shops, lodges and houses. A wooden cantilever bridge leads to more houses, and some hot springs.

Keeping to the north bank, the trail begins to climb through forest and gorges and past spectacular waterfalls, until of all things, you reach a huge new orchard surrounded by a big wooden fence. Just beyond this the trail crosses to the south bank of the Marsyandi Khola by a cantilevered wooden bridge. It turns right, but ahead on the hillside is Bhratang village, mostly abandoned, and a camping site.

From Bhratang the valley is steep and narrow and the trail corkscrews. A new section of trail is being blasted out of the vertical rockface on the other side of the river, like a tunnel with one side open to the valley. A very heavy frost had us all shivering and longing for the sun, but as it rose it paralleled a ridge and the trail remained in the shade for hours.

When at last the valley did open out, to the north were revealed some incredible smooth slabs rising more than 1500m (5000ft) from the river, bigger than the Glacier Point Apron in Yosemite. This is the Paungoa Danda rock face, a challenge to any climber. Enjoying the sunshine we walked on through meadows and pine trees to Pisang.

The Marsyandi valley here is wide and open with steeper forested slopes on the south giving to open ground by the river. The northern slopes are more open and rise to the snow-covered Pisang Peak and Naurchuli. On the south bank is the village of Lower Pisang with a huge new lodge, looking like a mill in a Lowry painting, a cluster of older lodges with campers on the flat roofs, and two small mills at work driven by Pelton wheels. A two-metre-high prayer wheel in a stone building of its own, we duly turned, as we did a line of smaller ones in the prayer wall. Across the river, men, women and children could be seen busily harvesting.

It takes half an hour to walk up to Upper Pisang (3290m, 10,791ft), but the climb is worth it to see the fine, long wall of prayer wheels, a *gompa,* the narrow alleyways and the flat roofed houses where the roof of one house serves as a yard for the house above, with ladders of notched tree trunks for access. After exploring for a while we returned to Lower Pisang to stay the night: good for acclimatisation once you are over 3000m (10,000ft) altitude.

There is a high-level route from Upper Pisang to Ghyaru, Ngawal and Braga where it rejoins the main route, but it's two hours longer (a lot of climbing, but super views of the Annapurnas) and the main route from Lower Pisang is recommended. Along the south bank of the Marsyandi Khola through pine and juniper, the trail climbs a spur to the upper Manang valley with Tilicho Peak (7132m, 23,392ft) at the head. At the little town of Ongre there's an airstrip and a trekkers' high altitude medical post staffed by American doctors. Stop by and ask about the medical aspects of crossing the Thorong La.

Yaks, goats, cows and horses can be seen grazing as you cross the Marsyandi to Munchi, then to Braga at 3505m (11,496ft). Braga is another village with houses stacked on top of each other, and has an important *gompa* perched on a crag that is well worth visiting.

Manang (3350m, 10,988ft) is now only half an hour away across level ground. Snow from the blizzards of a week ago (when we had rain down below) was still lying in some shaded corners of the town when we got there, but several trekkers confirmed that Thorong La was passable although they had had to wait several days for good weather. Manang is a useful place to take stock, to explore, assess your state of acclimatisation, the state of the route, guess about the weather, and buy provisions for the next few days if going on.

Stage 2: Manang to Muktinath

Half an hour beyond Manang is the last permanent settlement, Tengi, and beyond that the trail forks. Our trail turns north-west through barren country dotted with dead scrub juniper and up the tributary valley of the Jareng Khola. Keep looking back over your shoulder at the huge Annapurna massif! A small teahouse has sprung up on a spur that makes a good viewpoint above the deserted village of Gunsang.

Then there is a wooden bridge over the river that comes down from Chulu peak to the east and it's an easy-angled trail over meadows and along hillsides to reach Leder where there is now a substantial lodge and shop, whose owner speaks nine languages.

An hour beyond Leder there is a new covered wooden bridge and a new section of trail over unstable slopes. Finally the trail reaches camping grounds west of the river at Phedi and climbs to a level shelf where there is more room for tents, and a lodge offering the last food and shelter before the pass.

Now the trail becomes small, insignificant and steep compared with anything seen before. It climbs over interminable snow-covered moraines, the air becomes thin and very cold, and walking becomes an act of will. Even in fine weather the dangers of exposure and altitude sickness are very real, even for the local people. And there is no mountain rescue service, so think hard about going on or turning back should any of the factors of time, fitness, morale or weather, be against you.

As you climb, the views looking back become outstanding, peak after glaciated peak being revealed in the increasing panoramas. The nearby Chulu peaks are seen to be more complex than imagined (when walking under them at Manang) as the Great Himalayan Divide sweeps away from you. Tibet is to the north, Gangapurna and the Annapurnas are to the distant south, while immediately to hand an attractive snow and ice peak curves up from the top of the pass, un-named on the trekking map, at an altitude of 6485m (21,273ft).

When you reach the large stone *chorten* on the pass there is an abrupt change in the views––from the white and blue of snow and ice behind––to the brown and yellow of rock and semi-desert to the west and north. Being in the sun all day, the snow-peak's companion to the north, Thorungtse––of about the same altitude ––is a rock peak. The ridge running down from it is of spectacular yellow screes. If you have binoculars, search out the green oasis of Kagbeni far below to the west, on the Kali Gandaki river; a splendid place to overnight in two or three days' time.

The descent is a knee-straining drop down

more moraines, at first snow-covered, to Mukti-nath; a drop of 1600m (5200ft). After two hours there is a possible camp site but in another half hour is a tiny stream and three small summer farmsteads offering tea, food, shelter, and tourist souvenirs. Later, the holy shrines at Muktinath appear in a walled oasis of trees to your left and a wide new stone staircase leads down to the village with its lodges, shops, police check post, and serried lines of trekkers' tents. As it has been a long and hard day it is wise to spend the next day resting, eating and exploring the locality.

Muktinath is the extensive stone-walled compound housing Hindu and Buddhist shrines: a major pilgrimage site for Hindus from India and Nepal. It is a tranquil oasis of poplar trees, warm sun and cold air, little mountain streams, rectangular ponds reflecting surrounding snow peaks, pagodas, temples, prayer wheels turned by water, a wall of waterspouts where pilgrims bathe, a Buddhist *gompa* (where a rather fierce Tibetan lady caretaker demonstrates small natural gas jets alongside a spring of holy water), drystone walls, flagstones and peace. The village, ten minutes down the hill from the shrine, caters for the needs of tourist and pilgrim. The enterprising Thakili people, of Tibetan origin, cater well for travellers with a chain of local inns, small hotels, and lodges. The small towns and villages are full of interest, with people selling handicrafts and the ammonite fossils within slate-coloured pebbles for which the area is renowned. The scenery is varied and spectacular, the trail easy to follow, the gradients (after the Manang route) are gentle. It's like a holiday!

Stage 3: Muktinath to Ghorapani

Out of Muktinath, the trail heads west high above the Jhong Khola to the Tibetan village of Jharkot and then Khingar through pleasant country with meadows, streams and orchards. Then comes a dramatic change to the semi-desert of yellow ground and sparse vegetation. At a fork in the trail take the right branch, marked with many little dolmen-like cairns erected by pilgrims. Slant down towards Kag-beni at the junction of the Jhong Khola and the main river way below. When the Kali Gandaki is reached, it is seen to be a kilometre-wide level riverbed of stones with braided streams and steep yellow mud bluffs. The Jhong Khola brings irrigation water to Kagbeni and water-driven flour mills and farm buildings cluster outside the town. The fortress-like three-storey town wall with only very few high, tiny windows is penetrated by a square entrance tunnel. Houses of mud-bricks and wood with shuttered windows and ochre doors crouch together, penetrated by dark alleys, tunnels, steps, stairways and ladders. Our lodge is through a pitch dark opening, into a courtyard with horses, calves and a milking cow, up stone steps to a long-tabled dining room and large kitchen run by a laughing Tibetan lady. Sleeping is in a dormitory or in small rooms on the third floor. A red door leads to the lodges' private *gompa* where there is a 3m (9ft) high gilt Buddha.

From Kagbeni follow the Kali Gandaki river to Jomosom. The peaks of Nilgiri (7061m, 23,160ft) are to the south and Dhaulagiri and Tukuche to the south west with this impressive cut of a river valley between. On either side and behind you are steep, bare, brown and yellow mountains, desert country that heats up in the morning sun sending convection currents high into the sky. Cold air is drawn up the river valley to replace this, and mid-morning onwards you are battling against strong dusty headwinds. Jomosom is an administrative centre of little charm: it has a police checkpost to call at, a bank, post office, hotels, and an airstrip with regular flights to Pokhara and Kathmandu.

Marpha, the apple-town, an hour downriver, is a much nicer place to stay and explore. The trail through the town becomes a sinuous alleyway beautifully paved with large flagstones. A constant stream of travellers passes through. The jingle of bells announces another train of twenty or more pack animals, the lead pony decorated with bells and plumes. Whitewashed stone buildings have ornately carved wooden shutters, their roofs are flat, and firewood is piled neatly around them. Ochre painted doorways give glimpses of courtyards with animals. Narrow side alleys lead uphill, one to the *gompa* with newly repainted frescoes, the work of one master and four assistant monks over twelve months. Between the town and the river lie fields and orchards irrigated by water that is black with suspended rock dust. Flocks of Demoiselle Cranes fly past on their migration from Tibet to India for the winter. Just outside the town is a Government Agricultural Station with big orchards. Superb apples are sold in season, and the apple brandy, peach brandy, and apricot jam should not be missed.

Out of the town, the trail continues on the west bank—easy going—to the villages of Tukuche and Khanti (or Khobang). Khanti is built with narrow alleys, courtyards, and tunnels against the winds. The tree-line has been creeping down the hillsides, and beyond Larjung the trail climbs away from the river and passes through pine and juniper forests. The arid country is being left behind. The trail then descends and crosses the river to the east bank on a new suspension bridge, then shortly afterwards back to the west bank at a spot where the river narrows and at last falls over rapids—the bottleneck for all that shingle stretching way back to Kagbeni and beyond. At Kalopani 2560m (8400ft), roofs are now sloping and

Far left: **Trekkers descend from the Thorong La pass, the highest point on the Annapurna circuit (5417 m, 16,510 ft).**

Below: **A trekker looks up the gorge of the Marsyandi Valley towards Annapurna II.**

(Photos: John Cleare.)

A trekking party crosses the Thorong La pass which links the Manang valley to the headwaters of the Kali Gandaki river.
(Photo: John Cleare.)

slated. Views of the high peaks have changed in perspective, Nilgiri now shows three impressive peaks and the great wall of Annapurna I gleams with ice, but is partly hidden by the foreground, as is Dhaulagiri 1 (8172m, 26,795ft) to the West.

From Kalopani the trail passes through Lete, Kaiku and Ghasa and then, passing through forest, becomes narrow and difficult in sections where there have been recent slides although roadmen are already working on it. We get out of the way as an oncoming pony train reaches us—the beasts picking their way delicately, expecting to have right of way. Now we are descending, the weather is much warmer, and we are back in the lands of terraced fields, banana trees and thatched roofs. After passing through Kabre and Dana the small town of Tatopani is a good place to take a rest-day, for here the track begins to climb again (for the next week), and there is a good selection of lodges, a splendid choice of food, excellent views, but most important of all—natural warm springs where you may bathe and wash your clothes (be very careful to observe Hindu etiquette).

From Tatopani there are two routes back to Pokhara. One follows the main river, the Kali Gandaki; the other involves a long day's climb of 1500m (4500ft) to Ghorapani to meet our cross-country trail to Kimrong and into the Annapurna Sanctuary.

Tatopani ('warm water') to Ghorapani ('horse water'), although a long day's climb, is straightforward. Leaving Tatopani, you take the suspension bridge to the east side of the Kali Gandaki, and cross the tributary river Ghar Khola which comes from the south-east. At the

fork where the trail splits, take the left-hand trail up some steep steps (they set the standard for the day), through the groups of farm buildings and hamlets, past the big village of Sikha, over an extensive landslip area of slatey rock, past Chitre until the path, through forest and rhododendron trees, finally delivers you to the pass called Deorali at 2835m (9298ft).

Ghorapani itself is ten minutes down the other side, but there are many lodges clustered on the pass itself, and camping space in a clearing. The lodge we stayed at had a large room floored with huge planks of polished wood, with dormitory alcoves off; a log fire to snuggle round and huge plates of food. An excursion to Poon Hill (3193m, 10,473ft) to see the sunrise was recommended, so away we went into the frozen night at 5am on a path eroded a metre deep by trekkers' feet. About an hour's climb took us to the top of the hill which is clear of trees with excellent panoramas of the Dhaulagiri Himal, Tukuche Peak, the Kali Gandaki gorge, Nilgiri, Fang, Annapurna I, Annapurna South, Hiunchuli. As the sun rose, unfolding the natural spectacle, the only sound was of clicking camera shutters from the fifty or so assembled tourists.

Stage 4: Ghorapani to The Sanctuary

The cross-country trail we now want strikes out east from the pass, at first on a ridge that matches Poon Hill. The trail is small, winding, quiet, through beautiful magical forest with ferns, purple flowers, mossy steps and waterfalls that reminded me of New Zealand rain forest. A new teahouse in the middle of nowhere, called Derali, offers welcome refreshment before more forest trail leads down and up to Tadpani/Gurung Hill with three lodges and other buildings. Gurung Hill is another Poon Hill from which to see the Himalayan sunrise with the moving shadows. From here take the Kimrong trail (not Ghandrung) through more silent forest of mosses, backlit greens, flocks of birds and occasional small clearings, then out to a maze of metre-wide terraces, newly ploughed, brown and very neat, with green-mossed retaining walls. Kimrong can be seen a long way down, but the trail to it is steep and difficult to find along the terrace boundaries.

Kimrong, not marked on our Police Federation Trekking map, is a village at the bottom of the valley where the trail crosses the Kyamnu Khola which comes rushing down from the glaciers under Annapurna South. A very long, steep stone stairway leads out of the village to a ridge with remarkable views of Machhapuchhare ahead, with on its left the steep gorge of the Madi Khola draining from the Sanctuary. The river swings to the east of our vantage point and a very long way below, on its way south to join the Kali Gandaki. A lodge stands on the ridge, and another trail joins from Landrung. We take this when we return from the Sanctuary. But now we go north, level at first then down five hundred stone steps to Chumrong (1950m, 6400ft), the village in the next tributary valley. It is the last permanent settlement. There are large farmhouses and lodges, tumbling streams, and Annapurna South impressive above. When the sun goes off the valley at 3pm it becomes very cold.

From Chumrong the route goes down to the river, then over a beautiful little suspension bridge with tins of marigolds on the support pillars, and up, up, up, steep and narrow, through forest, with the unseen Modi Khola somewhere way below to our right. There are tea houses—bamboo and thatch structures—with a kitchen fire at one end and a dozen sleeping platforms, or straw on the floor, at the other. First the Hotel High Cliff and Lodge; then a lodge and farmhouse at Kholdi Ghar with, beyond, a smart Government place surrounded with barbed wire, and a sign pointing you on to Hinko. In general it's a steady climb through a bamboo forest tunnel. There are many travellers, including porters with enormous loads returning from climbing expeditions and as the trail is narrow, it is difficult to pass. After a rest at the teahouse at Doban, another two hours takes you to the Himalay Hotel Lodge with its bamboo mat sleeping stalls reminiscent of a manger. Here the gorge is so steep you can't see any peaks.

An hour's walking with legs of lead takes you to Hinko, which is a cave with sleeping platforms under a huge boulder but no tea house. Another half an hour's exhausting scramble over great blocks of ice and avalanche debris that has come down from Hiunchuli right into the river, takes you to the Hotel Dream Bagar, and there the forest thins out to present river terraces and a little beach. Huge 'open book' formations can be seen in the mountainsides to the east, and when the valley turns west the Sanctuary is reached. Climb a moraine and there are two bamboo lodges and another two by some boulders five minutes away. The trail continues for an hour, past yet another lodge, to more lodges well inside the Sanctuary. The demand for fuel must have a devastating effect on the local ecology. There were well over 100 tourists in the Sanctuary when we were there.

The valley is quite wide, with tussocky brown alpine grass, white everlasting flowers, inquisitive yellow-crested wrens, and a mind-blowing circle of mountains. It often snows in the afternoon, and it is a good idea to be up before dawn—the sun rises between the twin peaks of Machhapuchhare—to walk the moraines and meditate on the views and possibly, with binoculars, to spot climbers giving scale to the vastness of snow and ice.

Stage 5: The Sanctuary to Pokhara

The only part of this trek where steps have to be retraced is from the Sanctuary to Chumrong and then up the 500-step staircase to the lodge on the ridge. Ask which way to Landrung and take the trail behind the lodge, through terraces, small and steep but easy to follow. A small hamlet of three houses, Chimu Danda, is perched above the final steep cliffs down to the Mardi Khola but these barriers are side-stepped by the trail cutting down to the tributary valley of the Kyumnu Khola, which it crosses on a wooden plank bridge over large boulders. Up a little on the other side then down to the Madi Khola itself to cross at a suspension bridge not shown on the map. There are lodges nearby. The trail then very pleasantly ambles along the left bank of the river, through nice forests and past waterfalls. Climb a couple of thousand feet to the large village of Landrung. Some of the stone buildings in this village are round or oval-shaped, instead of the usual rectangle. There are fine open views of the river valley and the terracing, and the large Gurung village of Ghandrung on the hillside opposite—looking no distance at all as the crow flies, but a long way on foot.

To Dhumpus is an easy trail through agricultural landscapes and forests, rising to 2000m (8000ft) then an easy descent. There are quite a few forks in the trail, in general take the obviously major one, but if in doubt wait till someone comes along, and ask. Dhumpus is not the compact village one has come to expect, but scattered farms, shops and lodges on grassy slopes just east of a ridge of forest, with grand views north-east to the Mardi Khola valley.

The path continues along a ridge giving aerial views of villages below and excellent perspectives of Annapurna. Farmhouses doubling up as lodges are everywhere. Then the path drops down to the large braided river and gravel banks of the Yamdi Khola. There are monkeys!

The sound of internal combustion engines signals that the trek is over. Jeeps are waiting at a collection of huts to take you on a spectacular four-wheel-drive ride to the outskirts of Pokhara, near the Shining Hospital. From there a municipal bus every twenty minutes runs past the airport to the lakeside area with its immigration office, host of hotels, lodges, restaurants, cafes, taxis, souvenirs—everything a trekker could need!

Walk 15 PERU: The Cordillera Huayhuash Trek by John Gillies

The Cordillera Raura from Punta Cuyoc, at 5490 m (16,732 ft) the highest point on the trek. (Photo: John Gillies.)

A Spectacular Andean Walk across Eight High Passes

To anyone unnerved by the sheer immensity of the Himalayas, the Peruvian Andes offer more accessible vistas. Long as the subcontinent, narrow and stratospherically high, they meander like the condor's flight path through what was once the Inca heartland, an icy wall separating the dust-dry coastal belt from the jungles of the Amazonas. For many hundreds of miles they may be bare of snow, their vegetation worn sparse and lean by the wind, covered only with inhospitable tufts of ichu, the spiky Andean grass. Then, without warning, a peak towers above the uniformity, a glacier glistens and

brilliant blue lakes of snow-melt appear. Suddenly we are in the very finest of walking country, level with the glaciers, so close to the snows that the crashing of avalanches accompanies every step.

Such ranges and sub-ranges are a paradise for the keen walker; they are high enough, steep enough, demanding enough to test the strongest legs and lungs when tackled head-on. Generally, though, they have a softer side as well, permitting at least limited access to those with less to prove. Some of them, like the famous Cordillera Blanca, are quite large, and encompass many variations of scenery and climate. Sometimes,

The Cordillera Raura from Punta Cuyoc, at 5490 m (16,732 ft) the highest point on the trek. (Photo: John Gillies.)

though, small things have the most power to surprise, and of all the Andean ranges it is perhaps the Cordillera Huayhuash which represents the most remarkable alpine experience.

The Huayhuash is situated at the southern end of the Cordillera Blanca, at least eight hours by road to the north-east of Lima. It is a whole mountain range in miniature: a mere 40km (25 miles) in length, it offers a savage perfection of mountain grandeur, as peak after peak rises sheer and abrupt from the surrounding highlands. The skyline of Huayhuash is the Manhattan of mountains, its neck-craning sky-scrapers quite different in their impact from the massive but more delicate curves of the neighbouring Blanca.

But there is nothing miniature about the trekking circuit of the range. Few of the world's walks can be as rewarding to the eye or the spirit, but such rewards must be earned, and the Huayhuash trek is emphatically not a walk for the novice or the ill-prepared. Over the hundred or so miles of walking, there are 6000m (20,000ft) of climbing and eight passes, mostly of about 4700m (15,500ft) in height; once you are in, there is no easy escape route in case of mountain sickness or injury, and extremely little human habitation or even contact. Even other trekkers are seen only infrequently, for this is too serious an enterprise to feature on the map of the world's trekking highways.

The Approach

The normal starting place for the circuit of the Huayhuash is the town of Chiquian, on the western side of the range, from which a long valley leads directly towards the peaks. Chiquian lies some eight hours by road from Lima, four of them on the Pan-American highway, a fast but tedious drive along the bleak, barren desert of the coast, and another four ascending rapidly from sea level to the 4200km (14,000ft) Conococha pass, which leads into the famous valley known as the Callejon de Huaylas: the gateway to the Cordillera Blanca. At Conococha the main road continues to Huarás, the largest town of the Blanca area, while the Chiquian road, twenty miles of well-maintained dirt track, turns off to the south-east.

For a long, high trek such as this one a proper period of acclimatization is essential, and there can be few areas where one's body can adjust in such magnificent surroundings as in the Callejon de Huaylas. Chiquian itself is very small, and though pleasant enough, it has little of interest to recommend it for an extended visit. The most rewarding way to begin the trek would be to spend a few days in Huarás, a much bigger town, from which excursions can be made either on foot into the neighbouring hills, or by road to see some more spectacular close-ups of the Cordillera Blanca. The most popular visits from Huarás are to the pass and lakes at Llanganuco, overlooked by the massive snow-peaks of Huascaran and Huandoy, or to Lake Paron, or the pre-Inca ruins of Chavin and the great panorama from the Punta Callan. On the way back from Huarás to Chiquian there is a spot where you can see the giant Puya Raimondi, the world's tallest flowering plant, growing sometimes to a height of 10m (35ft).

Although Chiquian is the normal starting

Below left: **On the first day of the trek the valley of the River Pativilca leads from Chiquian towards the mountains.**

Below right: **Trekkers rest near Lake Mitacocha, overlooked by Jirishanca.**

(Photos: John Gillies.)

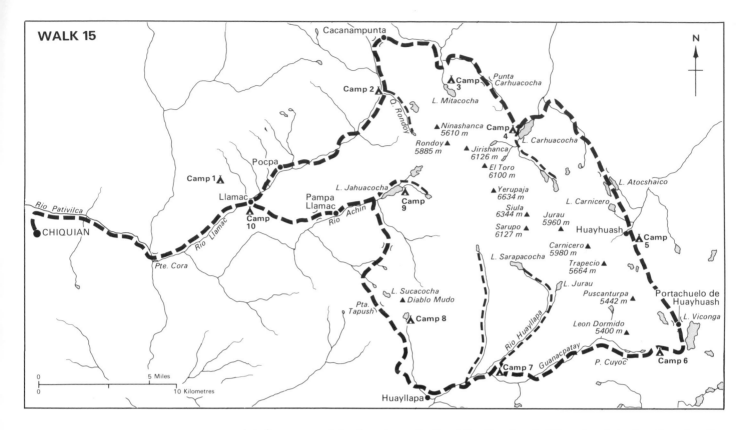

N

Distance: 166km (104 miles).

Time Required: 11 days.

Type of Walk: A high altitude walk through sparsely inhabited country for the experienced only.

Base: Chiquian (but see text).

Start: Chiquian.

Note: The trek is described in eleven daily stages, but it would in fact be unwise to attempt to complete it in this length of time. A more normal itinerary would include a spare day at the two lakes Carhuacocha and Jahuacocha, and probably a further day to visit the lakes of Sarapacocha and Jurau. The climbs of Leon Dormido and Diablo Mudo would add a further two days.

Best Time of Year: June–August. September and October are possible, though with the risk of some rain or cloud.

Guidebook: *Trails of the Cordilleras Blanca and Huayhuash of Peru*, Jim Bartle. Obtainable through Bradt Publications.

Maps: Instituto Geographico Militar - Lima, Peru, 1977, 1:100,000, sheets 21i (Chiquian) and Yanahuanca (21j). A simpler map showing the trekking trails is included in Jim Bartle's book, based on the maps produced by Ingemmet, the Peruvian Government agency responsible for the control of the glacial lakes.

point for anyone intending to walk the full circuit of the Huayhuash, the town of Cajatambo is a perfectly practical alternative, especially for shorter walks visiting only some of the lakes. Both towns are small, both have acceptable but very basic hotels and restaurants, and both have shops where a limited range of trek rations can be bought. Nonetheless, those wishing for a reasonably varied diet during their trek would be well advised to do their shopping in either Lima or Huarás.

The most salubrious of Chiquian's hostelries is the Hostal San Miguel, five minutes' walk from the main square; its façade is simple, scarcely different from that of any other house in the street, while behind lies a large traditional-style hacienda built around a central courtyard planted with flowering trees and bushes. The owners are friendly and welcoming, and the uneven red pantiles of the roof, the rickety balcony that serves the first floor rooms, and the simple communal facilities (the sexes equally catered for in that neither has hot water) combine to give the hotel a delightful atmosphere that owes much to ethnic charm and little to an abundance of life's comforts.

Day 1: Chiquian to Llamac

Chiquian, just over 3300m (11,000ft) high, lies on a wide plateau which overlooks the Rio Pativilca and the valleys that lead into the

Huayhuash. When the air is clear there is a fine view of Jerupaja and much of the rest of the range. The trail begins with a sharp descent from the town into the valley (the true significance of this steep 200m (700ft) drop is often not appreciated until the last day of the trek.) From the valley floor the mountains are for the most part invisible, but the landscape is soft-toned and attractive, well irrigated and heavily cultivated, often with intensive terracing. For the first 10km (6 miles) a road has been constructed, going as far as the Puente Cora, where the Rio Quero joins the Pativilca, but the summer rains not infrequently wash away sections of the road, and it is quite often impassable to vehicles. The Cora bridge is the lowest point of the trek—just over 2700m (9000ft)—and this section of the walk is usually hot and tiring, crossing a stretch of almost desert terrain, with sandy soil and scrubby acacia-like bushes. At the bridge the Pativilca river veers to the south, and the Huayhuash trail takes a left turn into the Rio Llamac, the *quebrada,* or mountain canyon, that will take you, the next day, in an increasingly rapid ascent to your first views of the mountains and the foot of the first pass of the trek.

For the most part, the first day's trail follows the course of the rivers, and, though quite long, is not difficult. Indeed, the absence of a pass, the warmth and the mostly lush, green vegetation may give a sense of complacency to the unwary trekker, a feeling which is reinforced on arrival at the village of Llamac at 3250m (10,660ft) where the first day's ending may be celebrated with locally-purchased beer. The horsemen often warn against the possibility of theft at Llamac, but this very likely stems from the fact that the horsemen who spread the rumour are usually recruited from the rival village of Pocpa, a little further on. Nevertheless, in Peru all such rumours are worth taking seriously, though Llamac is the last point for some time at which questions of security really need to be considered.

Day 2: Llamac to Cartelhuain

From Llamac the trail continues to Pocpa, climbing 200m (650ft) in only 3km (2 miles). Pocpa is smaller and more picturesque than Llamac, and its inhabitants certainly appear to be less commercially-minded than their neighbours. From Llamac, any earlier impressions that the trail will be a stroll are eradicated by the increasingly uphill nature of the walking: the next 11km (7 miles) rise by 550m (1800ft) while tantalizing glimpses appear of the snow-capped peaks of Rondoy 5878m (19,280ft) and Ninashanca at 5804m (19,040ft). The second camp site is normally close by the entrance to the Quebrada Rondoy, a spot known as Cartelhuain, at 4000m (13,120ft). Here the tops of the two mountains peek out from behind the closer hills, glistening in the reflected light of the sunset. Attractive though it is in daylight, Cartelhuain is a windy spot, and viciously cold at night.

Day 3: Cartelhuain to Laguna Mitacocha

For a closer view of these two mountains there is a pleasant side walk up the Quebrada Rondoy to a small lake known as Jancacuta, while the main trail continues up the Rio Llamac towards the first pass, the Cacanampunta, which is 4695m (15,400ft) high. Until now, the walk has been in a roughly easterly direction towards the northern extremity of the range; having crossed the Cacanam the next few days are spent walking along, and often very close to, the eastern wall. It is worth remembering, too, that now you have crossed the continental divide, the rivers on this side of the range flow into the Amazon, and ultimately the Atlantic.

The ascent to the pass involves about 3km (2 miles) of switchbacks, quite steep, but mercifully not too long. From the top the scenery is quite different from that of the Rio Llamac: to the north are some bare and jagged black mountains, with a bright orange lake, Pucacocha, draining down onto a wide open plain, swampy

in parts, below the pass. To the east the plain extends into the far distance, interrupted only by more dark mountains on the horizon. To the south are the snow peaks of the Huayhuash, but for the time being they are mostly obscured by the smaller, closer hilltops. It is an expansive, multicoloured landscape of impressive emptiness.

Descending, the trail crosses the wide valley, known as the Quebrada Caliente (warm valley), in the centre of which there is a small settlement of a few shepherds' shelters used in the dry months. From here, a smaller valley goes off to the right, towards the peaks. At the top of the valley the mountains form a semi-circle around a lake. It is here that the full majesty of the Huayhuash range, so far only a series of tantalizing hints and snatched glimpses, becomes breathtakingly evident, as Ninashanca, Rondoy and at centre stage the massive twin-peaked Jirishanca are suddenly revealed towering in glacier-clad splendour at the head of the valley. A fast flowing river, the Rio Janca, tumbles down the centre of the valley, which throughout its couple of miles of length provides any number of superbly scenic camping places right up to lake Mitacocha at its end. The streams and lakes here are stocked with fat, co-operative rainbow trout, which the local shepherds seem to be able to coax out of the water to order.

Day 4: Mitacocha to Laguna Carhuacocha

Back from the shepherd camp at the confluence of the several rivers of the Quebrada Caliente the trail heads down a valley that goes in a more or less southerly direction, parallel with the mountains. This valley is wide, its floor covered with thick grass, and the rather strange hard mossy hillocks, often a metre or more in diameter, that are typical of the area. There are frequently herds of sheep grazing, and even cows and the occasional bull. The next pass, the Carhuac 4634m (15,200ft), is an easy ascent; as we approach there are some excellent close-up views, particularly of the twin Jirishanca massif, and from the top we see the peak of Jerupaja for the first time at close range. At 6634m (21,760ft) Jerupaja is the highest mountain in the Huayhuash and the second highest in Peru; a more bulky and rounded peak than its neighbours, the snows of its glacier and its summit are separated by an almost sheer wall of black rock.

On the descent from the pass an impressive panorama unfolds, as each of the great peaks of the central Huayhuash becomes visible in turn. In the far distance there is a brief glimpse of one of the lakes fed by the melt from the glacier of

Lake Carhuacocha, with Yerupaja and Jirishanca above.
(Photo: John Gillies.)

Siula; for a few moments it shines out in brilliant contrast against the glaciers, before quickly disappearing as we descend. Finally the trail arrives at a large mound of moraine, from which is revealed a superb and totally unexpected tableau: at the top of the moraine the ground drops almost vertically down to a large oval lake 30m (100ft) below. About a mile and a half long, its shores are very steep on two sides, and the western end, to the right, is a flat and marshy area criss-crossed with little streams carrying the melt water into the lake from the glaciers which tumble from the two summits of Jerupaja directly down to the lake. Laguna Carhuacocha is one of the gems of the circuit, and its element of scenic surprise is quite overwhelming.

Day 5: Laguna Carhuacocha to Huayhuash

The trail from Carhuacocha leaves by the western end of the lake, and it is almost immediately necessary to wade across the stream, which can be anything from a trickle to a raging torrent. Climbing quite steeply up the first valley to the south, we are soon able to look down over the lake, which seems even more spectacular, if that is possible, from the increased altitude. This higher valley provides a pretty, pastoral landscape, with rushing streams, flocks of sheep, and even classical Andean shepherds with their pan-pipes. The climb is quite long and steady, but only becomes steep at the foot of the next pass, a point which is reached after a small lake, where the trail narrows and ascends like a staircase.

This next pass, the Punta Huayhuash, 4573m (15,000ft), is a complicated series of boulder-strewn tracks which lead over several increasingly large humps, revealing first one and then the other of the two Atocshaico lakes. The scenery undergoes a sudden change here: from rounded masses of rock and green pastures we find ourselves in a weird lunar setting of black, slaty crags; sharp and monochromatic, tingeing the waters of the lakes with a hint of menace and inhospitability not previously felt in the alpine paradise behind.

But the Grimms' fairy tale setting is short-lived, as the trail veers to the right and suddenly reveals a stupendous view of the eastern wall of the Huayhuash, with a new colossus at the centre, the broad-shouldered Butcher, Carnicero 5960m (19,550ft), named for its frequently fatal effect on those who have tried to climb it. To the left is Jurau at 5670m (18,600ft), and in the far distance Trapecio, the Trapeze, lower and sharper-peaked, overlooking the valley where the corrals and huts of Huayhuash village can just be made out. For a couple of miles we walk downhill, hanging in a heady limbo between the bare moonscape to the left and the shining ice-walls on the right. Halfway down is the Laguna Carnicero, reflecting the icy towers above it. Just in front is a house, simple enough, if bigger than the average shepherd hut, but enjoying a situation that in Switzerland would put it well into the millionaire class of real estate.

Day 6: Huayhuash to León Dormido

The name Huayhuash apparently means 'weasel' in Quechua, the language of this part of the Andes. If the village of Huayhuash is infested with weasels the fact is not immediately evident. Indeed the village itself is scarcely evident—certainly not the metropolis one might imagine having a mountain range named after it. Its few corrals and even fewer habitations are at best scantily populated, and then only for a few months of the year.

We continue southwards, passing a couple of small lakes and some good views of the splendid pyramid of Puscanturpa. The pass, the Porta-chuelo de Huayhuash 4756m (15,600ft) is not too demanding, and from the top there is a long view across to the big, rounded icecap of the Nevado Santa Rosa, at 5700m (18,700ft), one of the highest peaks of the Cordillera Raura, the next range to the south. On the downhill side of the pass in the distance lies another lake, the Laguna Viconga, the largest in the Huayhuash, which is the reservoir for an extensive hydro-electrical project; its calm and beauty, however, have been little disturbed, except that the level of the lake has dropped by several feet, with the result that the immediate shore-line is somewhat unattractive at close quarters. The trail around the lake, following the right-hand shore, is rather unclear, and some guesswork and scrambling is usually necessary in order to find the way to leave the lake at the bottom right hand corner. Here the main valley follows the river towards the town of Cajatambo, while your trail cuts back sharply towards the north-west and the looming peak of Nevado Puyoc, or León Dormido, the sleeping lion, as the Spanish called

it. Here there is a small camp—part of the hydro-electric scheme—surrounded by a sea of empty bottles which is the only adverse human influence on the whole trek; from here you head up towards the next pass, climbing towards the massive bulk of León Dormido.

Day 7: León Dormido to Quebrada Guanacpatay

Today sees the highest and the most spectacular pass of the trek, the Puyoc, 5030m (16,500ft) high. The ascent is steep, made bearable by the constantly magnificent scenery. The first stage of the climb takes you out of the valley to the foot of the pass, where a small lake is fed by the glacier that covers the flank of the Lion. The main path goes up to the left of the glacier, though the intrepid may skirt the right-hand side for a more strenuous and more alpine experience. The views to the south are towards the Cordillera Raura; here the mountains are of a different nature: their peaks are broad and rounded, completely snowcapped, with only a few of the jagged pillars that typify the Huayhuash. The views rapidly increase in splendour throughout the climb, and from the top of the pass—freezing and wind-whipped though it is—there is a 360-degree panorama of Raura to the south and Huayhuash to the north, with the lethargic Lion drooling his glacial melts only yards away from the trail.

León Dormido is a peak that can be climbed with only basic equipment in an extra day on trek; it is not a serious climber's peak, nor is it a trekker's excursion, but it can be managed fairly easily by a reasonably competent technical climber as the culminating achievement on the trek.

The descent from the Puyoc pass is violently abrupt, leading into one of the range's biggest valleys, the Guanacpatay, which descends in broad steps along the course of the rapidly flowing river. At the beginning of the descent are two huge eroded pillars of rock. Local legend has it that they are the remains of two star-crossed lovers, allowed by the gods to escape over the pass to a happy life, provided they did not at any time look behind them.

Day 8: Quebrada Guanacpatay to Huatiac

The pleasant green valley descends and narrows rapidly. Soon, in a steep cleft by a high waterfall and some intricate terracing, the Rio Guanacpatay, which you have been following, meets the Rio Huayllapa. A very good side walk is possible from here if you turn back along the Huayllapa river and ascend for about 11km (7 miles) to lakes Jurau and Sarapococha, which lie

The pass of Cacanum Punta is a narrow rib of limestone between sharp rock peaks; it is the continental divide. To the right, the Quebrada Caliente drains to the Amazon while on the left the Quebrada Cuncush leads to the Pacific. (Photo: John Cleare.)

at the very heart of the range, surrounded on three sides by mountains. From above these two lakes there are some fine views, particularly of the snow peak of Sarapo, which is reputedly the most beautifully shaped of all the mountains of Huayhuash.

The main trail continues to the village of Huayllapa, the first permanent habitation seen since Pocpa on the second day. It is a fair-sized community, with a few small shops and friendly inhabitants; it also provides another escape route down to the town of Cajatambo, some 20km (13 miles) to the south. It is also, at a mere 3597m (11,800ft), the lowest point that you have reached since Pocpa. This bronchial respite is short-lived: from Huayllapa the trail, now heading north, climbs 1067m (3,500ft) in the 7km (4½ miles) between the village and the next pass, an unremitting penance only relieved by an overnight stop at the little shepherd camp of Huatiac, a chilly but delightful water meadow below the pass and peak of Diablo Mudo, the Dumb Devil. Diablo Mudo is another mountain that can be climbed in an extra day without undue difficulty.

Day 9: Huatiac to Laguna Jahuacocha

The route from Huatiac to the Laguna Jahuacocha might well be done in two days, but it is perfectly possible, if a little masochistic, to accomplish it in one. From Huatiac to the first pass, the Punta Tapush (4800m, 15,750ft) is by now only a short distance (a fact that first becomes obvious from the night-time temperatures at Huatiac). The descent to the Quebrada Angocancha, past the other flank of Diablo Mudo and the Laguna Sucacocha, is undemanding enough to instil a sense of well-being and false security on reaching the possible camping ground at the foot of the valley. The desire to proceed is quite strong at this point, and by the time it has evaporated about two hours later, it is of course too late to turn back.

From the bottom of the valley the trail turns right and follows the narrow Quebrada Angocancha a little distance to the foot of a second, unnamed pass, (4847m, 15,900ft) by the side of the Cerro Escalon. This arm of the western-most massif of the range effectively prevents any good views from the approach side of the pass—a pity, since the occasional panorama might take one's mind off the fact that this slightly unexpected obstacle is not only high and extremely steep but largely scree-covered at its higher levels, requiring a considerably greater effort than any of the passes so far experienced. The top, however, does bring a panoramic reward: immediately in front of us is a magnificent view of the western faces of Jerupaja, with Jirishanca and Rondoy beyond, seen from exactly the opposite side than they first appeared at Lake Mitacocha.

On the far side of the pass the trail descends very steeply and not at all clearly in a tiring scramble into the valley below. It then turns left to follow the river, the Rio Huacrish, with a steep hillside to the right which obscures all views in the direction of our destination, until we suddenly skirt the far side of the slope to discover below us another wide valley, this time of the Rio Achin; away to the right, beyond a group of corrals, is lake Jahuacocha, nestling beneath a mountain backdrop of staggering immensity. From the valley floor, some 150m (500ft) below, the situation of the lake represents almost the perfection of alpine splendour: its shores are green and firm, making a perfect camp-site; a small hillock shuts out from view the valley behind, while in front the waters of the lake reflect both the brilliant blue of the Andean sky and the towering whiteness of the peaks behind it. To the far left is the triangular ridge of Rondoy, next the twin pillars of Jirishanca, then a perfect view of the smaller mountain known as El Toro (the bull) for its silhouette of two horns and curved bovine back. Finally on the right stands the great mass of Jerupaja. Across the front of the four is draped a huge glacier, one tongue of which falls directly down towards the lake.

From the left-hand shore of the lake the hillside climbs steeply. Covered with scrubby bushes at the higher levels, and nearer the water with rust-red Quenua trees with contorted branches like a witch's arms. From a small hut an enterprising *campesino* sells beer and the local *gaseosa,* a nauseous green-coloured fizzy concoction called Inka Cola.

Equally enterprising shepherds pull trout from the lake with the crudest of fishing equipment, or quite often with nothing at all except the inborn wiles of the natural poacher. Wildfowl of many species frequent the lake, though evidently the rigours of their alpine lives make them less than succulent, at any rate to western jaws. At the far end is an extensive water-meadow, with little streams of glacier-water rushing into the lake. Some way above

Trekkers rest on the last pass of the Huayhuash trek, the Pampa Llamac. (Photo: John Gillies.)

Jahuacocha, and invisible from the lake itself, is a second lake, only slightly smaller, called Solteracocha, a difficult climb around the glacier which is not always passable for walkers, where the mountain views are even more toweringly immediate, and which makes a good starting point for serious attempts on the summits.

Day 10: Laguna Jahuacocha to Llamac

The return journey takes you back into the Achin valley, and quickly climbs to another pass, the Pampa Llamac, providing on the way some final nostalgic looks back towards the lake and the surrounding mountains. The descent to the village of Llamac is the longest of the entire trek, falling 1070m (3500ft) in a very short time. An alternative pass close by would take you to Pocpa, but is higher, even steeper and rather longer.

Day 11: Llamac to Chiquian

The final day is a repeat of the first, with one crucial difference. On the first day the initial descent from Chiquian tends to go unnoticed in the general euphoria. On the return, coming at the end of a long, hard trek and a particularly long, hot day, it represents an obstacle that, even at such a low altitude, causes a quite disproportionate amount of suffering to lungs and limbs. The rueful consensus is invariably that it is the nastiest, most masochistic and least expected exertion of the entire trek, for which the only consolation is that convalescence can take place over an unlimited number of cold drinks, a hot meal and a comfortable bed.

145

Walk 16 AMERICA: The John Muir Trail
by Chris Townsend

Distance: 336km (210 miles).

Time required: 12 days.

Type of Walk: A wilderness trail for backpackers.

Start: Whitney Portal, California.

Note: This is a completely arbitrary itinerary, suitable only for a strong backpacker but having the advantage of only taking 12 days and only requiring nine days' supplies to be carried initially.

Maps: USGS Topo 1/62500 Lone Pine, Mount Whitney, Mt Pinchot, Big Pine, Mt Goddard, Blackcap Mtn, Mt Abbot, Mt Morrison, Devils Postpile, Mono Craters, Tuolumne Meadows, Hetch Hetchy Reservoir, and Yosemite. Note: the guidebooks contain adequate if limited maps for summer walking.

Guidebooks: *Guide to the John Muir Trail* by Thomas Winnett (Wilderness Press), *Starr's Guide to the John Muir Trail & the High Sierra Region*, by Walter A. Starr, Jr. (Sierra Club Books).

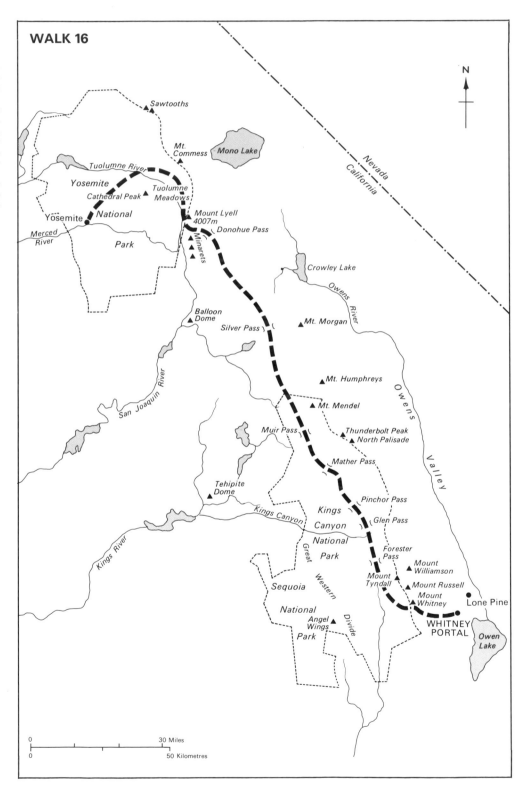

WALK 16

N

Sawtooths

Mt. Commess

Mono Lake

Tuolumne River

Yosemite

Cathedral Peak

Tuolumne Meadows

National

Yosemite

Merced River

Park

Mount Lyell 4007m

Donohue Pass

Minarets

Crowley Lake

Owens River

Balloon Dome

Silver Pass

Mt. Morgan

San Joaquin River

Mt. Humphreys

Mt. Mendel

Muir Pass

Thunderbolt Peak
North Palisade

Owens Valley

Mather Pass

Tehipite Dome

Pinchor Pass

Kings Canyon

Kings Canyon

Kings River

National

Glen Pass

Park

Forester Pass

Great

Mount Williamson

Sequoia

Western

Mount Tyndall

Mount Russell

National

Divide

Mount Whitney

Lone Pine

Angel Wings

Park

WHITNEY PORTAL

Owen Lake

Nevada

California

0   30 Miles

0   50 Kilometres

A Famous Walk through the High Sierra

Named after Scottish conservation pioneer John Muir, who came to California in 1868 to spend most of his time in the mountains of the Sierra Nevada, the John Muir Trail runs for almost 340km (210 miles) through these mountains from the summit of Mount Whitney to Yosemite Valley. The trail is a fitting tribute to Muir, a man whose writings led to the creation of the Yosemite and Sequoia National Parks in 1890, and who described the Sierra Nevada in his book *The Mountains of California* as 'the Range of Light, the most divinely beautiful of all the mountain-chains I have ever seen.' The Sierra Nevada covers a greater area than that of the French, Swiss and Italian Alps combined, being more than 640km (400 miles) long and about 110km (70 miles) wide. The highest section, known as the High Sierra, runs for 240km (150 miles) from the Mount Whitney area to Sonora Pass north of Yosemite National Park. This region is mostly over 2700m (9000ft) in elevation and 'alpine' in character. It is through the High Sierra that the John Muir Trail runs. Subject in the past to severe glaciation this is a region of u-shaped, deep canyons, polished granite rock walls and high lake-filled cirques with boulders and moraines everywhere; a harsh land of stone and water yet also a land of almost-magical beauty—a land for solitude and the joys of quiet reflection.

For most of its length the Sierra Nevada consists of one main crest which the John Muir Trail parallels rising to cross high passes where lengthy spurs jut out from the main crest towards the parallel crests that lie to the west and which themselves often reach 4000m (13,000ft) in height. Twelve peaks rise above 4250m (14,000ft), six in the Palisades and six in the Mount Whitney range including Whitney itself, at 4420m (14,494ft) the highest peak in the contiguous 48 states and whose summit is the starting point for the John Muir Trail. The trail passes through three National Parks (Sequoia, Kings Canyon and Yosemite), two designated Wilderness Areas (the John Muir Wilderness and the Minarets Wilderness), as well as the Devil's Postpile National Monument. But whilst these areas ensure the protection of the land along the trail from any form of development, ironically the John Muir Trail itself is a 'made' trail which, in places, includes whole sections that have been dynamited down cliff walls to form huge stone-built staircases. On more gentle terrain the trail is carefully levelled and drained. Each year after the winter snows melt, the various authorities responsible for sections of the trail send out work crews to repair damage and remove fallen trees or 'blowdowns'.

Passing, as it does, through the highest, remotest sections of the High Sierra the John Muir Trail is a wilderness mountain trail, a trail for backpackers and those who wish to escape all signs of civilisation. There are no Alpine-style huts, no hostels, no organised campgrounds. All equipment and supplies must be carried. Between Mount Whitney and Tuolumne Meadows 298km (186 miles) away, the trail constantly climbs over 3300m (11,000ft) passes before dropping down to 2400m (8,000ft) in the forested canyons and then climbing back up above timberline again. This switchback, which continually takes the walker from the dense

The Yosemite Valley is famous for its dramatic rock scenery, such as the 1000-m (3000-ft) granite monolith of El Capitan.
(Photo: Steve Pitcher.)

'climax' forest at the bottom of deep valleys up through the sparse, stunted trees at timberline to the stark, lifeless rock and snow of the bare mountains, is characteristic of this walk. But if the scenery is always changing, one factor is constant—the presence of water—whether in rushing, foaming creeks, placid, wooded pools or half-frozen cold cirque lakes. In all the panoramic views of the High Sierra seen from the John Muir Trail the sparkling brilliance of the myriad lakes and creeks gives light and life to the landscape.

For a mountain range, the weather of the High Sierra is remarkably benign. In summer it is usually hot with perhaps an afternoon thunderstorm and above the timberline a night frost. Early in the season—mid-June to mid-July depending on the size of the snowpack and the date when snow-melt starts—there may be snow at higher elevations and on the north side of the passes. During snow-melt, however, normally easily forded streams can turn into raging torrents, and then great care and perhaps a rope are needed. Camp sites abound but the trail is so popular that a little thought is needed in choosing pitches that will cause least damage to the environment. In particular, meadows, tempting though they are, should be avoided as their eco-systems are very fragile. Some sites are heavily over-used but it is easy, by wandering off the trail a little, to find solitude and unspoilt pitches.

Day 1: Whitney Portal to Crabtree Ranger Station

The John Muir Trail proper starts on the summit of Mount Whitney. Of course, the walker has to climb the mountain first to begin the trail and most people do so by ascending the Mount Whitney Trail from Whitney Portal, a road head 20km (13 miles) west of the town of Lone Pine in Owens Valley to the east of the Sierra Nevada. There is a car park, a campground, small store and cafe at the trail head. The elevation at the start is 2550m (8361 ft) and any walker starting out on the John Muir Trail and laden with a heavy pack is faced immediately with a 1870m (6133ft) climb. It would be wise to be fit when you set off!

Climbing steeply through Jeffrey Pine and Red Fir forest the Mount Whitney Trail soon reaches timberline and the idyllic Mirror Lake, where camping is forbidden, then climbs up steep switchbacks past Thor Peak to where Mount Whitney comes into view. From Trail Camp (where camping is permitted and where the last reliable water is to be found until the descent), 100 switchbacks climb 500m (1600ft)

to Trail Crest. Here for the first time there is a view westwards to the forests, peaks and lakes of Sequoia National Park. This is a good spot for a much-needed rest. Just beyond and below Trail Crest the John Muir Trail is finally joined and followed for two miles past huge granite pillars across a steep mountainside to the last pull up to the summit of Mount Whitney. Owens Valley, 3000m (10,000ft) below, appears at times through 'windows' between the rocks but the real eye-catching views are in the other direction, down to the shimmering lakes almost below one's feet and west and north to the miles of green forest and the wall after wall of snow-spattered mountains.

The summit, when reached, is a small plateau with a tiny stone shelter, a plaque and, incongruous but obviously necessary, a chemical toilet. The view is all-embracing but not very spectacular as everything else is so much lower and seemingly so far away. The chief impression given is of the awesome vastness of the High Sierra and the challenge of the long walk just begun. As you turn to head back down the mountain you are beginning at last the walk to Yosemite along the John Muir Trail. Below Trail Crest, steep switchbacks lead down into the lake-and-boulder-strewn tundra-like landscape below the mountain and soon afterwards timberline is reached again and the Crabtree Ranger Station (wardened in the summer) is passed. Camp sites can be found by Whitney Creek in the woods lining Crabtree Meadows.

Day 2: Crabtree Ranger Station to Bubbs Creek

Shortly beyond the meadows the direction of the trail, westerly until now, turns to the north where it will stay all the way to Tuolumne Meadows. Undulating in and out of the forest the trail crosses Wallace and Wright Creeks (both fords potentially difficult early in the season) before climbing to Bighorn Plateau. Views from this sparsely-vegetated gravel-covered 4000m (12,000ft) high flat expanse are comprehensive. Especially noteworthy in the panorama are the peaks of the Great Western Divide and the view back to Mount Whitney. After a descent to Tyndall Creek (again a dangerous torrent during snow-melt), the trail begins the long climb to Forester Pass, at 4018m (13,180ft) the highest pass on the John Muir Trail.

From a bleak landscape of bare rock and cold lakes the pass looms above the walker, the rock wall below it seemingly too steep to ascend. And so it would be but for the switchbacks cut into the granite that take you slowly and surely to the

tiny, often wind-swept, notch of Forester Pass. This is the gateway between Sequoia and King's Canyon National Parks, the latter now entered by the John Muir Trail. Northwards ever more mountains stretch out for mile upon mile until they fade into the sky. The descent from the pass is less steep and feels effortless after the climb up. It ends with a stroll along Bubbs Creek which has to be forded many times as the trail switches from bank to bank.

Day 3: Bubbs Creek to Woods Creek

To the east is the impressive jagged wall of the Kearsage Pinnacles, full in view as the walker climbs up steeply from Bubbs Creek, a climb that eventually leads to the next steep pass that has to be crossed, the 3650m (11,978ft) Glen Pass. Like Forester, Glen Pass is at the top of another blank rock wall ascended via very steep switchbacks. The descent, too, is steep enough to require concentration, but once it eases off above Rae Lakes you can admire the magnificent views of the multi-coloured, multi-textured ring of peaks at the head of these lakes; Dragon Peak and Painted Lady being particularly spectacular in their red, gold and purple livery. A longer descent than previous ones takes the walker all the way down to Woods Creek, where there is actually a bridge, deep in the forest at 2590m (8492ft) the lowest point since starting the Mount Whitney Trail, 88km (55 miles) back. The mixed 'climax' forest here of Incense Cedars, Red Firs, Lodgepole Pines and Ponderosa Pines plus Quaking Aspens and Willows by the creek, together with the birds, butterflies and flowers, feels very luxurious after the harsh world of the high passes and stunted timberline vegetation.

Day 4: Woods Creek to Lower Palisade Lake

Unfortunately the lower elevation only means a longer climb back up, this time to the 3698m (12,130ft) Pinchot Pass. The way is not too steep though because it takes just over 11km (7 miles) to climb the 1110m (3638ft). A string of sparkling lakes and lakelets lines the descent from Pinchot Pass to the South Fork Kings River and this necklace of water continues as the trail climbs through empty Upper Basin to the grim, rocky 3770m (12,100ft) Mather Pass, passing en route the red and white metamorphic rock walls of Striped Peak and Cardinal Peak. From Mather Pass the serrated peaks of the 4268m (14,000ft) high Palisades can be seen clearly. Lower Palisade Lake has many good camp sites beside it and makes an excellent overnight stopping place.

Day 5: Lower Palisade Lake to Evolution Creek

High spot of the descent of the pass is the 'Golden Staircase', a tight set of steep switchbacks constructed on the cliffs of the Palisade Creek Gorge below Palisade Lakes. The descent then continues to Middle Fork Kings River at only 2445m (8020ft). Slowly the average elevation of the trail is declining. In fact the next pass, named after Muir himself, is, at 3645m (11,955ft), the last point on the trail above 3354m (11,100ft). On the ascent up Le Conte Canyon to Muir Pass huge swathes of forest are missing where avalanches have crashed down from the heights above. Early in the season a tangle of twisted and torn trees intermingled with patches of hard dirt-covered snow may lie across the trail in this canyon. Crossing such avalanche debris is hard work. At times, though, the trail climbs up the shining water-washed granite right beside the creek, providing tempting scrambling opportunities for the more adventurous. The waterslides and cascades in Le Conte Canyon are powerful and dramatic, especially during snow-melt. At the head of the canyon, 3535m (11,595ft), high Helen Lake has good if bleak camp sites round its shores giving superb views east to the Palisade Crest. On Muir Pass itself is a stone hut, the only man-made shelter on the trail and built in honour of John Muir, which would provide adequate shelter for a night out, though water would need to be carried up to it.

A gentle descent wanders down from Muir Pass past more lakes including Wanda Lake (named, like Helen Lake, after one of John Muir's daughters), with splendid views of the multi-hued metamorphic rocks of the Goddard Divide; a colourful contrast to the stern granite of most of the High Sierra. Grand names have been given to the grand features hereabout. One descends into Evolution Basin where runs Evolution Creek and lies Evolution Lake. Above tower the heights of Mounts Darwin, Spencer, Haeckel, Wallace, Fiske and Huxley. The ford of Evolution Creek can be the most difficult along the trail, as high water often continues well into the middle of the season.

Day 6: Evolution Creek to Sally Keyes Lake

A long, pleasant and easy walk beside the creek, past waterfalls and through flower-filled forest meadows, leads to the South Fork San Joaquin River where there are many camp sites. Finally this lengthy descent ends at the junction with the Florence Lake Trail at only 2405m (7890ft). Two km (1½ miles) down this side trail lies the Muir Trail Ranch resort and 15km (9½ miles) beyond that a roadhead. Food supplies could possibly be sent to the ranch. (Write to Box 176, Lakeshore, CA 93634, USA for details).

Down here the bright reds and purples of Paintbrush and Lupin blossoms line the trail in early summer. For the first time you are out of the mountains, albeit briefly, because to the west only the flat wooded Sierra foothills can be seen, rolling away into the distance. A short, sharp ascent leads back to the mountains proper––600m in 3.5km––(2000ft in 2.2 miles) before levelling slightly for the rest of the climb to the 3323m (10,900ft) Seldon Pass, passing on the way forest-shrouded Sally Keyes Lakes where there are good camp sites.

Day 7: Sally Keyes Lakes to Mono Creek

From the pass Marie Lake, dotted with islands, beckons you down yet again into the forest and another ford, this time of Bear Creek. This too can be hazardous early in the summer — when we crossed it in June, three of us had to link together in a triangle and even then we only just made it. Bear Creek is followed for a while until the trail begins a steep switchbacking climb up to Bear Ridge with good views back up the Creek to the peaks at its head, of which Mount Hooper at 8843m (12,349ft) is specially impressive with its Matterhorn-like shape. From Bear Ridge seventy switchbacks lead down through thickening forest to Mono Creek at 2362m (7750ft) where camp sites abound.

Day 8: Mono Creek to Duck Creek

The climb up from Mono Creek is enlivened by the crossing of Silver Pass Creek at a point both below and above a series of cascades. A fall here would be fatal and my companion and I roped up and belayed each other across. (We only in fact had 9m (30ft) of line so we had to belay on some rocks in the middle of the stream as the rope wouldn't stretch the whole way! For creek fords at least 18m (60ft) of rope is needed.) The creek is then followed to Silver Pass Lake from where you climb the 3323m (10,900ft) Silver Pass itself. A somewhat tortuous descent leads down to Fish Creek where you encounter for the first time graceful stands of Mountain Hemlock, one of the most beautiful of conifers. Tully Hole, above Fish Creek, has many good camp sites. From here the trail climbs above the Cascade Valley in which Fish Creek lies to Lake Virginia from where it contours round the hillside high above the valley, eventually descending to pass Purple Lake before arriving at Duck Creek.

Day 9: Duck Creek to Reds Meadow

Unusually, there is no water on the trail for the next six miles as the trail stays above the Cascade Valley. Deer Creek provides the next water and the start of the descent to Reds Meadow where there is a summer resort with a small stores and a campground, the first supplies on the trail and very welcome after the 256km (160 miles) since Whitney Portal. Being only a seasonal resort Reds Meadow doesn't open until

The dramatic eastern ramparts of Mount Whitney and its satellites. (Photo: Steve Pitcher.)

Two walkers set out on the trail to Mount Whitney from Whitney Portal. (Photo: Chris Dickenson.)

after the snow-melt so early in the season it may still be closed. The John Muir Trail itself actually bypasses the resort but few if any backpackers do. As well as supplies the resort also has some hot springs in which one can soak off the sweat and grime accumulated over the previous days.

Day 10: Reds Meadow to Rush Creek Forks

Just past Reds Meadow is the popular tourist attraction of the Devil's Postpile National Monument. Its popularity is justified, for this massive cliff of polygonal andesite columns is well worth a look. The pillars were formed when molten basalt was forced through a crack in the earth's surface by volcanic forces nearly a million years ago. As the basalt cooled it cracked into these 'posts' which average two feet in diameter and have four to seven sides. The highest columns reach 20km (60ft). Around the base of the Postpile lies the rubble of broken columns looking like the cast-offs of a mason in Ancient Greece. Glacial ice smoothed down the top of the columns to form a polished basalt pavement in which the sides of the posts can be seen clearly, looking like a huge honeycomb.

The climb up from the Devil's Postpile takes the walker into the Minarets Wilderness as the lake-spattered slopes of Volcanic Ridge are traversed, high above the Middle Fork San Joaquin River. When the descent down to Shadow Lake is begun views appear of the Minarets and in particular Mount Ritter 4011m (13,157ft) and Banner Peak 3946m (12,945ft).

Throughout the section from the Devil's Postpile to Donohue Pass the John Muir Trail follows a complex, undulating route across many ridges, past many lakes, both above and below timberline. Lakes are everywhere, but dominant is the large, aptly-named, 1000 Island Lake with its fine views of Banner Peak. Above the lake lies the 3110m (10,200ft) Island Pass, an unusually wide pass with stands of Lodgepole Pine and Mountain Hemlock amongst its meadows and pools. Below it is the icy Rush Creek which has to be forded three times, and which can be deep early in the season.

Day 11: Rush Creek Forks to Tuolumne Meadows

A meandering trail leaves Rush Creek to climb 3370m (11,056ft) Donohue Pass, gateway to Yosemite National Park. The route to Tuolumne Meadows is seen clearly from here as it goes straight down Lyell Canyon. As the walker descends to the canyon, Mount Lyell, Yosemite's highest peak at 4007m (13,144ft)

comes prominently into view. Its glacier is the largest one visible from the John Muir Trail. Soon you arrive at the headwaters of the Lyell Forks River and the start of the long but easy walk down this massive canyon.

Many camp sites line the trail along the west bank of the river and as you near Highway 120 (the first road across the Sierras encountered on the trail), and Tuolumne Meadows, facilities start to appear in the camps; in particular steel cables strung between trees from which to hang your food out of reach of the bears. Bears, are a serious problem from here to the end of the trail.

The massive usage of the area is evident from the multi-tracked trail, reminiscent of the start of the Pennine Way in Edale Meadows. Here too, soft, wet grassland has been carved into muddy trenches by the boots of thousands upon thousands of hikers. Shortly before the highway, the turn-off for the Tuolumne Meadows Campground is reached, where most John Muir Trail trekkers spend a night, even though it is three quarters of a mile off the trail. Actually, on Highway 120 there is a store and Post Office——but again, like the one at Reds Meadows, it is seasonal only. In 1982, a year of late, heavy snowfall and late snow-melt, they didn't open until the second week of June. For those who've had enough of camping it is possible to stay at the Tuolumne Meadows Lodge where showers and meals are also available.

Day 12: Tuolumne Meadows to Happy Isles

The John Muir Trail itself turns away from the campground trail to cross Lyell Forks River and then the Dana Fork of the Tuolumne River from where the paved highway is paralleled until it is joined, just past the Tuolumne Meadows Ranger Station and car park, where there is a booth from which, in summer, wilderness permits can be obtained. Those who have used the campground will rejoin the trail here to enjoy the views of Lembert Dome, a huge curve of rock that tells walkers they are in Yosemite, home of the domes.

From Tuolumne Meadows the John Muir Trail turns west and ceases its northward journey. Ahead lie the Horned Peaks, Unicorn and Cathedral, dramatic on the skyline. The trail makes its last major climb up to the 2966m (9730ft) Cathedral Pass. The views of Cathedral Peak, the Echo Peaks, the Cockscomb and Unicorn Peak draw one along the undulating but always slowly climbing trail. The pass itself gives wide views in all directions. The highest point of this last section of the trail is, though, just beyond the pass on the east slopes of

Tresidder Peak, a wonderful viewpoint for the southern half of Yosemite National Park.

A long walk down the appropriately named Long Meadow follows, concluded by a steep descent beside the headwaters of Sunrise Creek which is then itself followed as it heads for Little Yosemite Valley. Mighty Half Dome can be seen through the trees during this descent telling you that your High Sierra trek is nearly over. You are in Yosemite Valley. The trail round Half Dome is passed as rich 'climax' forest is reached and Sunrise Creek runs into the Merced River.

Follow the Merced to the top of the incredible Nevada Fall where it plunges 181m (594ft). Our descent is on a paved, walled-in section of trail stuck to the side of a precipitous granite cliff. Now that you are in the heartland of Yosemite Valley, popular trails branch off on every side and the views of the falls and domes are superlative. Finally the John Muir Trail ends at Happy Isles from where a free shuttle bus runs down the valley. The magnificent mountain journey that has taken the walker from the summit of Mount Whitney over the savage high passes, past the cold glacial lakes and tumbling, cascading creeks, through the rich forests of the canyons down to the domes of Yosemite Valley is over.

Permits

Two permits are needed. The first, valid from Whitney Portal to Tuolumne Meadows, can be obtained from The Chief Ranger's Office, Sequoia-Kings Canyon National Park, Three Rivers, CA 93271, USA. The second permit, valid from Tuolumne Meadows to Yosemite Valley can be obtained in Tuolumne Meadows.

Supplies

There are no supply points between Whitney Portal and Reds Meadow, a distance of 257m (161 miles). At an average daily mileage of 28km (18 miles) per day, as in my itinerary, the Trail takes nine days and therefore (at approximately 2lb of food per day) requires the carrying of about 8kg (18lb) of food per person plus adequate amounts of stove fuel (wood fires are banned along much of the trail). The only alternative to this involves making long detours, either on foot or by hitch-hiking, off the trail.

Bears

Black Bears are a serious hazard along the whole of the trail and precautions must be taken to safeguard food supplies. At least 15m (50ft) of strong cord is required plus tough bags to contain supplies (nylon stuffsacs are ideal). Food must be hung at least 3m (10ft) above the ground and 2m (6ft) below the branch used and 2m (6ft) away from the tree trunk. The other end of the cord must also be kept out of reach as bears have learnt that if they find a nylon cord and break it a bag of food appears! The method of avoiding this happening is called counterbalancing. Two food bags of equal weight are needed. The line is tossed over a high branch by attaching it to a stone then one bag is hauled up to just below the branch. The other bag is tied to the end of the line and then thrown up in the air so that, hopefully, it ends up level with the other bag and at least 3m (10ft) off the ground. If this sounds tedious and difficult, it is, but the alternative is a nightly visitor and the loss of your supplies. Bears regularly visit popular camp sites along the John Muir Trail. It is best to camp a few hundred yards downwind of the food bags and never cook or keep food in your tent. If a bear does get your food let him keep it. If you try and retrieve it you could end up seriously injured. Finally, don't leave food or your pack unattended even for a few minutes during the daytime and if you come across a she-bear with cubs stay well clear. If the mother thinks you're a threat to her cubs she'll attack.

A walker on the trail in Evolution Valley. Mount Haeckel rises in the background. (Photo: Steve Pitcher.)

Walk 17 KASHMIR: The Concordia Trek
by Alan Rouse

K2, the world's second highest mountain, seen from Concordia. (Photo: Alan Rouse.)

A Difficult and Dangerous Walk into the Heart of the Karakoram

K2, Broad Peak, the Gasherbrums, Hidden Peak and Chogolisa surround the desolate meeting of glaciers called Concordia in the heart of the Karakoram: a remote and inaccessible place which can only be reached by an arduous trek through deserts, dangerous rivers and long glaciers. Those who make the effort will be well rewarded by the most inspiring collection of the world's highest mountains that can ever be seen. K2, the world's second highest mountain, only a few hundred feet lower than Everest, is a mountain of dreams. Elegant, steep and standing alone: the epitome of inaccessibility. Glaciers pour down from the heights to join at Concordia before continuing for another 40km

(25 miles) like a giant highway through the mountains. The raw forces of nature dominate the landscape. You can feel the erosion and the gradual but constant change of the surrounding slopes of rock and ice. Nothing lives here except for an occasional spider on the ice. You get the feeling that nothing will ever live here, yet here lies the source of Pakistan's wealth, for these glaciers contain the water that will eventually flow down into the great Indus river and irrigate the plains of the Punjab, giving life to millions.

Skardu, the starting point for expeditions in the area, used to be reached most easily from Srinagar but after the partition of India this became politically impossible. Until the last few years the only access to Skardu was by a flight from Islamabad, that although scheduled to run

every day, was often delayed by weeks. Fortunately, the construction of the Karakoram Highway, linking China with Pakistan, with a branch up the Indus River to Skardu, now allows the traveller to journey by bus in just thirty hours from the capital. The roads are a remarkable feat of engineering in this inhospitable area of constant geological change. Landslides sometimes close the road for a few days but it is always reopened by the army as it provides an important strategic link to the border areas with India.

The daily bus service goes via Gilgit along the KKH (Karakoram Highway) and then branches eastwards along the narrow confines of the Indus Gorge through extremely hot and inhospitable terrain. Sometimes the road hugs the river but at other times it climbs up for 300m (1000ft), its pathway blasted across cliffs of solid granite. Frequently, huge unstable boulders are perched delicately above the road, waiting for one of the not infrequent earthquakes which severely affect the area. Eventually the road comes out on a small plain dominated by a rocky mound topped by Skardu Fort.

Skardu is quite a busy town and a welcome relief from the oppressive gorge. Dusty and dirty, Skardu is not a particularly interesting place but after supplies have been bought a rapid exit can be made by hired jeep to the end of the road at Dassu. This takes about six hours along a rough track, which passes through the pleasant oasis of Shigar, where houses are Nepalese in style, perhaps because of the Buddhist influence which existed before Islam took hold of the people. A visitors' rest house has been constructed in Dassu. The granite walls have angular lines of protruding cement, and the windows and doors are painted in primary colours This solid building is the last point of outside interference. Bureaucrats do not walk and the road ends here. Apricot trees abound, carefully irrigated by meltwater from the permanent snows high above. Locals do not bother much with the fruit but prize the kernels which taste bitter like almonds.

From Dassu a three-day walk up the Braldu Gorge leads to the last village, Askole. After Askole a further eight or nine days takes you to Concordia.

Above left: **Trekkers near Askole, the last permanent settlement before the Baltoro Glacier.**

Above right: **Walking between Liligo and Urdukas.**

(Photos: Alan Rouse.)

155

Distance: 100km (63 miles).

Time required: 20 days.

Type of Walk: A strenuous walk for the fit.

Base: Skardu, Baltistan.

Start: Dassu.

Permits: Required from Islamabad.

Best Time of Year: May – August.

Maps: AMS Series U502 Sheets NI43-3 and NI 43-4 1:250,000.

Guidebooks: *The Trekker's Guide to the Himalaya and Karakorum* by H. Swift. Brief reference only. The best modern description of this trek is contained in Galen Rowell's *In The Throne Room of the Mountain Gods* (Allen and Unwin).

WALK 17

N

CHINA

Ogre
Latok
Skyang Kangri
K2
Mustagh Tower
Broad Peak
Biafo Glacier
Panmah Glacier
Lobsang Group
Gasherbrum Group
Trango Towers
Baltoro Glacier
Concordia
Paiju
Sia Kangri
Dassu
Braldu Gorge
Askole
Masherbrum 7925 m
Chogolisa
Pioneer Peak
INDIA

PAKISTAN

Shigar

River Indus

SKARDU

Some of the borders shown on this map are disputed

0   20 Miles
0   40 Kilometres

Days 1 – 3: Dassu to Askole

Leaving Dassu early in the morning and carrying brollies in anticipation of the midday sun, a road was followed for a mile or so before a 300m (1000ft) climb warmed us up. We reached the col at about nine in the morning and emerged into harsh sunlight. It is tempting to drain the contents of your water bottle, but beware—there is hardly ever any water available on these walks except for the filthy sediment of the Braldu river, grey and completely opaque.

A pleasant amble across hillsides, gradually descending, leads to the first of many *nullahs:* steep muddy stream beds, studded with glacial boulders. They are always worrying, being crossed by paths hacked out of the now dusty mud and threatened by boulders defiantly denying the forces of gravity. When the Braldu is regained easy going takes you to Chakpo, although an interesting side diversion can be undertaken to the village of Biano, where mature walnut trees offer welcome shade. The great heat will be encountered for the first time on the flat barren areas of a terrace above the river. We raised brollies but still sweated in the midday sun. The observant will find a clear water spring just before crossing the glacial river into Chakpo. Clogged with algae it is not as

attractive as you might imagine!

Chakpo is a primitive village, typical of the area. Apricot trees abound, irrigated by muddy channels cut laboriously right back to the main river. Houses are not too evident to a casual inspection, being largely below ground and roofed in dust. Small stone circles are the visible evidence of occupation below. The inhabitants are noticeably poor and wary of the strange travellers who pass by each year during the season. Travellers have no impact here; they are incidental to a life which is already fully occupied with the business of survival. Only the children take any notice, curious and smiling, perhaps trying to cadge or sell. Like all visitors we camped in a dusty field and counted the porters straggling in at the end of a long day. They disappeared quickly from the landscape without fuss and without explaining to us that the fields are flooded each day (including the one we were in!) by diverting the irrigation ditches.

The next day took us through part of the Braldu Gorge and through genuinely dangerous terrain made oppressive by its lack of escape routes and the pervasive heat. Endless moraine slopes stretched all around us, but particularly above us, offering a disturbing sight to those who know. The porters may not walk if rain is

The view westwards at dusk from Urdukas across the great Baltoro Glacier, towards the peaks of the Paiju Group. (Photo: John Cleare).

imminent as they understand that rain in the mountains above will bring boulders and mud sliding down in a dangerous landslide. A friend of ours, Pat Fearneough, was killed on this section when boulders rolled down the slope and knocked him into the river.

A welcome break arrives in the form of hot springs, where two pools have been constructed. Small caves behind are decorated with encrustations and variegated algae thrive in the oasis. A mile or so further on the gorge opens out and a small stream tinkles down the dusty slopes, peppered with thorny bushes and boulders that have come to rest. We stopped for lunch by two cottage-size granite blocks that fell down just four years before.

There is a choice here: if the Braldu is low some logs will have been placed across the river and it is easy. If however the weather is bad or the river is in full spate, you will have to climb 300m (1000ft) and go around the cliffs. We crossed the river, grateful to avoid the climb, and strolled on to the pleasant village of Kurpe, where we settled down to sleep on the grass without our tents. The other route crosses

exposed cliffs on paths made of flat stones, that rest on old dry logs, and are jammed miraculously between cracks in the rock. The last part of the route entails hopping down a steep mud gulley from one embedded stone to another. Dislodged rocks slither down and fall free into the river a few hundred feet lower, reminding you of the consequences of a slip. Fertile fields bring you into the village of Chakpo and the camp site.

The third day is easy, pleasant, and almost entirely through cultivated land, which is dotted with clusters of houses and people working in the fields. Three or four hours suffice to reach Askole, the local capital, with its cobbled streets, shops and houses piled one on top of the other. Beautiful and awful at the same time, it is the last habitation you will see for at least two weeks. Supplies can be bought here, but *atta,* the flour for chappattis, is best carried from Skardu as in the villages it tends to contain grit which gives stomach trouble. The headman Hedji Medhi was friendly, greeting us with boiled eggs and cups of tea outside the optimistically called Post Office. Each year more women in the

157

village appear to passing strangers but you should not photograph them, as it is forbidden by law. Islam rules here and pictures of Ayatollah Khomeni decorate rooms.

Days 4 – 7: Askole to Paiju

The following three days to Paiju, pass through very dry areas. A flat plain leads to the Biafo glacier, which cuts across the valley, stopping just in time to allow the river through. It is necessary to pick a way over boulder-strewn ice slopes with little trace of a path before dropping down to Korophon. Prickly bushes survive near a resurgence from under the mounds of glacial debris. It is quite an agreeable place, with brightly coloured flowers everywhere the water reaches—insignificant on the scale of things but very important to human eyes.

An early start is essential the next morning if the Panmah river is to be crossed before the sun touches the glaciers which feed it. I kept my boots on in the thigh-deep water. Later in the season it is necessary to walk a few miles upstream to swing across on a wire-and-pulley system run by Askole ancients who charge ten rupees for the dubious privilege of being pulled across in an old wooden seat, 30m (100ft) above the river. Later that day Bradumal is reached. Why this spot is dignified by a name is a bit of a mystery as it looks identical to all the rest of the terrain around here. Anyway a few boulders offer some welcome shade but the only water is the Braldu itself which is not very good for the insides!

Paiju is reached the following afternoon. For the first time dramatic mountains can be seen and the contrasting lushness of Paiju makes for a beautiful sight. A few hundred naturally occurring trees grow from a bed of grass and bushes. Real shade is available for the first time and a tranquil afternoon can be spent here. When we were there, the place was covered in litter, so Doug Scott organised our 140 porters into a line to sweep through the wood picking up the rubbish. When they had finished however, they were all clutching twigs and leaves—no one had thought to explain just what our sensibilities had indicated to be rubbish! The porters relaxed, taking the opportunity to make bread and chappattis in the last place where wood would be available.

Days 8 – 9: Paiju to Urdukas

The character of the walking changes completely as the Baltoro glacier is finally reached. From now on you will be following a highway of stones and ice cutting through some of the most dramatic mountains on earth. Paths are indistinct and change from year to year, or

even day to day in some areas. At the end of the first day on the glacier we exited to another non-place: Lilligo. A small level platform just off the glacier is delineated by an occasional river and vertical walls of mud behind. The walls of mud contain boulders the size of houses, waiting their turn to return to the glacier and be carried off, eventually to be ground away to silt to cover the plains of the Punjab. Gentle drizzle obscured the view and the porters huddled tight into the walls of mud.

A fine dawn brought us views of the dramatic rock spires which offer the gateway to the higher mountains. We were away long before colours had resumed their individual identity. The sharp grey half light of early morning hurried us along as we tried to get as far as we could before the great heat resumed. I felt queasy as we neared Urdukas. A mixture of altitude, heat and effort I suppose. It seems to happen to everyone once on any long walk in the mountains.

Urdukas is a fine place: a secure balcony from which to view the surrounding mountains, safe in the comfort of grassy slopes, unthreatened by natural disaster. In May pockets of snow still occupied secluded hollows and the grass was beaten and yellow from lying under the winter snows. Later, on our return, the place was filled with flowers and grass growing furiously in the short season in which life is permitted. Tent platforms are conveniently sited all over the slopes: they were first constructed by the Duke of the Abruzzi in the 1890s. Now they have blended into the environment, appearing more or less natural to the casual observer.

Opposite Urdukas lie the rock spires for which this region is famous. Red granite spires like Trango or Uli Biaho fulfil a child's dream of mountains: sharp needles piercing the clouds. Rising sheer from the glaciers to heights of 7000m (10,000ft) they offer fascinating mountaineering possibilities for the experienced climber. We decided to spend some time here and make a few first ascents in the Lobsang Spire Group before moving on to the higher mountains.

Days 10 – 13: Urdukas to Concordia

For a couple of weeks we climbed a series of interesting mountains, returning each time to an increasingly verdant camp site, which was coming to life with birdsong and insects. It was with some regret, but a great sense of anticipation, that we turned towards the wastelands of the upper Baltoro glacier. The porters, quite understandably, do not like this stage of the journey. It can be done in two days to Concordia but it is three official porter days. In May much of the glacier is covered in deep snow from

Far right, top: **The second day in the Braldu Gorge is quite dangerous. It was here that Sheffield climber Pat Fearneough was killed when falling rocks knocked him into the river.**

Far right, middle: **Paiju is the last oasis of greenery before the Baltoro Glacier.**

Far right, bottom: **The Cathedral Group typifies the rock towers for which the lower Baltoro is justifiably famous.**

(Photos: Alan Rouse.)

Urdukas onwards, but later in the year the surface snow melts revealing hard ice painted with lines of stones. The frozen river undulates continuously now as glaciers pour into the main stream from each side. Each side glacier is squeezed onto the main Baltoro to form another parallel ridge of ice. There is no shelter except for pathetic stone circles perhaps two feet high where previous parties have made shelters for the porters. Fifteen porters will cram in, covered by a polythene sheet.

High mountains start to appear; Masharbrum, just under 8000m (26,000ft) on the right, Mustagh Tower, over 7000m (23,000ft), is a beautiful mountain on the left. At the head of the glacier, getting larger each day is the magnificent Gasherbrum 4, until eventually it dominates Concordia with its fine steep pyramid. The scenery changes slowly on this 24km (15 mile) stretch of glacier. Distances are much further that they appear in the crystal clear air. The mountains look like models. Photographs of them cannot convey their mass—that only comes from knowing them. The climber feels the presence of the mountains, he understands their scale intuitively.

The walking is easy enough though a little dangerous as Concordia is approached. Flat areas of snow hide deep crevasses in the ice. The first pair at least should be roped up at this time of the year. Eventually Concordia is reached and K2 can be seen at last, 16km (10 miles) away, up the Goodwin Austen Glacier. Standing alone it looks very high. Clouds racing across the summit slopes, when everything is still on the glacier, show that it is a different world up there. Broad Peak's massive bulk grows out of the Gasherbrum Group to the left, while on the right Chogolisa's endless snow slopes offer a certain harmony. Concordia is not one spot but an area of meeting: a junction for mountaineers, who from here will turn towards their chosen mountain for the next month or two. We turned towards K2 and three weeks later were standing on the summit of Broad Peak. We never made the summit of K2; that will have to wait for another time.

Days 14 – 20: Concordia to Dassu

The return journey is faster: a return to life spread over a week. Urdukas is teeming with life, sensations and smells. Askole is attractive, the squalor is forgotten in the joy of seeing people again. Skardu is like a metropolis and home never seems quite the same again.

ADDITIONAL INFORMATION

Maps and Guidebooks

The commoner ones (especially for Europe) are available in many outdoor equipment shops. More comprehensive stocks are held by:

Edward Stanford Ltd, 12-14 Long Acre, Covent Garden, London WC2E 9LP, (Tel: 01.836.1321).

McCarta Ltd 122 Kings Cross Road, London WC1X 9DS, (Tel: 01.278.8278).

Cordee Books, 3a De Montfort Street, Leicester LE1 7HD, (Tel: 0533.543579).

Magazines

The Traveller. This quarterly magazine is the journal of WEXAS, an organisation devoted to long-distance travel, especially of the more adventurous kind. Offers reduced air fares to members. Details from the Membership Director, WEXAS International Ltd, 45 Brompton Road, Knightsbridge, London SW1 1DE.

Climber. A monthly mountaineering magazine which frequently carries features on trekking. It also carries advertisements from all the leading equipment manufacturers, retailers and trekking companies. Readily available in most outdoor equipment shops, or on subscription from Subscription Dept, Holmes McDougall Ltd, Ravenseft House, 302 St Vincent Street, Glasgow G2 5NL.

Books

The following practical books are inexpensive and informative, particularly useful for anyone organising their own trek:

Off the Beaten Track. Various authors. WEXAS.

The Tropical Traveller. John Hatt. Pan Books.

500 Inside Tips for the Long Haul Traveller. Richard Harrington. WEXAS.

The Walker's Handbook. H.D. Westacott. Penguin Books.